# The SCOTLAND of Robert Burns



ISBN 0-907526-67-5



Printed in Scotland by
Walker & Connell Ltd., Hastings Square, Darvel, Ayrshire.

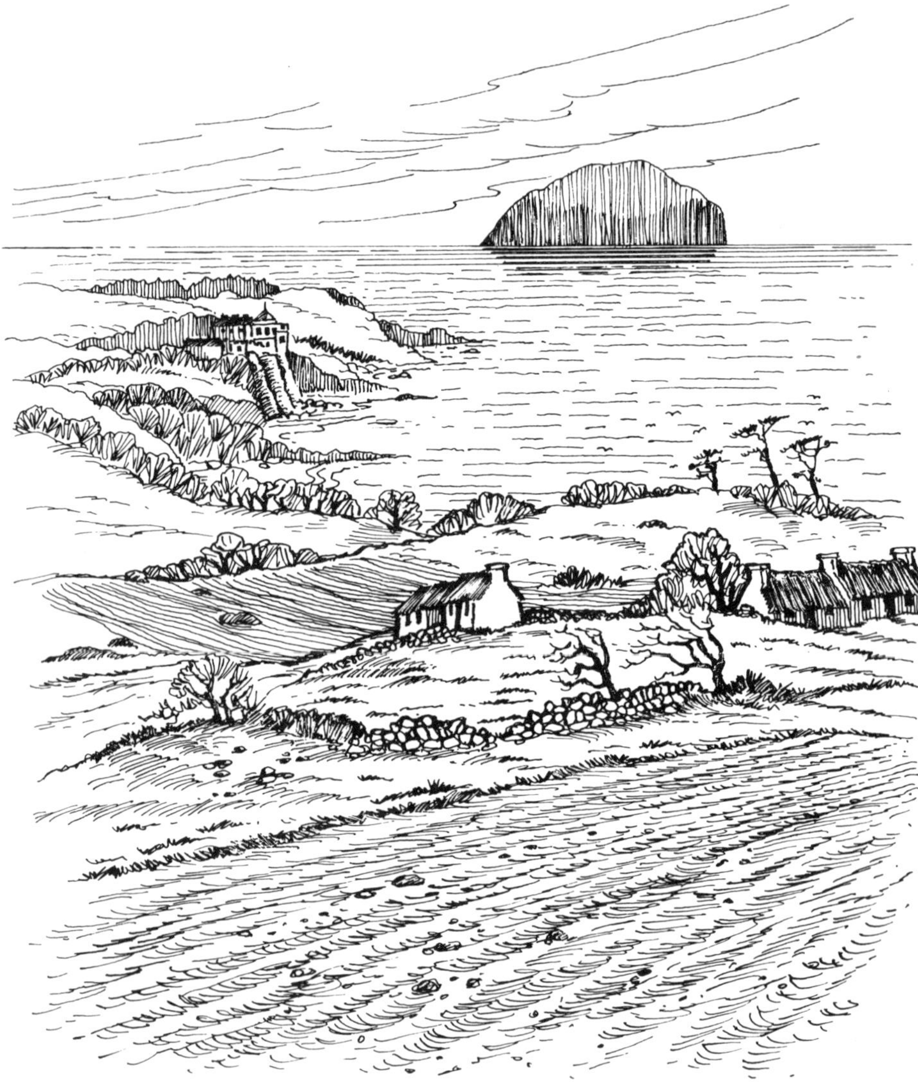

# The SCOTLAND of Robert Burns

**John Strawhorn**

with
Illustrations by Christy Danielles

*dedicated to Danny & Sarah*

Alloway Publishing

*DARVEL • AYRSHIRE • SCOTLAND*

# The SCOTLAND of Robert Burns

## Contents

# Foreword

Social history is like science fiction – a work of imagination, trying to make real an alien environment. The dangerous difference is that what a historian writes is often uncritically accepted as truth. All history involves a selection of facts. Sometimes the information available is incomplete and the historian has to work with evidence he may suspect to be one-sided or biased. Or if his materials are ample, he has to make a choice in interpreting the data, and this may involve prejudice, conscious or unwitting. A social historian in trying to depict life in a past generation has a special difficulty. The picture which emerges may be of a 'bleak age' or the 'good old days', depending on his philosophy or the state of his liver. And where a well-known figure is involved – like Robert Burns – pre-conceived notions of the man may colour the impressions of his background.

The Scotland of Robert Burns was undergoing many changes. That at least is undisputed. There were economic changes which, from one point of view, can be described as improvements and progress. These involved social difficulties whose character and extent must always be a subject for argument. Yet it was a time when someone like Robert Burns could overcome adversity and win fame.

The career of Robert Burns can be conveniently summarised. Born at Alloway on 25th January 1759, the first-born son of William Burnes and Agnes Brown, he moved with them in 1767 to nearby Mount Oliphant farm, then in 1777 to Lochlea near Tarbolton, where his father died in 1784. Robert and the rest of the family then moved to Mossgiel near Mauchline. His *Poems Chiefly in the Scottish Dialect* were published in Kilmarnock in 1786 and an Edinburgh edition followed the next year. With his wife Jean Armour of Mauchline he took the farm of Ellisland in Dumfriesshire and he also started in the Excise. In 1791 he moved into Dumfries as a full-time exciseman, and died there on 21st July 1796 at the age of 37.

This is not another biography of Burns, but an account of the circumstances in which he lived. Apart from visits to Edinburgh and trips to the Highlands and the Borders, his entire life was spent in Ayrshire and Dumfriesshire. That is the Scotland which Robert Burns knew. In this book are presented studies of the varied aspects of the environment in which his genius flowered.

First it is desirable to sketch some of the main features of his time.

The second half of the 18th century was an age of progress, in certain respects.

It was an era of agricultural improvements. New crops like potatoes and turnips; new animal breeds like Ayrshire dairy cattle and Clydesdale horses; increased output stimulated by rising prices: but rising rents and evictions for 'poor tenant bodies scant o cash'. Those who, like the Burns family, lacked capital, faced disaster.

The 18th century saw the beginnings of industrialisation. In the year after the Kilmarnock edition, the great Catrine Cotton Works opened and in the same year Muirkirk Iron Works was set up. Deep pits were being sunk, weaving villages growing up, manufacturing towns expanding. When Burns was born there were only three towns in Ayrshire with more than a thousand inhabitants – Kilmarnock, Ayr and Irvine – and a score of smaller villages. 75% of the population lived in the country. Within a generation Kilmarnock and Ayr had more than doubled in size. A swollen population had moved into forty other town and village communities, some of them new creations. The rural population declined both numerically and proportionately to less than 50%. In 1759 most people lived in the country; by 1796 most lived in towns and villages.

The whole social fabric was thus transformed by the economic changes. There were ensuing difficulties.

Society was vexed, as ours is, by recurrent complaints. Mauchline Kirk Session records of the 1780s report not only immorality but murder, theft, assaults, street disturbances, vandalism, and juvenile delinquency. People were concerned, as we are, with the problem of poverty and its alleviation. 'It is very difficult forming a plan that would provide for the poor, without encouraging in them either inattention, indolence, and waste.' So wrote Rev. William Auld of Mauchline in 1791. People were concerned then too with health – at that time smallpox and infantile mortality. People were concerned, as for long after, with issues like revitalising the Highlands; pollution of the Rivers Ayr and Irvine; the declining influence of the kirk; the rising price of whisky; the absorption of immigrants of an alien culture, with the influx of beggars from Ireland; the problem of unemployment. In a letter from Lochlea to his uncle Burns wrote: 'This country, till of late, was flourishing incredibly in the manufacture of silk, lawn and carpet weaving . . . but much reduced from what it was; we had also a fine trade in the shoe way, but not entirely ruined, and hundreds driven to a starving condition on account of it . . . this country has been, and still is decaying very fast.'

Inflation was another 18th century problem. During Burns's

life-time prices trebled. These figures for an Ayrshire parish (Kilwinning) in 1742 and 1791 are typical:

| 1752 | | | 1791 | | |
|---|---|---|---|---|---|
| butter | 3d | (1¼p) | 9½d | (4p) | per lb |
| beef | 1¼d | (½p) | 4½d | (2p) | per lb |
| cheese | 1¼d | (½p) | 4d | (1½p) | per lb |
| eggs | 1d | (½p) | 6d | (2½p) | per dozen |
| shoes | 2/- | (10p) | 6/- | (30p) | per pair |
| coal | 2/- | (10p) | 5/- | (25p) | per ton |

(Modern currency equivalents shown in brackets).

The 18th century was an era of extremes of wealth and poverty. The Earl of Eglinton took from his estates an annual income of £20,000. The poor in Mauchline parish received from the kirk session a subsistence of less than £5 a year. Tenant farmers would be doing well with £70.

Yet, like today, the 18th century was not all black. That century was an age of opportunity. A range of 18th century Ayrshiremen won fame, and sometimes fortune: James Boswell as a biographer, John Loudon McAdam as a roadmaker; and others below the rank of laird as well: William Murdoch of Bello Mill as engineer and inventor, Charles Tennant from Ochiltree who founded the St. Rollox Chemical Works, James Shaw from Riccarton who became Lord Mayor of London, David Dale from Stewarton who became one of Scotland's great captains of industry, John Galt from Irvine winning distinction as a colonist and fame as a novelist, Robert Burns from Alloway – poet.

Burns, like these others, was born into an environment of opportunity. It was a community centred on the kirk: from his father Burns inherited the Calvinist ethic of hard work, deep thinking, and ambition. It was a community where education was valued: the 1696 Education Act of the old Scots parliament was now creating unique opportunities for self-advancement. It was a rural community with rich traditions of song, verse, and dance. And the new industries were offering opportunities of a new sort. In particular, as far as Burns was concerned, the establishment of Wilson's printing press in Kilmarnock around 1780 made it possible for a local poet to gain a national reputation. Had Burns been born ten years earlier his poems might have never reached print, and all that survived might have been some anonymous songs, preserved by folk singers. The opportunity he was afforded to put his work into 'guid black prent' was the prerequisite for his immortal memory. J.S.

NOTE: Quotations from Burns poems in this book are printed with a reference which refers to the page number where the complete poem appears in all editions of Alloway Publishing's *Complete Poetical Works.*

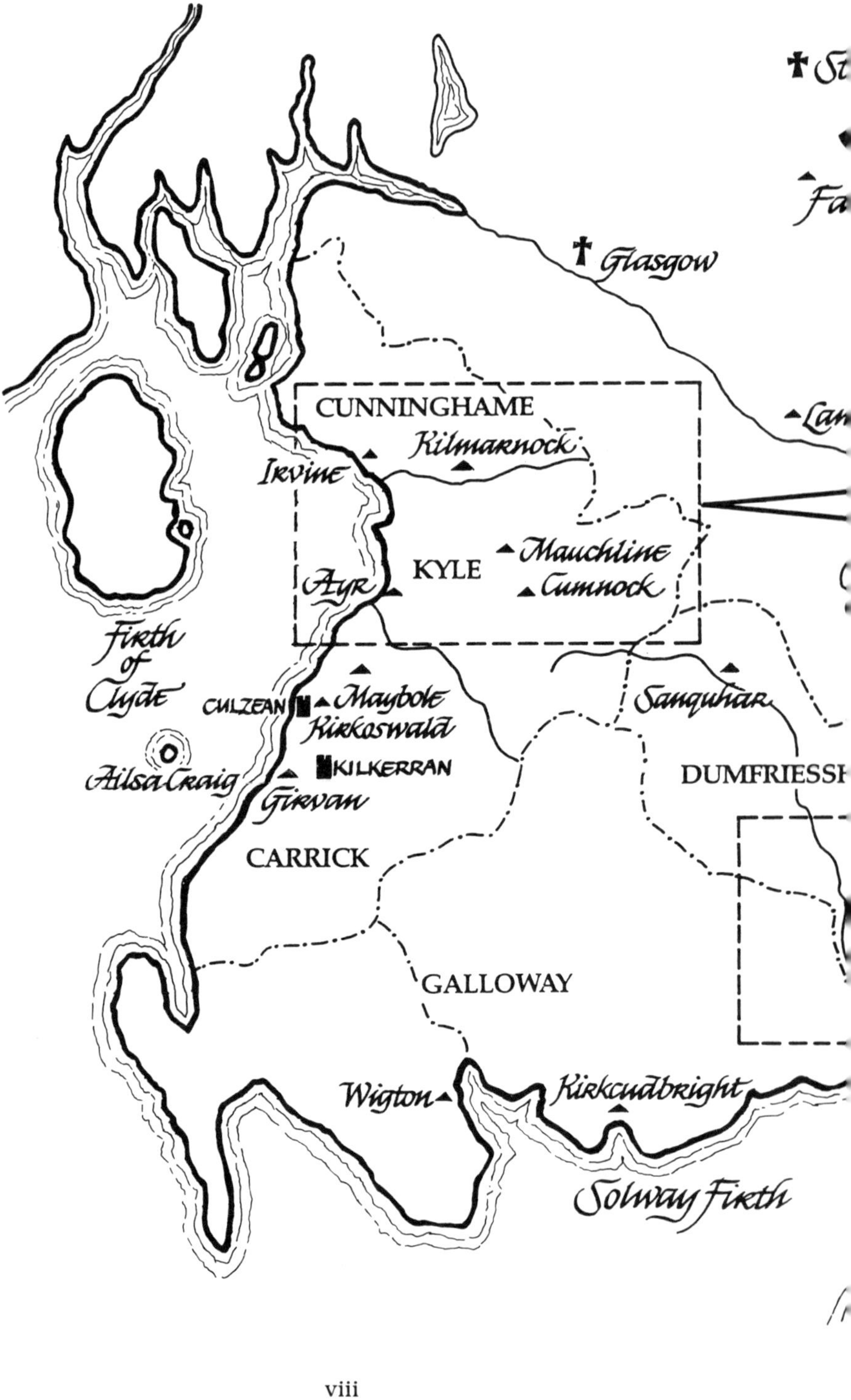
Glasgow
CUNNINGHAME
Kilmarnock
Irvine
KYLE
Mauchline
Cumnock
Ayr
Firth of Clyde
CULZEAN
Maybole
Kirkoswald
KILKERRAN
Ailsa Craig
Girvan
Sanquhar
CARRICK
GALLOWAY
Wigton
Kirkcudbright
Solway Firth

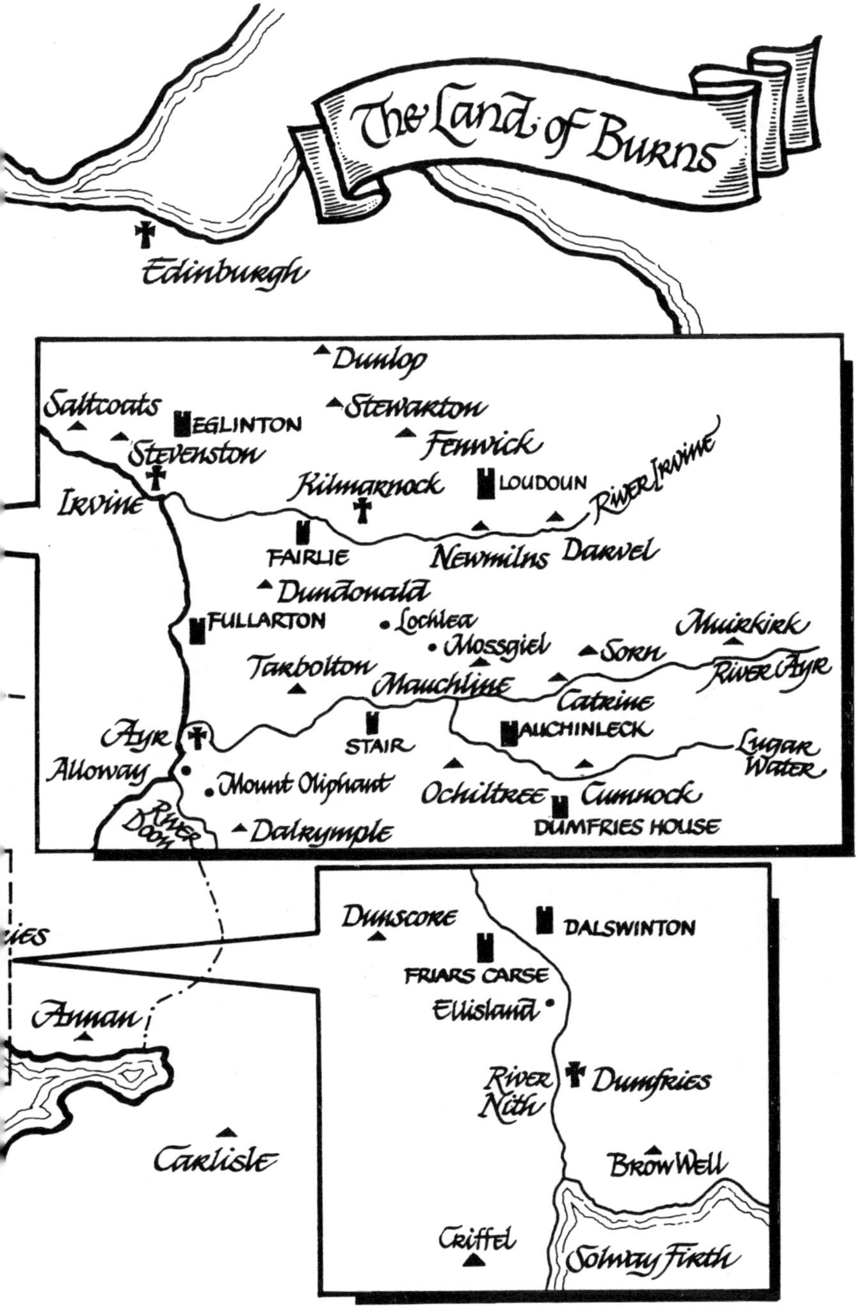
The Land of Burns
Edinburgh
Dunlop
Saltcoats
Eglinton
Stewarton
Fenwick
Stevenston
Irvine
Kilmarnock
Loudoun
River Irvine
Fairlie
Newmilns
Darvel
Dundonald
Fullarton
Lochlea
Muirkirk
Mossgiel
Sorn
Tarbolton
Mauchline
River Ayr
Catrine
Auchinleck
Ayr
Stair
Lugar Water
Alloway
Mount Oliphant
Ochiltree
Cumnock
River Doon
Dalrymple
Dumfries House
Dunscore
Dalswinton
Friars Carse
Ellisland
Annan
River Nith
Dumfries
Carlisle
Brow Well
Criffel
Solway Firth

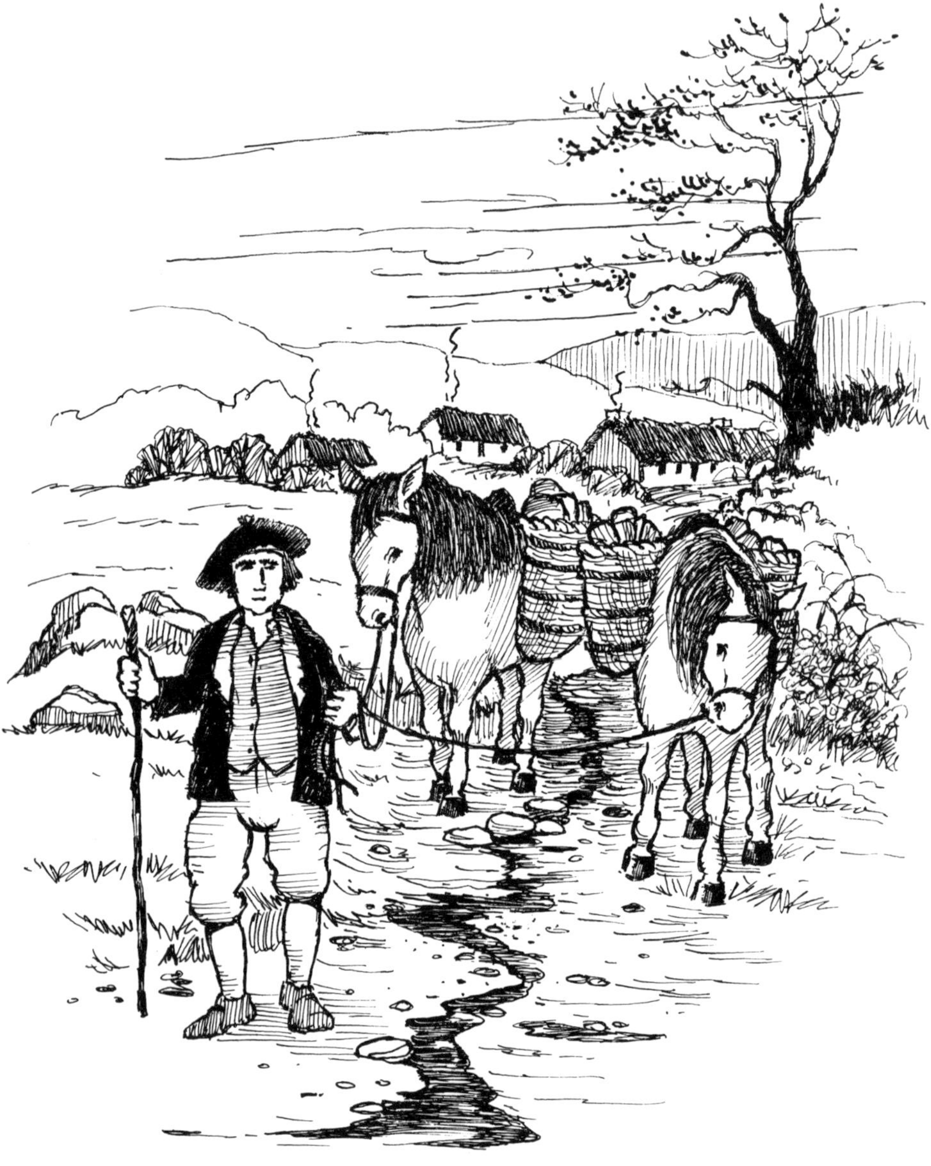

CHAPTER 1

# LANDSCAPE 1759

Scotland at the time of Burns, two hundred years ago, was a different sort of place from what it is now, in many ways. To begin with, the whole landscape was different. Let us look at the Ayrshire countryside as it is now – the rectangular fields, the tidy hawthorn and beech hedges, the plantations of trees, the neat whitewashed farmhouses, the well made country roads. All these are man-made, created since the time of Burns. The very fields are different. Generations of liming and manuring and draining have transformed them. The fields of Ayrshire are greener than they were in Burns' time. Ayrshire is a bonnier place than it used to be.

Some things have not changed – the skies so often obscured with the clouds that presage the sudden shower; the coast with its sandy bays and rocky outcrops; the hills in the background; the deep covering of brown boulder clay that clothes the bedrock, puckered and wreathed up into undulations throughout the lowlands; furrowed by the burns and waters that drain westwards into the Firth of Clyde.

But the surface of the land has been transformed. In the 18th century it was a bleak land, as it had been for long generations before, and the contemporaries of Burns make repeated reference to the great changes they saw under way, fashioning the ancient 'state of nature' into the green and fruitful countryside of later years.

The ministers and others who contributed to the Statistical Account near the end of the 18th century noted the changes. In Tarbolton the 'ancient and natural aspect has evidently been sufficiently rude and wild, bare and unsheltered; varied with frequent inequalities of surface, marshy in the hollows, on the heights overgrown with heath. But the rude aspect of nature has here, long since, given place to the beauties and the wealth of industrious cultivation.' In Symington: 'About fifty years ago, this parish, like others in the neighbourhood, was almost in a state of nature. At that period there were no inclosures, except the glebe or a few acres adjoining, were enclosed with hedge rows. The country in winter was naked waste, scarce a tree appearing to gratify the wandering eye, except a few about the seats of resident heritors; and the roads were all deep and unformed.' In the same area, at Stair: 'The general appearance of the parish, as well as the productiveness of the soil, has been greatly improved since the year 1735, when the present incumbent was settled. At that period there was no fence of any kind, excepting one small enclosure of fir near Barskimming and some coppices of natural wood.'

It was the same in north as in central Ayrshire. Around Kilmarnock, 'till about 35 or 40 years ago . . . no inclosure was to be seen, except, perhaps, one or two about a gentleman's seat, in all the wide, extended and beautiful plain of Cunninghame. Hence, at the end of the harvest, when the crop was carried from the field into the barn-yard, the whole country had the appearance of a wild and dreary common, and nothing was to be seen, but here and there a poor, bare and homely hut, where the farmer and his family were lodged. But now the scene is completely altered and infinitely to the better.' Near Ardrossan: 'Forty, even thirty years ago, the land was almost in a state of nature, very low rented, and the parish almost destitute of enclosures . . . Its present state, however, compared with that in the remembrance of some old men, shows that the farmers have not been altogether idle or ignorant.'

Only in the remoter areas, in south Ayrshire particularly, was the landscape unaltered. 'As to improvements of any sort, it may be said to be in its natural state,' was the description of Barr.

In his 'Memories of Ayrshire about 1760' Rev. John Mitchell later summed it up: 'The face of the country was far from being cultivated or inviting. On the contrary, it appeared rough and dark, consisting greatly of heath, moss, patches of straggling wood and roughly cultivated grounds. The roads, made entirely by statute labour, were not smooth, irregular in their line, and far from being level in their track. The ditches which bounded them were seldom cleared out, and the hedges with which they were skirted being allowed to shoot forth into all their wild luxuriance were seldom cut and almost never pruned or clipped. Young trees were rarely planted, except perhaps in the hedge-row, in short the work or rural improvement had not yet begun, the country presented upon the whole a bleak and somewhat repulsive appearance.'

Until the 18th century, then, and for centuries before, Ayrshire was a bleak land, with mosses and muirs covering not only the uplands but much of the lowlands as well. Areas now improved were barren; and many of the farm names, like Mossgiel, commemorate their former state. There were lochs and marshes, many of them shown on early maps, which have silted up or been drained in comparatively recent times. Lochlea actually had a loch when the Burns family tenanted it; it was drained in the 19th century – when, incidentally, the remains of a prehistoric lake-dwelling were exposed. And though the countryside before the 18th century was not entirely devoid of trees, as is sometimes stated, nearly all the present-day woodland had still to be planted. The roads were mere tracks, unfit for wheeled traffic. When William Burnes's coffin was taken from Lochlea to its last resting-place in Alloway Kirkyard, it was carried on poles, between two ponies.

Roy's Military maps of 1755-1767 show extensive areas of cultivated land only on the more fertile lowland areas. Throughout the county were isolated touns, clusters of cottages whose tenants farmed scattered patches of land. Colonel William Fullarton described them as 'mere hovels, moated with clay, having an open fireplace in the middle, the dunghill at the door; the cattle starving; and the people wretched.' The lairds to whom the lands belonged lived meagrely off sparse rents in bare, bleak, and ancient tower houses until late 18th century agrarian improvements and widening opportunities enhanced their living style. Three quarters of the Ayrshire population, estimated at 59,000 in 1755, lived in this primitive country environment.

Of the minority who lived in nucleated communities, most were in Ayr, Irvine and Kilmarnock. The royal burgh of Ayr had been created in 1205, and had hardly extended beyond its restricted medieval extent of Sandgate and High Street. Its population in 1745 was estimated at a mere two thousand, and Ayr was described as 'a fine beauty in decay' and though the county town it had been surpassed by rivals. Irvine, the other royal burgh further up the coast, only a few years younger, had had a similarly modest growth, with around 3,000 population in mid-18th century. Inland, Kilmarnock had been created a burgh of barony as recently as 1592, but after a meteoric growth had reached 2,500 in mid-18th century and was continuing its expansion.

Apart from these three quite small towns there were thirteen smaller burghs of barony, none of which could have contained more than five hundred inhabitants. Three were quaint little crofter-craftsmen communities – Newton-on-Ayr with 36 freeman, Prestwick with 48, and Kilmaurs with 40. Largs, Saltcoats, Kilbirnie, Newmilns, Mauchline, Tarbolton, Cumnock, Dalmellington, Maybole, and Girvan each carried on weaving and other crafts. Markets were held at other parish centres, where still smaller groups were settled.

The distribution of the population can be assessed as 7,500 in the three towns; 4,500 in smaller townships, villages, and hamlets; with 47,000 in the countryside. Of Ayrshire's 46 parishes, eight held more than 2,500 inhabitants, while four held less than 500. The main social unit of mid-18th century Ayrshire was the parochial congregation, averaging around a thousand in number, drawn normally from a wide rural hinterland.

CHAPTER 2

# DAILY LIFE

What was it like to live in 18th century Ayrshire? Everyday life in all but the most-sophisticated societies is always circumscribed by the elemental needs for shelter, food, and clothing. So here is certainly the place to begin.

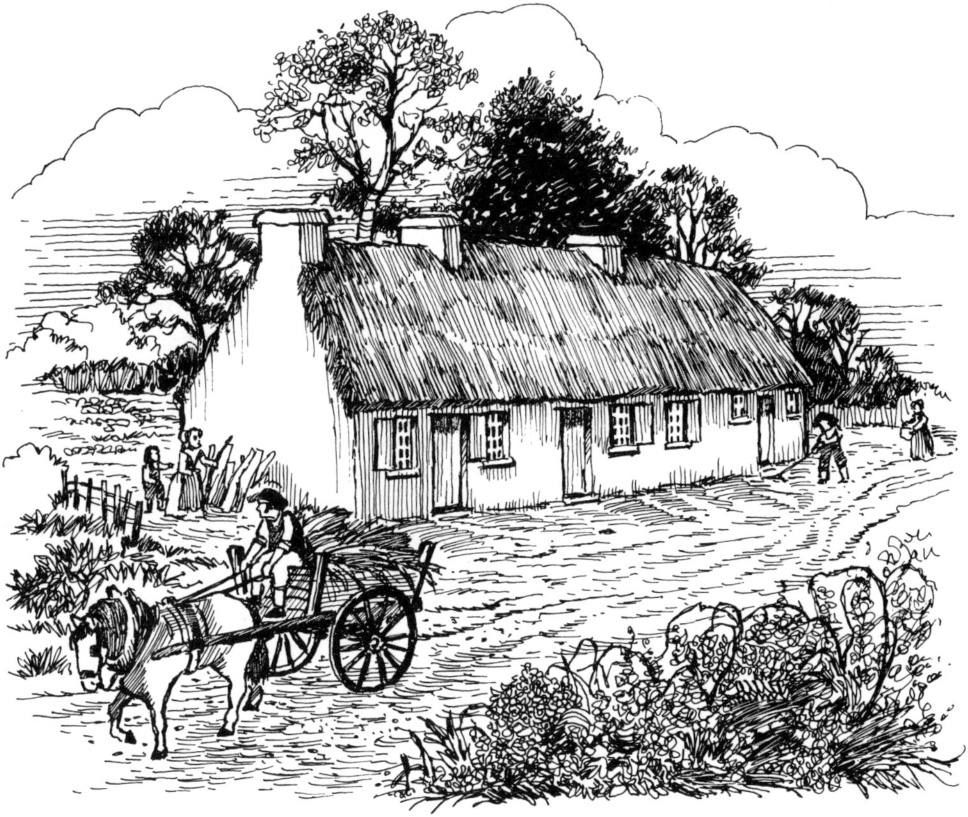

What were the houses like? The best way to answer this question is to think of Burns Cottage at Alloway, and remember that it has been renovated and improved since that 'auld clay biggin' was built by Burns's father, with his own hands. Building materials were of course obtained locally. There were low walls of undressed stone, fitted together with clay and lime; rafters and doors and shutters of wood; a roof-covering of thatch or turf. Many of the 59,000 inhabitants of mid-18th century Ayrshire must have lived in much more primitive conditions than the decent new cottage William Burnes erected at Alloway in 1757.

Inside a typical cottage were two rooms – the but and the ben. The latter formed the living quarters for the family; in the other the beasts were kept every night and throughout the winter, or else was the workroom where the handloom weaver or other craftsman carried on his trade. Folk and beasts lived together under one roof – with a division sometimes only breast-high, at best with a cobbled passageway leading from front to back door. Always they were low-walled thatched cottages, with a low door, sitting on the side of a rough track that was the only roadway, with a midden at the doorstep and the kailyard at the side.

Enter at the front by the foredoor. You might find yourself in the but or in the ben or in a passage leading to the backdoor, with heck door leading to the but and trans door into the ben. The living room is from twelve to fourteen feet square. In larger dwellings – like Burns cottage – there was a second living apartment called the spense, of similar dimensions, entered through the in-seat door. But most families lived in a single ben. Under your feet is an earthen floor, packed together by constant tramping. The roof is low, with no ceiling but rough wooden rafters where all sorts of odds and ends are stacked and sometimes the hens are perched. The side walls are never more than five feet high, and it is a dark interior because the windows are so small. Glass is expensive, and sometimes wooden shutters form the only protection. At one end is the big open hearth and fireplace in which peat is burned. In older dwellings the hearth is actually in the middle of the floor and the only chimney a hole in the roof.

In the centre is a rough wooden table with a couple of wooden forms. There are a few three-legged stools, a meal chest, a wash tub, some sort of dresser for storing utensils, perhaps a wooden cupboard or press. At the side are the built-in beds. There are no mattresses, for the family

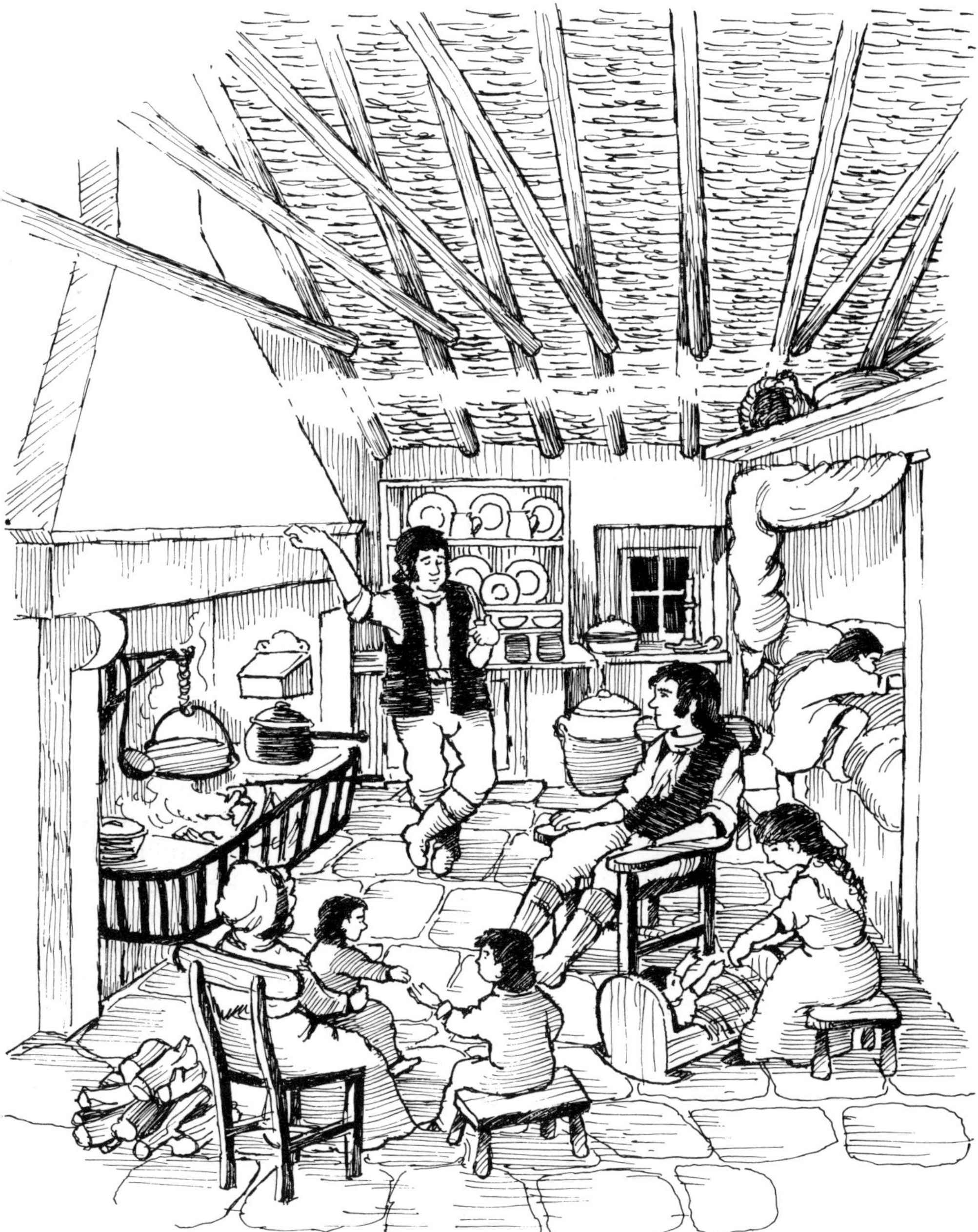

sleep on piles of straw evenly spread out and covered with coarse linen sheets; bolsters filled with chaff; blankets of wool; coverlets of patchwork stuff. It is a dark and draughty place. The fire is always smoking.

*There, lanely by the ingle-cheek*
*I sat an ey'd the spewing reek,*
*That fill'd, wi hoast-provoking smeek,*
*The auld clay biggin;*
*An heard the restless rattons squeak*
*Aboot the riggin.* CW 115

When it is windy the door keeps rattling on the sneck. There is no lock to fasten it.

During Burns's lifetime things were improving. Additional pieces of furniture were added to the households of those who could afford it – a big wooden dresser, chairs and sometimes an armchair for the guidman, a looking glass above the fireplace, occasionally an eight-day clock. The better houses had flagstones on the floors and perhaps even one of the new carpets made in Kilmarnock. As the population of Ayrshire grew, from 59,000 in mid-century to 75,000 forty years later, the masons were kept busy with the building in towns and villages of cottages and two-storey tenements, like that in Mauchline where Robert Burns set up house with Jean Armour in 1788. But on the farms, it was said, often the cattle were provided with up-to-date new accommodation, while the tenants continued to live in ancient hovels.

In no ways was life in Burns's time more different from that of today than in the manner of food. Two hundred years ago the menu of the folk of lowland Scotland consisted almost entirely of three things – oatmeal, some milk, and kail. A remarkable number of items which we nowadays take for granted as necessities were not available three hundred years ago, and rarely available two hundred years ago. Sugar, tea, potatoes, bread itself, and meat – in Burns's early days these were used rarely or not at all. The diet was made up almost exclusively of what could be produced locally – oatmeal and some barley from the fields; milk from the kye; kail from the kailyard kitchen garden plus few other vegetables.

Oatmeal took the place of bread. The bread we eat is made of wheat, which does not grow very well in Ayrshire; and loaves are made in ovens, which were unknown in the but and ben cottages. What took the place of bread was porridge, served at two out of the three daily meals, and bannocks of oatmeal baked on the girdle over the fire, served at each meal. Occasionally you could have barley bannocks or mashlum bannocks, the latter including peasemeal or beanmeal. Some variety was obtained by using the meal in other recipes. Brose could be made quickly for dinner when the wife came in from working in the fields, with oatmeal or peasemeal stirred up into a paste with hot water. Sowens was a delicacy and the measure of a good cook. Recipe: steep oatmeal in water for several days; drain off the sour liquid; boil the residue for several minutes; serve with milk. And there was haggis, composed mainly of oatmeal, highly spiced to give it flavour. In years of famine at the end of the 17th century some families subsisted by draining blood from their cattle, mixing it with oatmeal, and making black puddings.

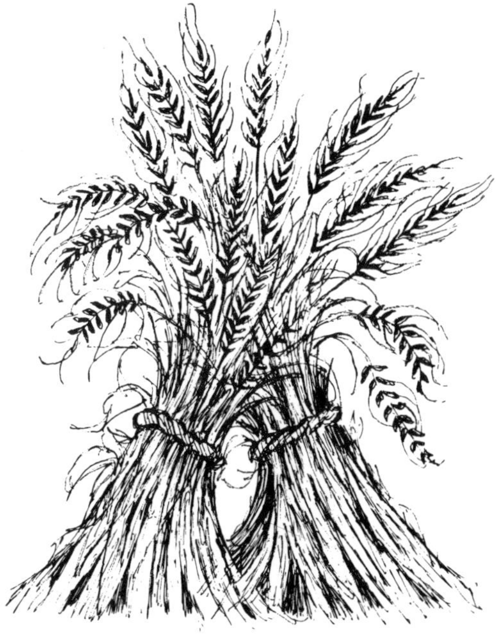

*Barley*

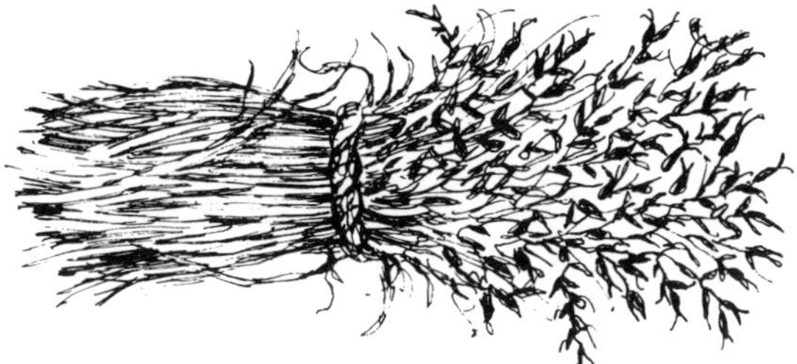

*Oats*

Milk you might expect to have been used a lot, but in fact the folk drank far less milk than now. For one thing the cattle were small half-starved creatures which yielded much less than the more recent Ayrshire breed. And for three months of the year they were dry, so that during the winter months there was no milk at all. Most of the milk was made into cheese for the winter – the 'weel-hained kebbocks'. Butter was something of a luxury. The usual drink at meals was ale, made from barley.

Three or four times a week there was broth. It was made principally of kail, with pease, beans, and barley to thicken it. Sometimes meat was boiled in the broth and eaten separately, but meat of any kind was comparatively little used. In the town of Ayr at the time that Burns was born, fewer than fifty beasts were slaughtered annually. Most of the folk had meat only if a cow or sheep happened to die of accident or disease, or in wintertime if there was no fodder to keep it alive. It was indeed customary for killings to take place at Martinmas and the meat to be salted down and used throughout the winter. Only a few cattle could be maintained through each winter, and every spring there was a ceremony called the 'lifting' when the cattle, weakened by their meagre diet, had to be lifted up and carried out to the grazings.

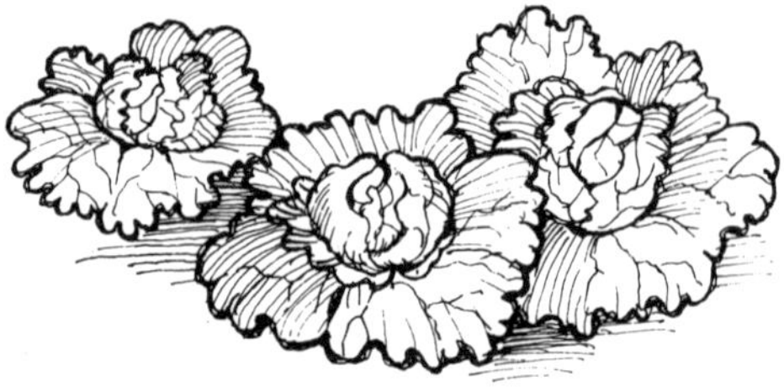

*Kail*

Meat was rare. Gilbert Burns, brother of the poet, remarked of their life at Mount Oliphant that 'for several years meat was a stranger in the house'. Not only were beef and mutton uncommon, but pork and bacon – even the later-famed Ayrshire bacon – were virtually unknown. In Ayrshire as in the rest of Scotland there was a prejudice against pigs – for had not evil spirits been cast into the Gadarene swine? On the other hand, the occasional hare might be trapped on the laird's preserves; and rabbits (or coneys as they were called) were being introduced as a domestic animal in enclosed warrens on several estates. Then there was always fish. Salmon indeed were so common that farmworkers were reputed to stipulate that it should not be served too often. Even in Ayr Poorshouse salmon was served once a week and herring one other day. Poultry were kept, but Burns mentions eggs only once. They were sometimes part of the rent paid in kind and thus had a restricted common use. The gentry had their wildfowl, and most estates had a doocot for the supply of pigeons.

For most people there was a monotonous diet and at times a slender one, but one which kept body and soul together and even bred many hardy men – though it seems likely that the early death of Robert Burns and many of his contemporaries was partly attributable to childhood malnutrition. It was at worst an adequate diet. Oatmeal supplied sufficient constituents for body-building and energy, and what was lacking was made up by the cheese and kail, even to the extent of vitamins. The serious deficiency was in fats. There were few pies or pastries.

Even after Burns' day this remained the staple diet. A sample farmworkers' menu for 1811 offered three meals a day:

| | |
|---|---|
| Breakfast, two courses: | porridge with milk or whey; cheese or herring with bannocks. |
| Dinner, two or three courses: | broth three times a week; meat boiled in broth or cold; or cheese; or fish-with boiled or champed potatoes; bannocks and milk. |
| Supper, two courses: | sowens; or porridge; or champed potatoes with milk; bannocks. |

During Burns's lifetime the menu was being extended. The greatest single advance was the introduction of potatoes. They were known as an occasional garden crop, but it was not till after 1750 that farmers began to grow them and by the end of the century had come into general use. The popularisation of the potato was perhaps the most important event of 18th century Scotland - more important than the Union of the Parliament, than James Watt's steam engine, than even Burns's poems. An easily-cultivated crop, they banished the formerly ever-present threat of famine.

Turnips too were introduced, but were regarded at first with as much suspicion as potatoes. It is curious to note that they were originally grown in gardens and served as a delicacy in mansion houses - eaten as a dessert like pineapples. By the end of the century they were being grown not only as a vegetable for human consumption but increasingly as a fodder for cattle. With turnips for winter feeding the cattle became stronger and healthier and yielded a greater quantity of milk and could be maintained throughout the winter. With turnips a greater cattle population could be maintained, and milk and meat became regular items of diet.

During Burns's lifetime tea was introduced. At first it was regarded not only with suspicion but with absolute horror. Ministers preached sermons against it and kirk sessions and other public bodies tried to check its use. Part of the trouble was that it was regarded as being somehow akin to the wines and brandies along with which it was often smuggled into the country, and like these it was blamed for sapping vitality and ruining the character. In 1744, for example, Kilmarnock council passed the following resolution: 'We the Earl of Kilmarnock, the Bailies, Treasurer and members of the Town Council all convened in council being deeply sensible of the pernicious consequences of the immoderate use of French wines and spirits in public houses and the drinking of tea . . . which is carried to sic an excess to the great injury of the nation and the detriment of the constitution of the people, do hereby promise and resolve that after the first of July next we and each one of us will moderate and discourage the drinking of tea in our families; and will not drink in any public house.'

In his *Annals of the Parish*, John Galt makes Rev. Micah Balwhidder report for the year 1761: 'Before this time the drinking of tea was little known in the parish save among a few of the heritors' houses on a Sabbath evening; but now it became very rife; yet the commoner sort did not like to let it be known that they were taking to a new luxury, especially the elderly women who for that reason had tea-drinking parties in outhouses and byplaces and they made their tea for common in the pintstoup, for very few among them had cups and saucers. Well do I remember one night in harvest in this very year, as I was taking my twilight daunder aneath the hedge along the back side of Thomas Thorl's yard, meditating on the goodness of providence and looking at the sheaves in the field, I heard Thomas's wife and two three old women in the inside of the hedge. They were at their tea and no doubt had a wee lacing of brandy in it, and were cracking away like pea-guns. But I gave them a sign by a loud host that providence sees all; and I heard them like guilty creatures whispering and gathering up their pots and cowering away hame.' But soon he gave us preaching against tea-drinking, and in 1779 in Edinburgh for the General Assembly: 'Mrs. Balwhidder bought her silver teapot, and other ornamental articles; but this was not done she assured me in a vain spirit of bravery which I could not have abided but because it was well known that tea draws better in a silver pot and drinks pleasanter in a china cup than out of any other kind of cup or teapot.'

Sugar was also becoming familiar, though still expensive. Until the 18th century the only sweetener known was honey – bee-keeping was common. But honey, and sugar when it became better known, was used as a medicine, and so also was jelly, for which the sugar was mainly used. But they were still rare. Burns never mentions jam or jelly. Galt, however, remarks on the innovation under the year 1787:

'I should not forget to mark a new luxury that got in at this time. By the opening of new roads and the traffic thereon with carts and carriers and our young men that were sailors going upon the Clyde and sailing to Jamaica and the West Indies heaps of sugar and coffee beans were brought home while many among the kailstocks and cabbages of their yards had planted grosset and berry bushes; which two things happening together the fashion to make jam and jelly, which hitherto had been only known in the kitchens of the gentry, came to be introduced into the village. It was found that jelly was an excellent medicine for a sore throat and jam a remedy as good as London candy for a cough or a cold or a shortness of breath. It occasioned great fasherie to Mrs. Balwhidder for there was no end to the borrowing of her brass pan, till Mrs. Toddy of the Crosskeys bought one, which saved ours.'

Young women and girls wore closely-fitting short gowns called jupps, and older women long gowns of the same basic pattern. These were sometimes of coarse linen, more commonly plain woollen cloth, or in stripes of different coloured woollen cloth called drugget. Under-garments were of harn, coarse home-produced linen. On their heads older women wore a mutch, a close cap of linen or flannel, while young women went always bare-headed. Home-knitted woollen stockings were sometimes worn, and plain leather shoes fastened by leather thongs. Younger women went barefoot. On special occasions they would carry shoes and stockings, and don them only as they approached the kirk or market. In inclement weather women would wear a cloak with a close hood which fitted the head, perhaps of local wool, perhaps of imported duffel, or – their greatest pride – a scarlet cloak of fine woollen imported material. Clothes were hard-wearing, long-lasting, and were handed down so long as they were serviceable. A garment of holland – fine imported linen – might be treasured though discarded from a wardrobe in the

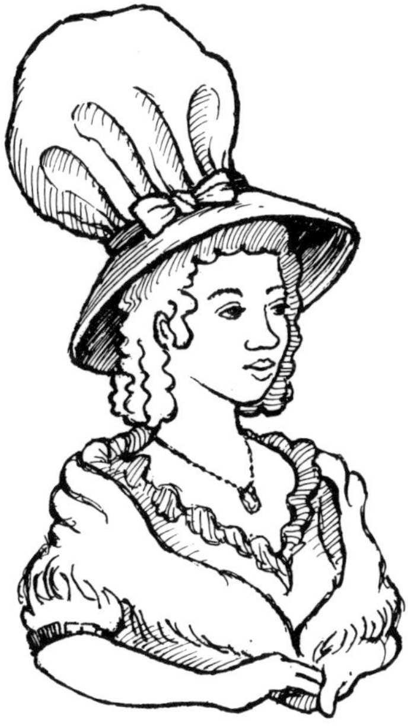

*Lunardi Bonnet*

mansion house. A scrap of brocade or silk or fine lace would be carefully preserved and stitched on to a workaday dress for a wedding ceremony. Fashions changed little, save where someone with dressmaking skill sought to copy some mode of the local gentry.

Men and older boys wore a jerkin or short coat, and breeches of 'hodden grey' woollen material. Small boys wore a one-piece kilt-like loose tunic. Undergarments were of harn. The collar of the shirt was left open, or buttoned, and with a knotted napkin on occasion. On their heads older men wore, often indoors as well as out, a Kilmarnock bonnet. This would also be grey, but when going to kirk or market they would don their 'guid blue bonnet' and, if they were well-enough-off, a suit of 'true blue.' Stockings and shoes were worn when occasion required, and riding boots if owned. As with the women, footwear was plain leather, or blackened with soot and spittle. For outer protection men wore a thick woollen plaid, normally plain though latterly with a checked pattern, wrapped round the body or folded and hung over one shoulder.

Just as diet was being revolutionised in the second half of the 18th century, so also was dress. That native woollen and linen industries in Scotland were being expanded – for a time Burns worked at the flax-dressing in Irvine – and improved communications were increasing the supplies of imported fabrics. But the greatest alteration was wrought by the importation of exotic raw materials. First of all silk was brought in, and silk weaving started in several Ayrshire villages. But silk was scarce and expensive. Then in the 1780s cargoes of raw cotton were brought across the Atlantic and what became for a time Scotland's greatest industry was established. In Ayrshire the Catrine Cotton Works was set up in 1787. Within ten years over six hundred persons were employed there spinning cotton, and the yarn was distributed to several thousand handloom weavers who had set up in every parish throughout north Ayrshire. Much of the cotton cloth manufactured went for export but a good deal of it found a ready market at home. And the bonnie lasses whom Burns knew must have greeted cotton with the same enthusiasm that their modern counterparts have given to nylon and the subsequent range of other synthetic fibres. Cotton, though less durable than wool and linen, was cheap. Garments could be more easily washed, and more readily replaced. Clothing became healthier. And greater variety in fashion became possible.

The minister of Symington, writing near the end of the 18th

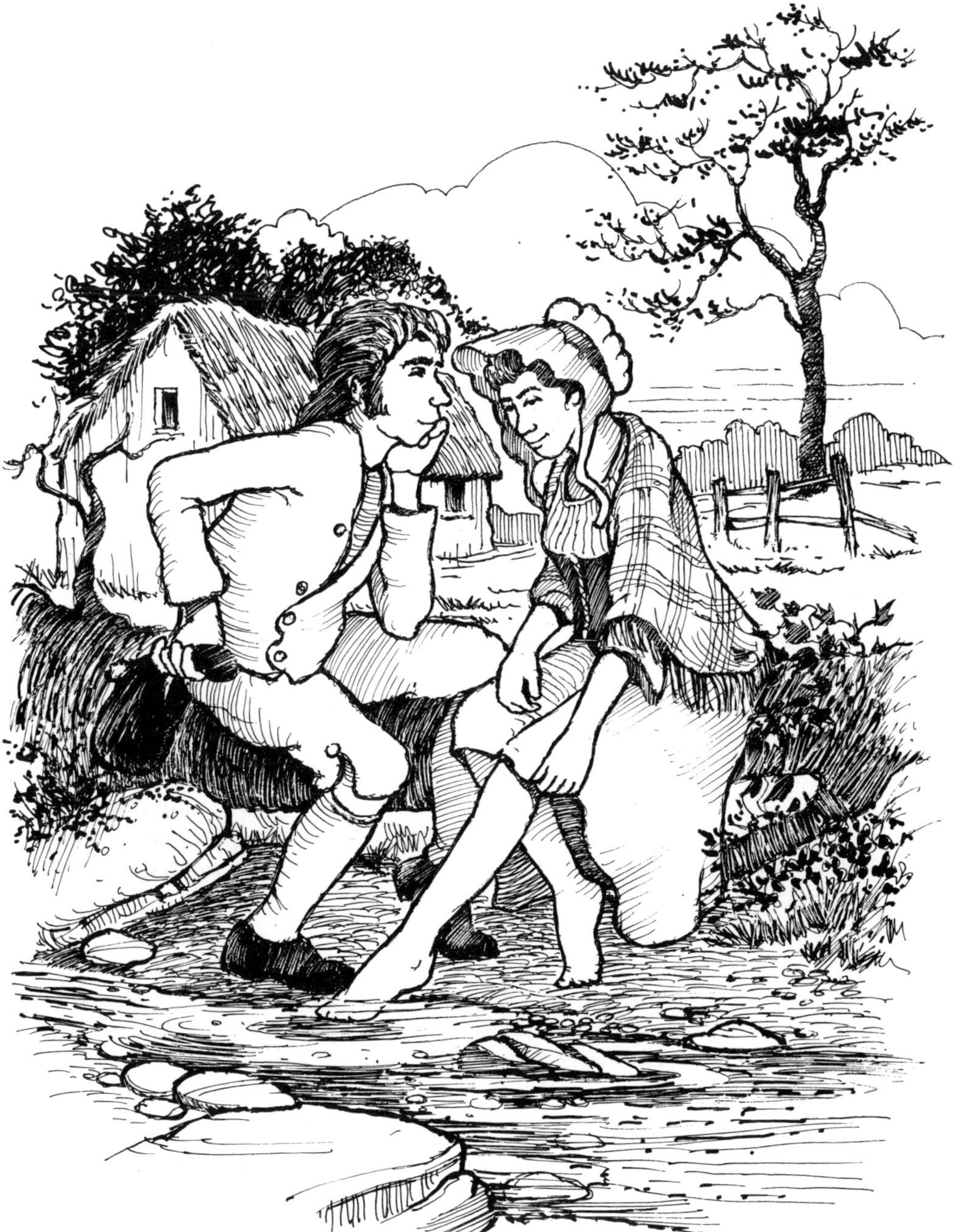

century, noted the changes which were taking place: 'Young women of the middle and even of the lower ranks would now blush to be seen in the blue cloaks, red plaids, and plain caps which only twenty years ago adorned their sex. Nay, even the scarlet mantle which was a badge of distinction among the daughters of the farmers is now despised; and the silkworms of the East must be pillaged to deck the heads and shoulders of our milkmaids. The bonnetmakers of Kilmarnock no longer find demand for their manufacture from the servant men and labourers; but hats are worn both by men and boys of all ranks. Our young men are not to be seen at church or market in a coat of their mothers' spinning but dress themselves in English broadcloths, fashionable cotton stripes, and fine linen. Every stripling must have a watch in his pocket, whereas only forty years ago there were but three in a parish.'

Rev. William Auld had the same story to tell of the social advances: 'The manner of living and dress is much altered from what it was fifty years ago. At that period there were only two or three families in this parish who made use of tea daily; now it is done by at least one half of the parish and almost the whole use it occasionally. At that period good twopenny strong ale and home spirits were in vogue but now even people in the middling and lower stations of life deal much in foreign spirits, rum punch, and wine. As to dress about fifty years ago there were few females who wore scarlet or silks. But now nothing is more common than silk caps and silk cloaks; and women in middling station are as fine as ladies of quality were formerly. The like change may be observed in the dress of the male sex, though perhaps not in the same extent.'

The rapidity with which new fashions were coming into vogue can be instanced by one example. In 1785 Vincenzo Lunardi made several flights in a balloon in the east of Scotland. A bonnet in the shape of a balloon, and named after him, came quickly into fashion. Before that year was out Robert Burns noted 'Miss's fine Lunardi' being worn in Mauchline kirk and recorded it in his poem 'To a Louse.' Daily life was never easy, but while the social changes of the later 18th century brought difficulties to many and disaster to some, there was a general rise in the standard of living. New housing, healthier clothing, better feeding all contributed to provide better health and a reduced mortality which was the major factor in increasing the population during Burns' lifetime.

CHAPTER 3

# THE GENTRY

In the changing condition of the 18th century, population was growing, general standards of living were improving, but the prime source of wealth and power remained ownership of land. Society remained essentially feudal, with social prestige based on land. Most of Ayrshire belonged to some 180 landowners most of whom had inherited rank and were acquiring increased wealth.

Among the landowners the most influential was a group of peers. There were ten earldoms based on Ayrshire - Cassillis, Dumfries, Dundonald, Eglinton, Glasgow, Glencairn, Kilmarnock, Loudoun, Stair; and the earldom of Carrick which since 1469 has been one of the titles of the eldest son of the monarch.

Most prominent were the Earls of Eglinton and Cassillis. The Montgomeries and Kennedys had set themselves up locally in the 12th century, acquired lordships in the 15th century, and earldoms in the 16th. By the 18th century Eglinton and Cassillis were leaders of Ayrshire county society.

Alexander Montgomerie, 10th Earl of Eglinton was 'the first nobleman, in point of rank and opulence in the county, may be justly considered the reviver of agriculture in Ayrshire' (Fullarton). He owned Eglinton Castle in Kilwinning parish, had lands in a dozen north Ayrshire parishes, and more in Renfrewshire. He could afford to spend much of his time socially in London; he died at Ardrossan in 1769, shot by Mungo Campbell, an exciseman whom he discovered poaching. His brother, Archibald, succeeded him as 11th Earl, continued agrarian improvements, patronised Burns by subscribing for 42 copies of the Edinburgh edition, and was appointed lord lieutenant of the county when that office was resuscitated in 1794. He was succeeded in 1796 in the earldom and lieutenancy by his cousin, Colonel Hugh Montgomerie of Coilsfield and Skelmorlie, whom Burns knew as

'Sodger Hugh.'

Sir Thomas Kennedy of Culzean succeeded as 9th Earl of Cassillis in 1762 after three years of litigation, acquiring extensive lands throughout Carrick, the biggest estate in the county, though some of it was poor upland territory. His brother David succeeded as 10th Earl in 1775 and engaged the famous architect Robert Adam to build the magnificent Culzean Castle. Like so many other of the Ayrshire gentry he put his name down as a subscriber to Burns's Edinburgh edition. Archibald, 11th Earl of Cassillis, was a distant relation who succeeded in 1792; his son followed in 1794 and would become first Marquess of Ailsa in 1832.

A third great landowner was William Crichton, 4th Earl of Dumfries and Stair, taking the first title from his mother in 1742, and the second from his brother in 1760. The Crichtons of Sanquhar had in the 17th century acquired Ayrshire lands in the Cumnock area and been awarded the earldom of Dumfries. Near Cumnock Earl William erected Dumfries House, the first major commission of the Adam brothers, John, Robert and James, who signed the plans in 1754. A nephew, Patrick, succeeded in 1768 as 5th Earl of Dumfries and continued his uncle's improvements; his son who followed in 1803 would inherit the title of Marquess of Bute.

The influence of other Ayrshire noble families – Loudoun, Glencairn and Kilmarnock – in the 18th century was limited in a variety of ways.

The Earls of Loudoun traced their family history from the 12th century. The Craufords and later the Campbells of Loudoun had been hereditary sheriffs of Ayr and within three generations in the 17th century acquired a lordship and then the earldom. John, 4th Earl, was a distinguished soldier and improver. But after his death in 1782 his cousin, the 5th Earl, James Mure Campbell of Rowallan, faced difficulties. Burns tells that he 'shot himself out of sheer heart-break at some mortifications he suffered, owing to the deranged state of his finances.' After his suicide in 1782 the six-year-old orphan Countess Flora was a ward of the Earl and Countess of Dumfries till she married the Marquis of Hastings in 1804.

Another old local family, the Cunninghams, had acquired the titles of Lord Kilmaurs, then Earl of Glencairn in the 15th century, and could claim precedence among the Ayrshire peers. William, 12th Earl, however chose to marry a wealthy commoner, Elizabeth McGuire, and though her dowry enabled him to extend his estate by purchasing the extensive lands of Kilmarnock, the marriage was not a happy one. An anecdote reveals the contempt he suffered for having married one who for all her wealth was stigmatised as a fiddler's daughter. The Earl of Glencairn at a ball, on praising the music, received a snide comment from the Earl of Cassillis that Glencairn was known to be fond of the music of the fiddle. Glencairn however appropriately riposted that Cassillis' favourite tune would certainly be 'The Gypsy cam tae our lord's gate', reminding him of the legendary countess of Cassillis who had eloped with Johnnie Faa the gypsy. James, 13th Earl of Glencairn, succeeded in 1775. It was he who more than anyone else sponsored the Edinburgh edition of Burns's poems. After his death in 1791 at the age of 42, Burns wrote a 'Lament' acknowledging 'I'll remember thee, Glencairn, And a' that thou hast done for me.' Within five years a younger brother, John, 14th Earl, died without issue, and the earldom became dormant.

Another Ayrshire earldom had already disappeared. The Boyds had obtained a lordship in the 15th century and the earldom of Kilmarnock in the 17th. The 4th Earl of Kilmarnock, alone among Ayrshire lords, supported the Jacobite cause; he was executed for high treason on Tower Hill in 1747 and the earldom extinguished.

The remaining three Ayrshire earldoms - Dundonald, Stair and Glasgow - were quite recent creations.

The Cochranes of Dundonald achieved in the 17th century a lordship and then an earldom. But in the 18th century they disposed of most of their Ayrshire properties, though Archibald who became 11th Earl in 1778 helped promote coal tar manufacture in Ayrshire as one of his varied scientific speculations.

The Dalrymples of Stair, an old local family whose members were much involved in 17th century Scottish politics, won a viscountcy, an earldom in 1703, and extensive acquisitions furth of their native county. From 1760 till 1768 the title went to the Earl of Dumfries, thereafter reverting to the Dalrymples, but they were mainly absentees, and for twenty years Stair house was let.

More local in their interests were the Boyles of Kelburn, who suddenly won a lordship, and then the earldom of Glasgow only four years later in 1703. John, 3rd Earl, was a soldier; his son George was 4th Earl for the long period from 1775 till 1843, contenting himself with extending his estates around Largs and with public affairs in the west of Scotland.

The biggest estates in Ayrshire in the 1790s were those attached to the earldoms of Eglinton, Cassillis, Dumfries, Loudoun, Stair and Glasgow. It was estimated in 1793 by Colonel Fullarton that with rising rents these could produce each up to £10,000 a year; and with lands outwith the county, peers like the Earl of Eglinton would have an annual income of some £20,000.

Eglinton, Cassillis, and Dumfries were not only leaders of Ayrshire society and prominent in Edinburgh, but throughout the century had established close links with London society as well. Genuine interest, as well as self-interest, encouraged them to devote themselves to estate improvement, involving themselves in agrarian experiments and often mineral and manufacturing enterprises as well, and as patrons of the arts. All had sufficient resources to overcome temporary financial setbacks which ruined some of the less-well-off landowners. Many of the noble families, however, seem to have had more than their fair share of personal difficulties which dislocated normal succession. There were surprisingly many bachelors among them; and many others died suddenly or without sons to succeed them.

Three female members of these noble families deserve special note. Elizabeth McGuire, Countess of Glencairn, has already been mentioned. Hugh McGuire, a carpenter in Ayr who augmented his income by playing the fiddle, befriended an Ochiltree-born orphan called James McCrae. McCrae went to sea, made his fortune in India, returned and bought estates in Kent and Ayrshire, including one at Monkton which he renamed Orangefield in 1734. In the same year he presented Glasgow with a statue to William of Orange. He also lent Glasgow £1,500 to make up the sum levied by Prince Charles in 1745; and he repaid McGuire by gifts to his daughters (or perhaps they were grand-daughters, it is not quite certain). The eldest, Elizabeth, had purchased for her Ochiltree estate in 1744 at a price of £25,000, and given as a dowry with £45,000 worth of diamonds when she married the 12th Earl of Glencairn. Margaret McGuire, her sister, married James Erskine who became Lord Alva. The third sister, Macrae McGuire, inherited Orangefield and married James Dalrymple, Sheriff-clerk of Ayr, who befriended Burns especially by introducing him to his brother-in-law, the 13th Earl of Glencairn. Elizabeth McGuire outlived her husband, and as Dowager Countess of Glencairn, continued to live at Ochiltree and latterly in Edinburgh till her death in 1801.

The second notable dowager was Susanna Kennedy, daughter of the wicked Sir Archibald Kennedy of Culzean, third wife of the 9th Earl of Eglinton, and mother to the 10th and 11th Earls. Lady Susanna was a renowned beauty, and a patroness of literature, to whom Allan Ramsay dedicated his 'Gentle Shepherd.' In her latter days she lived at Auchans house near Dundonald, where she was visited by Dr. Samuel Johnson and James Boswell. In her old age she continued her cosmetic custom of daily washing her face with sow's milk, and tamed and made pets of the rats which abounded in the old mansion. She died in 1780 aged 91.

The third dowager countess was the daughter of the first Earl of Stair and widow of the 3rd Earl of Loudoun, who occupied Sorn Castle from 1731 till her death in 1779 aged 99. She was an enthusiastic improver of agriculture, like her son, and when Andrew Wight visited her in 1778 he declared: 'There perhaps does not exist in the world such another woman.' Of less exalted rank than these three dowager countesses was another remarkable woman. Frances Ann Wallace, daughter of Sir Thomas Wallace of Craigie, married John Dunlop of Dunlop. She was born in 1730, eloped at seventeen, had seven sons and five daughters and survived till 1815. Her husband died in 1785 and the widowed Mrs. Dunlop the following year began a ten-year correspondence with Robert Burns.

It was also through a woman that another great Ayrshire estate was in process of creation in the last decades of the 18th century. Beginning in 1786, the Kilmarnock lands of the Glencairns and properties in adjacent parishes were purchased by the trustees of a Fifeshire heiress, Henrietta Scott. In 1795 she married the Marquis of Titchfield who in 1809 became 4th Duke of Portland and the wealthiest Ayrshire landowner of the 19th century.

Nearly thirty landowners below the rank of peers were very wealthy, enjoying a considerable thousand pounds a year or more from their estates. These, like the peers, became heavily committed to agrarian and other improvements in the latter half of the 18th century. Some strained their more limited resources and indeed only about half of them successfully retained their possessions. Several of the large estates which remained intact are listed in alphabetical order.

Auchinleck: the celebrated James Boswell followed his father Lord

Auchinleck in 1782 and was himself succeeded in 1795 by his son Sir Alexander Boswell, antiquarian, poet, and promoter of the Burns Monument as Alloway in 1820.

Carnell or Cairnhill in Craigie parish: William Wallace, advocate and song writer, was succeeded in 1763 by his son William Wallace, Master of St. David's Lodge, Tarbolton, and Sheriff of Ayr from 1775 till his death in 1786, when Captain Thomas Wallace succeeded.

Dunlop: John Dunlop made a runaway marriage with Frances Anna Wallace of Craigie, who survived his death in 1785 and became a correspondent of Burns; one son inherited through his mother the estate of Craigie, which he had to sell; another son, who inherited the north Ayrshire Dunlop estate, became General Andrew Dunlop.

Enterkin: on the banks of the River Ayr, owned by another branch of the Cuninghame family, where William Cuninghame celebrated his coming-of-age in 1788 by a Fete Champetre which Burns commemorated poetically.

Fullarton: Colonel William Fullarton, soldier, adventurer, politician, and agriculturalist succeeded to this Troon estate at the age of five in 1759, was noted in 'The Vision' as 'Brydon's brave ward', himself commended Burns in his *View of Ayrshire Agriculture;* after he died in 1803 the Fullarton estate was purchased by the Marquis of Titchfield, later Duke of Portland.

Grange, near Kilmarnock, and Kerelaw near Stevenston: Alexander Hamilton who succeeded in 1774 had a cousin and namesake who helped form the United States Constitution; a new Kerelaw House was built, and Grange sold to Henrietta Scott, later Duchess of Portland.

Kilkerran in south Ayrshire: outstanding among this group of important landowners was Sir Adam Fergusson of Kilkerran. Member of a long-established and distinguished Carrick family, the third baronet was a great advocate – noted by Burns in 'The Vision' as 'the aith-detesting chaste Kilkerran' – M.P. for Ayrshire 1774-1784 and 1790-1796, and for Edinburgh in the intervening period. He inherited Kilkerran from his father in 1759 and successfully improved it before his death in 1813. In 1796 he unsuccessfully claimed the title of Earl of Glencairn.

Some considerable landowners went under, because of financial difficulties, particularly following the collapse of the Ayr Bank in 1772 – like Sir John Whitefoord of Ballochmyle, William Wallace of Sauchrie, and Sir Thomas Wallace Dunlop who had inherited Craigie from his maternal grandfather in 1770 and had to dispose of it only twelve years afterwards.

Lands which came on the market were purchased by new men who had made money in commerce, the law, or abroad: land was an investment, and just as important ownership of land guaranteed a social prestige that money by itself did not afford. Early in the century James Macrae, late Governor of Madras, bought from the impoverished Hugh Baillie of Monkton those lands he renamed Orangefield. Later from India there returned to his native county Claud Alexander who purchased Ballochmyle and set up the Catrine cotton works; Dr. William Fullarton who acquired Rosemount; his brother Major General John Fullarton who bought Kerse, and whose son later built there the village called Patna. Across the Atlantic, from his West Indies estate John Hamilton brought negroes to his new Ayrshire property of Sundrum; John Loudon McAdam returned from New York to purchase Sauchrie and become famous as a roadmaker; Richard Oswald, London merchant and owner of lands in America and the West Indies, became owner of Auchincruive in 1764.

How new blood enriched Ayrshire stock can be exemplified by the case of John Miller of Glenlee in Kirkcudbrightshire who in 1708 acquired Barskimming not far from Mauchline. A successor Thomas Miller became Lord President of the Court of Session and a baronet in 1788; and his son who succeeded in 1789 was Sir William Miller, Lord of Session and Lord Glenlee. To the former Burns paid tribute as one who knew him as a fellow-parishioner: 'An aged judge, I saw him rove, Dispensing good'. His brother Patrick Miller, after an adventurous youth became a director of the Bank of Scotland, purchased Dalswinton estate in Dumfriesshire, where he conducted an experiment in steam navigation, and let the farm of Ellisland to the now-famous poet.

There was a group of about eighty lesser lairds, considered well-off with incomes of over £200 a year. Some were cadet branches of noble families or long-established local stock, who could associate socially with the others of greater wealth. One such was Hugh Logan, the 'Laird of Logan', a celebrated wit. As a heritor in Cumnock parish he objected to the expense of maintaining the kirkyard: 'It's time enough to repair the dykes when the tenants complain.' Though educated in Edinburgh with Hugh Montgomerie, later Earl of Eglinton, and John Hamilton of Sundrum, he retained the traditional Scots speech which so many of his class were abandoning in favour of English. J.D. Carrick described the appearance of this well-known character: 'His stature was tall, and his form remarkably handsome... His weight varied from eighteen to twenty stones. Though not fastidious about his clothes, he was always appropriately dressed, wearing generally a blue or brown coat, with light-coloured shorts, having buckles at the knees... considering his associates and the scenes of dissipation in which he but too frequently mingled, only one instance of an illicit amour has been laid to his charge.' Like others of his class, the attempt to maintain a high social standard on the limited resources of a small estate was beyond him. Ruined by the Ayr Bank crash, he had to sell Logan to a Glasgow merchant. Many of these smaller estates were passing into such hands.

Occasionally the new owner himself got involved in financial difficulties. David McLure, an Ayr merchant, purchased the Tarbolton estate of Shawwood sometime before 1774, and carried out some notable improvements, but was impoverished by the failure of the Ayr bank. He was forced to press his tenants, including William Burnes in Lochlea, with whom he became involved in a law suit. Of his father in these circumstances Robert Burns wrote: 'a venerable parent in the jaws of a jail; where, but for the Poor Man's last and often best friend, Death, he might have ended his days.' McLure himself had to give up his estate and leave the district in 1788. His son William was more successful. Emigrating to the United States he won fame as 'Father of American geology' and fortune as an entrepreneur.

More fortunate were those Ayr merchants who took advantage when Ayr town council sold off its Alloway lands in 1754 at what were bargain prices. New estates were laid out at Mount Charles, Cambusdoon, Doonholm, Rozelle and Belleisle, which added to Newark, Doonside, Belmont, Castlehill, Craigie, and Blackhouse, encircled the county town with a constellation of mansions, most of which were occupied by merchant-lairds. Among these was Provost John Ballantine of Castlehill, promoter of Ayr New Brig and of Ayr Academy, and correspondent of Burns. William Burnes came to Ayr to work on Doonside estate. In 1755 'William Burns at Doonside Mill' obtained a contract to lay out what became Greenfield Avenue. Then he worked for William Ferguson, later provost of Ayr, at Doonholm. In 1756 'William Burns, gardener at Doonside Miln' feued, from Dr. Alexander Campbell of Belleisle, the seven acres he called New Gardens and built his cottage there. In 1766 he rented Mount Oliphant from Provost Ferguson of Doonholm.

There was no comparable estate development in north Ayrshire around Irvine or Kilmarnock, though in parts of north and even central Ayrshire some Glasgow merchants bought small country estates for themselves. Robert Simson, professor of Mathematics at Glasgow University and restorer of Euclid, had a residence at Kirktounhall in West Kilbride from 1735 till his death in 1768. Catrine House and estate was inherited by Matthew Stewart, professor of mathematics at Edinburgh University, and after his death in 1785 by his son, Dugald Stewart, professor of moral philosophy, also at Edinburgh. It was here that Burns first 'dinner'd wi' a lord.' He was introduced by Dr. John Mackenzie of Mauchline who later moved to Irvine and became laird and magistrate. Another surgeon, Patrick Douglas from Ayr, inherited Garrallan, had property in Jamaica, and arranged Burns' proposed emigration to Jamaica.

All of this is sufficient to indicate how widespread was the movement of business and professional people into land. Even in little Mauchline, Gavin Hamilton sub-let to Robert Burns the farm of Mossgiel which he held as a kind of summer residence. And another Mauchline merchant, Henry Richmond, acquired the farm of Little Montgarswood and went to live there.

Each landowner sought to provide himself with a mansion house appropriate to his station. Sometimes the old tower house was renovated – examples still survive at Killochan, Cassillis, Sorn, Cessnock and Hunterston. Sometimes a more imposing structure was formed around the old shell; often a new building was erected on a new adjoining site. Most magnificent were Culzean Castle and Dumfries House; followed by Eglinton Castle and Loudoun Castle which were completed in the early 19th century. And there are dozens of smaller but still fine creations, from Auchinleck and Ballochmyle to Auchincruive and Kilkerran.

Some of the gentry still retained a town house in Ayr which was, about 1800, as Lord Cockburn recalled, 'a gay, card-playing, dancing, scandal-loving place. There seemed to be a dinner, or a tea, and card party, every day at several houses of Kennedys, and Boswells, and Crawfords, and Dalrymples; lots of old colonels and worthy old ladies; and to get up a ball, nothing was wanted but for somebody to suggest it, and they would be footing it away in a few hours.' For social

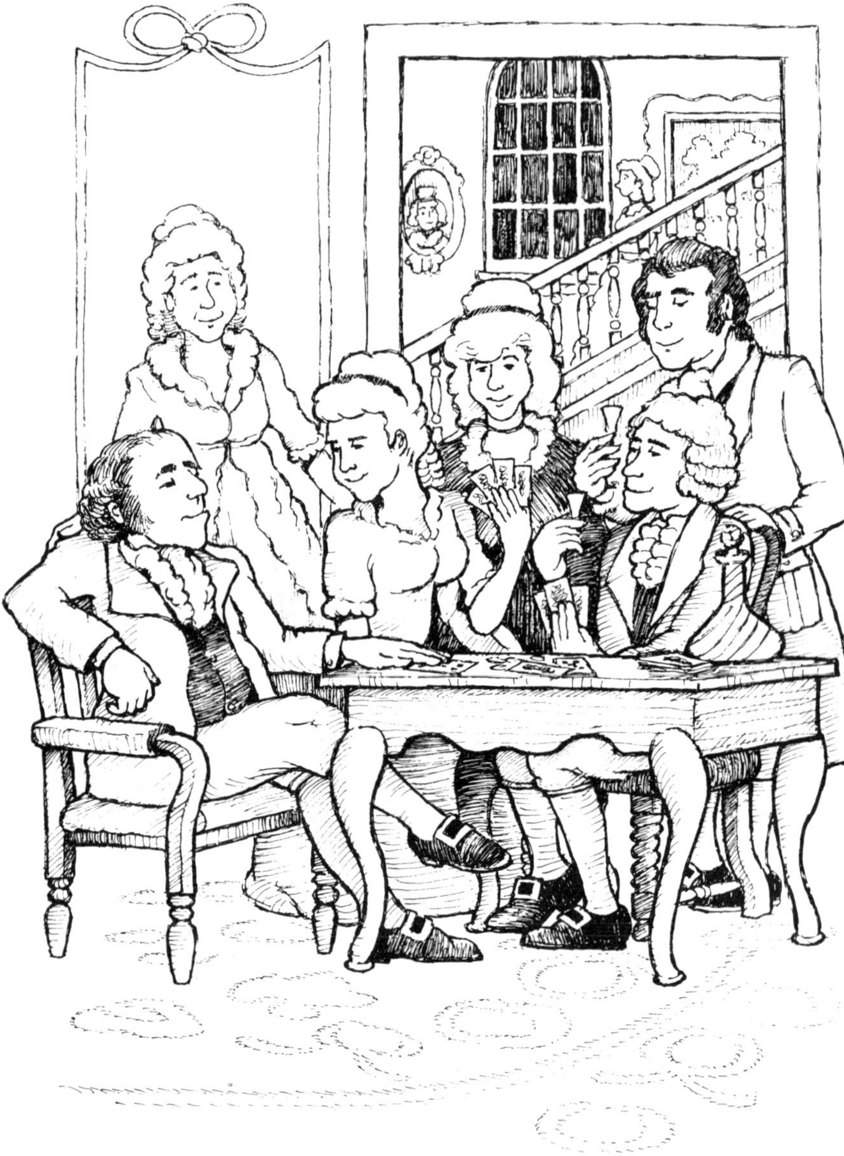

gatherings there was an assembly room in the town hall.

Horse racing was popular throughout the county and among all classes – Mauchline had its races annually in April on the Mossgiel road. But for the county society, important social occasions were the races at Bogside, on a course provided by the Earls of Eglinton, and those at Ayr. Racing at Ayr in the 17th century had been on the sands, with the town council awarding in 1698 a prize of a silver disc. In 1770 the council was approached by a committee of local 'noblemen' who were the 'Stewards of the Races' and agreed to the laying-out of a racecourse on the Town's Common. In 1787 it was improved by the rooting-out of whins and the construction of a five-foot stone dyke to enclose it. And in 1789 a Viewhouse or grandstand was erected. Just about the same time another horse sport was organised with the formation of the Ayrshire Hunt in 1792.

Still another sport in which the gentry and others participated was golf. It was played on the sand dunes by the shore at Ayr, and probably other places along the coast. Inland a golf course was laid out at Loudoun by the Earl. His factor, John Arnot of Dalwhatswood, a correspondent of Burns, seems to have played. In the ledger of Tam Samson, the Kilmarnock seedsman, are listed for 1789 purchases of seed by 'Mr. Robert Burns, farmer, Ellisland' and Arnot was supplied with '2 Golf Balls, at 6d.' Tam Samson himself was, like so many others, an enthusiast for the winter sport of curling.

A new fashionable and supposedly health-giving pastime was sea-bathing – Burns was prescribed this treatment at Brow Well in July 1796. At that time, 'Saltcoats is the principal watering place in Ayrshire. From 300 to 500 people usually resort there, during the Summer months, for sea-bathing, especially from the towns of Paisley, Glasgow and Hamilton.'

Socially separate from all the landowners mentioned was an inferior range of small land-holders. Bonnet-lairds they were called, for they owned only their own farm and were adjudged too poor even to possess a three-cornered hat which was the mark of a gentlemen. About eighty of these were comfortable enough with incomes above £100 a year. There were at least twice as many who were no better off than tenant farmers. Altogether there must have been about two hundred and fifty of them, especially numerous in north Ayrshire. Like Burns and other tenant farmers they were regarded as belonging to the middle rank in society.

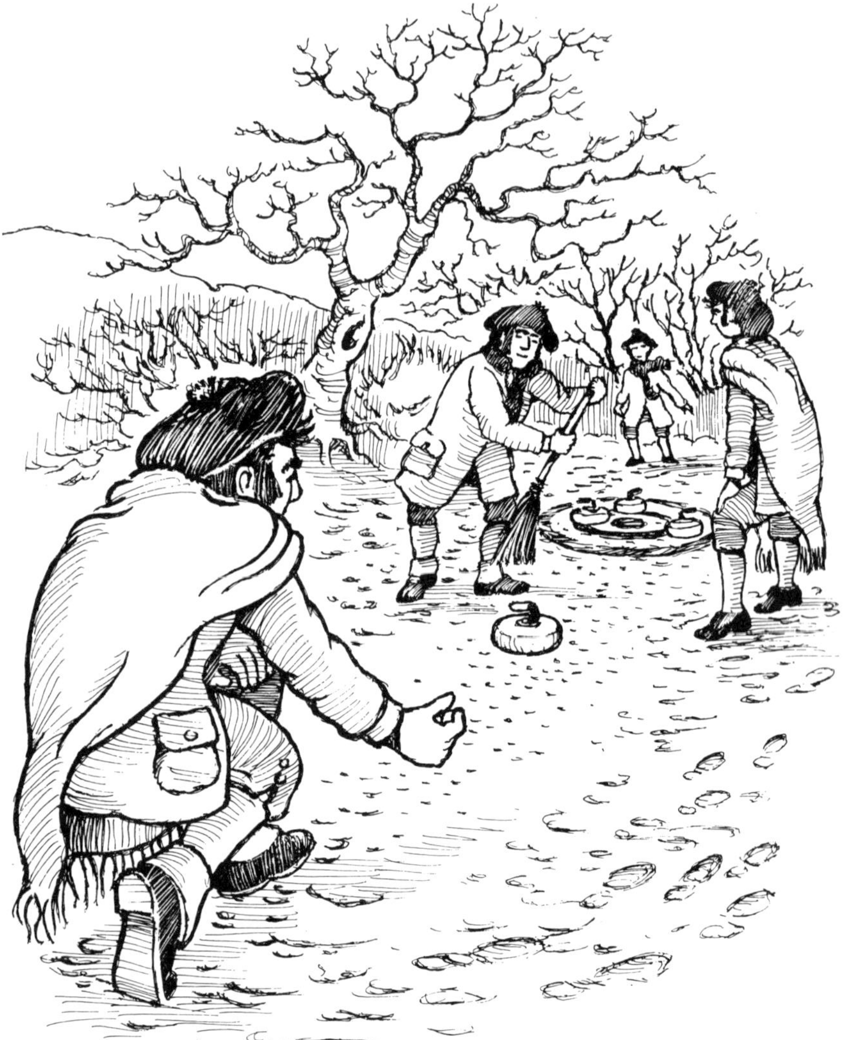

## CHAPTER 4

# THE MIDDLE RANK

People of the middle rank in society included tenant farmers, estate factors and surveyors, small merchants, master craftsmen, lawyers, surgeons, ministers, schoolmasters, excise officers, innkeepers, millers and the like. Such associations as they had with the landed gentry, however friendly, were always based on a concept of social inequality - a tacitly accepted caste system. Within the middle rank there were of course differences in status and wealth. Certain groups in the 18th century were advancing, with some members able to purchase their way into the ranks of the landowners. Others were faring less well in an era of inflation.

Many tenant farmers were finding things difficult. In 1760 good land could be had for 25p-50p per acre; a generation later it was costing four times as much. Those who had capital to stock and run an improved farm could do well enough by selling their produce at the new inflated prices, and earn up to £100 a year. But not all were successful in getting a new farm and making a success of it. Holdings might be monopolised, a new tenant granted the lease, and the former occupants displaced. Burns, who appreciated the experience of eviction, in the first poem of the Kilmarnock edition, 'The Twa Dogs', took up just this topic of the relations of landlord and tenant and how the latter might meet with

*. . . sair disasters,*
*Like loss o health or want o masters.*
*Poor tenant bodies, scant o cash,*
*How they maun thole a factor's snash:*
*He'll stamp an threaten, curse and swear*
*He'll apprehend them, poind their gear;*
*While they maun stan, wi aspect humble,*
*An hear it a', an fear an tremble!* CW 142

He returned to the same theme in 'Man was made to Mourn', lamenting over the

*. . . poor, o'erlabour'd wight,*
*So abject, mean, and vile,*
*Who begs a brother of the earth*
*To give him leave to toil.* CW 124

The difficulties besetting tenants of limited means can be illustrated from the history of the Burns family. William Burnes, born in Kincardineshire in 1721, was a man of farming stock whom circumstances forced into a series of jobs in estate gardening. Moving into Ayrshire in his early thirties he worked successively for Alexander Fairlie of Fairlie in Dundonald parish, then William Crawford of Doonside and William Ferguson of Doonholm. On his own he took a feu of a plot at Alloway where he built his cottage in 1757, took a wife and started a family, managing a little dairy with two or three cows.

In 1765 William Burnes became a full-time tenant farmer, leasing from Ferguson the 60 acre farm of Mount Oliphant, to pay £40 rent

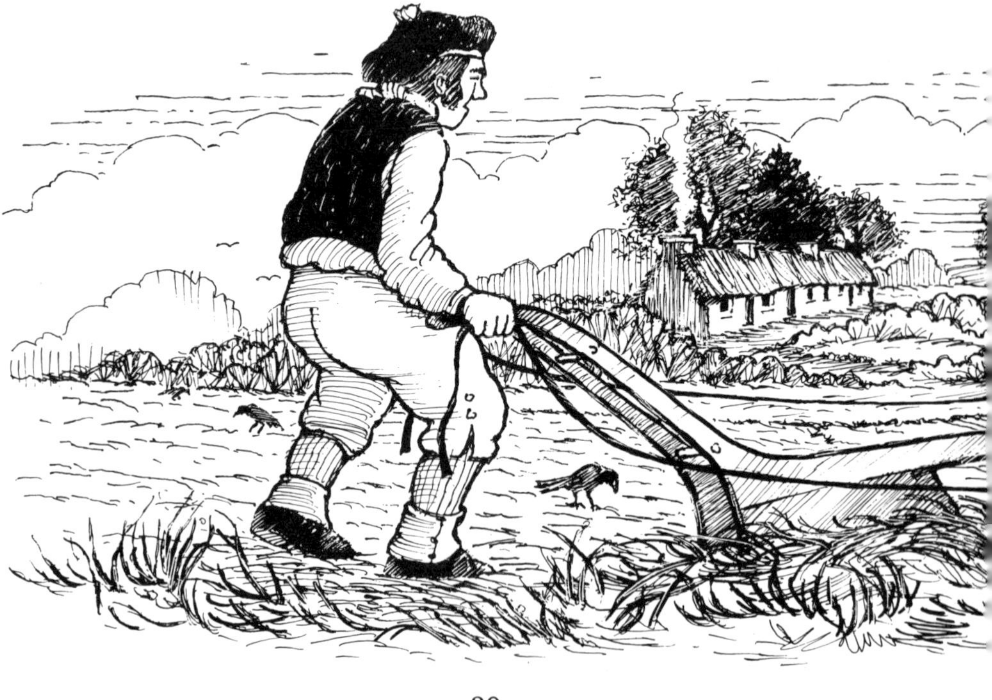

annually for the first six years till Martinmas 1771, and then to continue if he wished for a further six years at £45 a year. He made a bad start: unable to sell his feu at Alloway he could stock his farm only by a loan of £100 from his 'generous master.' Even so he could not hire help, the soil proved unproductive, and cattle were lost through accident and disease. The lease had to be continued after the first six years, because there was no alternative of moving elsewhere, and the difficulties of paying the augmented rent were increased when Ferguson died in 1775 and his property was thereafter administered by a less indulgent factor who was the original for the one depicted in 'The Twa Dogs.'

Before the lease came to an end in 1777 William Burnes was able to secure the 130-acre farm of Lochlea from David McLure, an Ayr merchant, who contributed to stocking the farm. For the first few years from Whitsun 1777 things went reasonably well, but Burnes began to fall behind in the payment of the £130 annual rent. In 1781 a dispute with the landlord began. Young Robert went to Irvine to the flax-dressing. After he returned home, in 1782 the dispute was

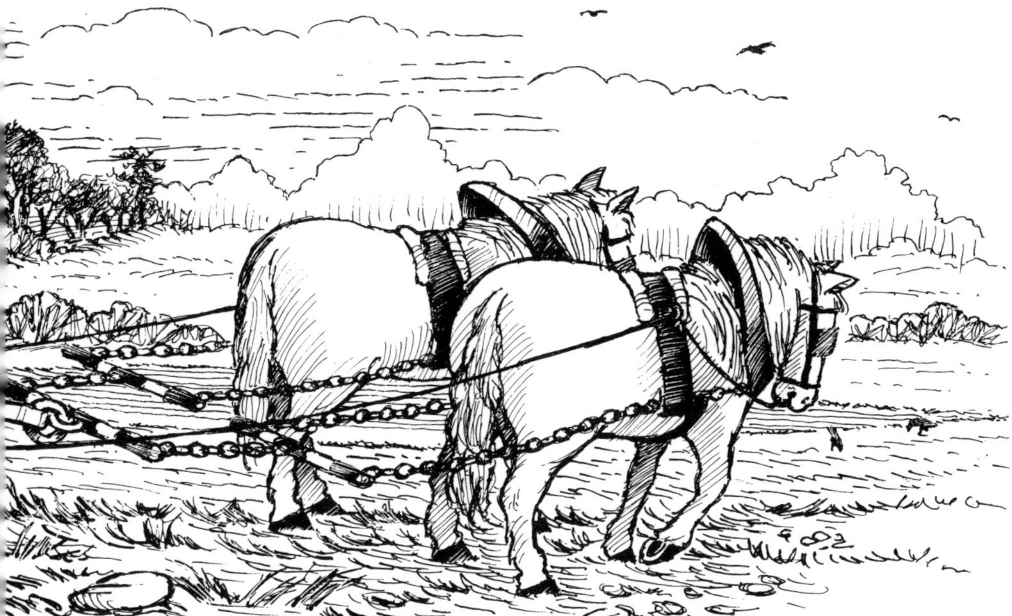

referred to arbiters. There was no written lease, and as McLure was himself in some financial difficulties he took out in 1783 a warrant of sequestration against the plenishings at Lochlea. Burnes was already far gone in consumption, and died early the next year.

Under the pretext that they had been employed by their father, the oldest members of the family were able to present themselves as creditors and secured enough to make a start in 1784 on the 118-acre farm of Mossgiel for which they were to pay £90 per annum to Gavin Hamilton, the Mauchline solicitor, who leased the farm from the Earl of Loudoun. Mossgiel was run as a sort of joint enterprise, stocked by the individual savings of the whole family, and each received wages, Robert and Gilbert getting £7 per year each. Here again they were unsuccessful. Wrote Burns: 'I entered on this farm with a full resolution – Come, go to, I will be wise! I read farming books – I calculated crops – I attended markets – and, in short, in spite of the devil, the world, and the flesh, I believe I should have been a wise man; but the first year, from unfortunately buying bad seed, and the second, from a late harvest, we lost half our crop.' When Robert went off on his own he had to subsidise the rest of the family at Mossgiel (which in 1786 was purchased from Loudoun by Claud Alexander of Ballochmyle). Eventually in 1798 Mossgiel was given up when Gilbert Burns secured a post as factor on Lord Blantyre's estates in East Lothian.

There is no evidence that the Burns family were inefficient farmers. William Burnes seems to have been well regarded as a gardener and worked hard to make his farming ventures succeed. Even Alexander Tait, the Tarbolton versifier, who scurrilously reviled them at the time of their failure at Lochlea, did not accuse them of incompetence. Robert himself was conscientious enough, unless his literary activities be accounted as unwarrantable distractions. At any rate when it came to the point later, at Ellisland, he was practical enough to realise that he couldn't run two jobs successfully, and gave up the farm to become a full-time exciseman. Yet had he been willing to continue, the evidence would seem to suggest that he might have made a good job of it, perhaps even an outstanding success. He was accounted by his contemporaries as a keen exponent of the new farming. Gilbert and he were ambitious enough to try some flax growing at Lochlea, for which a prize of £3 was won. They were also at Lochlea experimenting with the growing of wheat and keeping of sheep. His views on the improvement of cattle were considered sufficiently meritorious for

Colonel Fullarton to mention in his Board of Agriculture Report of 1793: 'In order to prevent the danger arising from horned cattle in studs and straw yards, the best mode is to cut out the budding knob or root of the horn while the calf is very young. This was suggested to me by Mr. Robert Burns, whose general talents are no less conspicuous than the poetic powers which have done so much honour to the county where he was born.' This suggestion was not taken up till the 20th century, when it has become universally adopted. Then in the Statistical Account the parish minister of Dunscore authoritatively quotes 'Mr. Robert Burns, a gentleman well-known by his poetical productions, who rents a farm in this parish' as to the merits of the new Ayrshire dairy cattle. William Clark who worked for him at Ellisland 'thought he was as good a manager of land as the generality of the farmers in the neighbourhood'. That he should be nominated in 1789 as a candidate for the professorship of agriculture at Edinburgh University was not altogether as 'fantastic' as has been suggested.

The trouble with the Burns family was their lack of capital. They could not afford to stock and rent one of the best improved new farms and had to try their efforts in more modest and less advantageous circumstances. Ferguson and McLure had not the resources themselves to improve their farms, and Mossgiel was an outlying property of the Earl of Loudoun leased to Hamilton. None of these farms seems to have been enclosed, on the evidence that herd boys had to be employed at Lochlea and Mossgiel, while the family themselves performed this obsolescent task at Mount Oliphant. In acquiring farms the Burns family were extraordinarily fortunate – in having Ferguson as a patron to instal them at Mount Oliphant, in leasing Lochlea without a written tack, in getting Mossgiel presumably through Robert's masonic connections with Hamilton. And their landlords cannot be charged with rack-renting – Mount Oliphant at 67p to 75p, Lochlea at £1, and Mossgiel at 75p an acre were not exorbitant rents; at Lochlea, and perhaps Mount Oliphant, rather higher than the land justified, but a case could be made for landlords who were really subsidising indigent tenants, and were recouping themselves through the rent. Though well-placed in one respect, the Burns family were really contemplating something beyond their resources. With no funds to speak of, to avoid the dispersion of his family and satisfy what was almost a lust to be a farmer in his own right, William Burnes committed himself and his family to a burden of excessive toil and a starvation diet in what could hardly be otherwise than a hopeless attempt to make ends meet. At Mount Oliphant, Gilbert Burns remembered: 'To the buffetings of misfortune, we could only oppose hard labour and the most rigid economy. We lived very sparingly, and for several years butcher's meat was a stranger in the house; while all the members of the family exerted themselves to the utmost of their strength – and rather beyond it – in the labour of the farm. My brother, at the age of thirteen, assisted in the threshing of the crop of corn and at fifteen was the principal labourer on the farm – for we had no hired servants, male or female.' It is almost terrifying to read how the strictest economy was made more strict and, said Robert, 'we retrenched our expenses and lived very poorly.' There can be no doubt that the privations suffered at Mount Oliphant shortened the life of the father who bore the responsibilities, and of Robert the eldest son who shared so much of the heavy burden. And there was no future in it, for as the boys grew up they could not all be supported on the family farm and were without adequate savings to get farms of their own.

As a contrast to all this, later on Robert was much better placed when he took over Ellisland for himself in 1788. This farm also was unenclosed and unimproved, and in a poor state altogether, but for this farm of over 100 acres Patrick Miller granted him a long lease on generous terms. He would pay up to £300 to cover costs of building a farm house and enclosing the land, and would himself plant necessary shelter-belts. For the first six months Burns might sit rent-free; for three years thereafter there would be a modest yearly rent of £50 to pay; thereafter £70 annually till the end of 19 years; and could be renewed thereafter. A rent beginning at 50p and rising to 70p an acre was a bargain. And even after giving the Mossgiel folk £180 from his Edinburgh edition, Burns had £300 left. He did quite well. Despite the upkeep of a wife, weans, sister Agnes, cousin Fanny, menservants and a maid, and the entertaining of visitors and vagrants; despite literary and social distractions; despite the excise job which took up so much of his time; despite the typical farmer's grumbles at the state of the soil; despite all this the farm came along quite well. He built up a stock of nine or ten milk cows, some young cattle, four horses, and several 'pet sheep'; and discovered that by 1791 the land was yielding well. In that year he gave up the farm – but not because he had to. The standing crops were rouped in August, realising well over the average, and at the Martinmas sale in November the livestock and implements fetched equally satisfactory prices. One cow in calf went for nearly nineteen pounds, as compared with the usual price of seven to twelve pounds for an Ayrshire cow. Had the excise not proved more tempting, he might easily have continued at Ellisland and done well enough as a farmer.

The key to success as a tenant farmer in the later 18th century was the possession of sufficient funds to stock the farm with the improved cattle, purchase the better strains of improved seed that were coming on to the market, acquire up-to-date implements, purchase vast quantities of lime, and hire sufficient staff to bring the land into good heart; with a surplus laid by to cover a bad harvest or a temporary drop in grain prices. Such a man could be fairly confident of a steadily increasing yield from his farm and a rising income as the price of his produce slowly rose through the years. Those tenants who started off in difficulties had a limited scope for taking advantage of the opportunities and usually had to give up the struggle and join the ranks of hired labourers.

A subtle assessment of how well people in the middle ranks were doing can be guessed from their nomenclature as defined in kirk session and similar records. A landowner is always precisely defined as for example, Mr. David McLure *of* Shawwood; a tenant as William Burnes *in* Lochlea. But a tenant farmer who is accounted of rather superior status is sometimes awarded the honorific title of Mr. When Robert Burns first is named in Mauchline kirk session records, acknowledging paternity, on 18th June 1786 it is as 'Robert Burns in Mossgiel.' Two years later and a person of more than local repute, he had his irregular marriage to Jean Armour acknowledged on 5th August 1788, whereupon 'Mr. Burns gave a Guinea note for behoof of the poor.'

All Burns's friends and close acquaintances were drawn from the middle rank to which he himself belonged. Most of them were people who were doing quite well financially. There were tenant farmers like John Rankine in Adamhill, in whose home Burns first encountered a carpet; and George Reid in Barquharie who lent him a pony to go to Edinburgh. There were factors. John Tennant came from Laigh Corton near Alloway to Glenconner to manage the Countess of Glencairn's Ochiltree estate. John Arnot in Dalwhatswood was factor to the Earl of Loudoun, and John Kennedy was factor to the Earl of Dumfries. Bruce Campbell, factor for Cessnock and Grougar, acquired ownership of the small estates of Mayfield and Milrig for himself. Surgeons were also doing well. Dr. John Mackenzie of Mauchline acquired some properties in Mauchline and later in Irvine, and eventually retired to Edinburgh. Dr. Patrick Douglas owned not only Garrallan but also estates in Jamaica.

Lawyers at a time of extensive land transfer were kept busy and prosperous. Gavin Hamilton of Mauchline was well-enough-off to rent Mauchline Castle and other properties from the Earl of Loudoun, and to defy the kirk session; the 'poor man's friend', he assisted Burns who dedicated the Kilmarnock edition to him. Robert Aiken, solicitor and surveyor of taxes in Ayr, subscribed for 145 copies of the Kilmarnock edition; David McWhinnie, also from Ayr, took another twenty. John Richmond, son of a Mauchline merchant, became acquainted with Burns as clerk to Gavin Hamilton; in 1765 he went to Edinburgh, where Burns lodged with him for a spell; in 1789 Richmond returned to set up business in Mauchline.

Ministers were also well-off professional people. Rev. William Auld of Mauchline had in 1791 a stipend which amounted to about £100, composed of £39 cash, 91 bolls of oatmeal, 51 bolls of bear (coarse barley), plus a six-acre glebe. The glebe was farmland attached to the manse, and some ministers were noted agriculturalists. One such was Rev. George Lawrie of Loudoun, who sent a copy of the Kilmarnock edition to Edinburgh, entertained the poet at Loudoun manse in the autumn of 1786, and was instrumental in changing his plans for the future. Rev. Andrew Mitchell of Muirkirk and later Monkton had his own estate in Cumnock parish. Rev. John Steele of Stair married the heiress of Gadgirth and became a noted agricultural improver – early in his career reprimanded by the presbytery for visiting the theatre in Edinburgh, he died a respected 'father of the church' in 1804 at the age of 93.

Much less exalted, and with often a penurious existence, were the schoolmasters. The statutory minimum stipend of 100 merks was not augmented till 1803 and even with fees, perquisites, and augmentations sometimes granted, things were far from easy for the schoolmasters in an age of inflation. The Scottish average in the 1790s was assessed at a miserable £15 per year. Andrew Noble who was appointed to Mauchline school in 1763 at the age of seventeen (and continued over half a century till his death in 1821) was given more than the minimum, which with supplements gave him an estimated £30 a year.

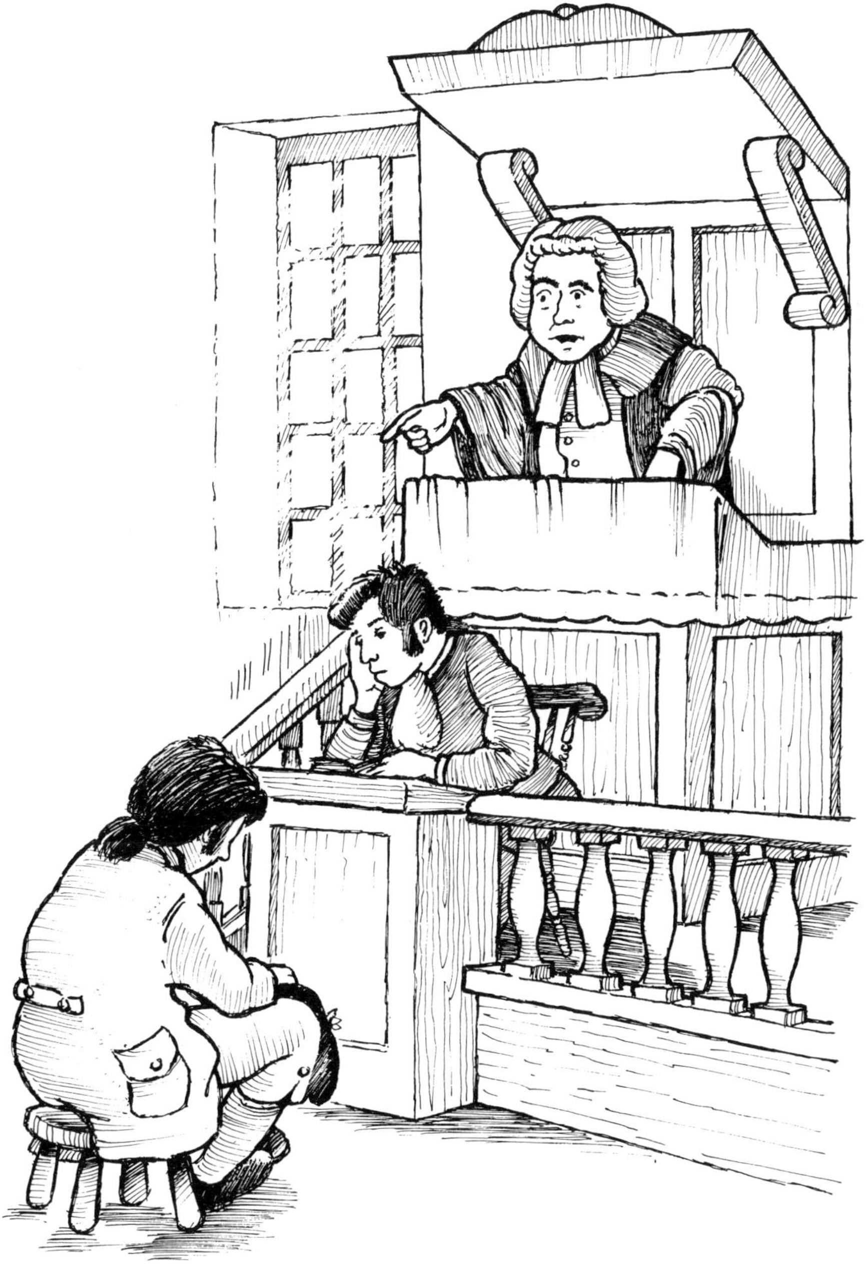

*Public pennance in the Kirk*

He was certainly among the half-dozen best-paid Ayrshire dominies. When Ayr Grammar School was in 1798 converted into an Academy the rector was granted a salary of £100. John Wilson in Tarbolton eked out his income by keeping a grocer's shop and acting as an apothecary – 'Dr. Hornbook'. David Sillar, a contemporary of Burns in Tarbolton, taught there and elsewhere, became a grocer in Irvine, went bankrupt and returned to teaching; then fortunately inherited money. John Murdoch, hired in 1765 as a young man of eighteen to teach the children at Alloway, got a post in Dumfries, then at Ayr Grammar School, but 'overtaken in liquor' was dismissed and went off to London. It was a career with few prospects – the rare hope was that a young graduate might be presented by a patron to a charge as parish minister. And even the distinction that graduates had of being addressed as 'Mr' was no longer reserved for them alone.

Merchants and master craftsmen had the opportunity to do well for themselves in the expanding economy. Luck and acumen could bring them in well over £100 a year; more than that and they were investing in land and setting themselves up as gentry. Burns struck up a close association with some of the businessmen of Kilmarnock. With John Wilson, bookseller and printer, it was a strictly business relationship. More cordial were his friendships with Thomas Samson, nurseryman and seedsman; Robert Muir, wine merchant, who subscribed for 72 copies of the Kilmarnock edition and 40 of the Edinburgh edition; and John Goudie, cabinet-maker then wine merchant, speculator, mathematician and theologian. In the town of Mauchline in 1791 there were 10 merchants, 20 weavers, 20 masons, 12 wrights (carpenters), 12 shoemakers, 10 tailors, and several other craftsmen. Some of these must have been quite well-off, including James Armour, a mason whose family firm is reputed to have helped in the building of Dumfries House, Howford bridge, and other works as far afield as Dalmellington. An impoverished tenant farmer was not really a good match for his daughter Jean. Some of the craftsmen, like 'Clockie' John Brown, the clockmaker, must have been much less wealthy. Lesser business folk were of limited means – innkeepers like John Dow and George Gibson, millers like William Muir. A general assessment might be – well-off at £100 a year; doing well at £70; comfortable at £50.

One new career with prospects was that of exciseman. After the Act of Union a joint system of customs and excise had to be devised. Smuggling along the coasts was widespread. The introduction of new levies like the Malt Tax of 1724 created an administrative problem for inland areas as well. It was only after William Pitt became prime minister in 1783 that a concerted effort was made to reform and organise the system of collection and police.

Landings of excisable goods were made all along the Ayrshire coast. John Galt in *The Annals of the Parish* recorded it under the year 1761: 'It was in this year that the great smuggling trade corrupted all the west coast, especially the laigh lands about the Troon and the Loans. The tea was going like chaff, the brandy like well-water, and the wastrie of all things was terrible. There was nothing minded but the riding of cadgers by day, and excisemen by night – and battles between the smugglers and the king's men, both by sea and land. There was a continual drunkenness and debauchery; and our session, that was but on the lip of this whirlpool of iniquity, had an awful time o't. I did all that was in the power of nature to keep my people from the contagion: I preached sixteen times from the text, 'Render to Caesar the things that are Caesar's.' In 1775 young Robert Burns spent three months staying with his uncle Samuel Brown at Kirkoswald, attending Hugh Rodger's school. 'I spent my seventeenth summer on a smuggling coast, at a noted school, to learn mensuration, surveying, dialling, &c., in which I made pretty good progress . . . The contraband trade was at this time very successful, and it sometimes happened to me to fall in with those who carried it on. Scenes of swaggering riot and roaring dissipation were, till this time, quite new to me; but I was no enemy to social life...' In fact, when the British government in 1765 took over the government and sovereignty of the Isle of Man that marked the beginnings of a decline in the coastal smuggling. Inland, the Malt Tax imposing a levy of threepence per bushel meant that 'twopenny' could no longer be sold at twopence per Scots pint (which was equal to half an English gallon) and the brewing of ale diminished. To enforce the regulations gaugers were appointed for 'searching auld wives' barrels' and 'grinding the faces of the publican and the sinner on the merciless wheel of the excise.'

There is evidence that in 1786 Burns was exploring the possibility of an excise appointment through some of his Ayrshire friends. After his visit to Edinburgh he was able to solicit directly the help of Robert Graham of Fintry, one of the Commissioners of Excise; concurrently with his negotiations with Patrick Miller of Dalswinton for the tenancy of Ellisland farm. In March 1788 he completed his arrangements with

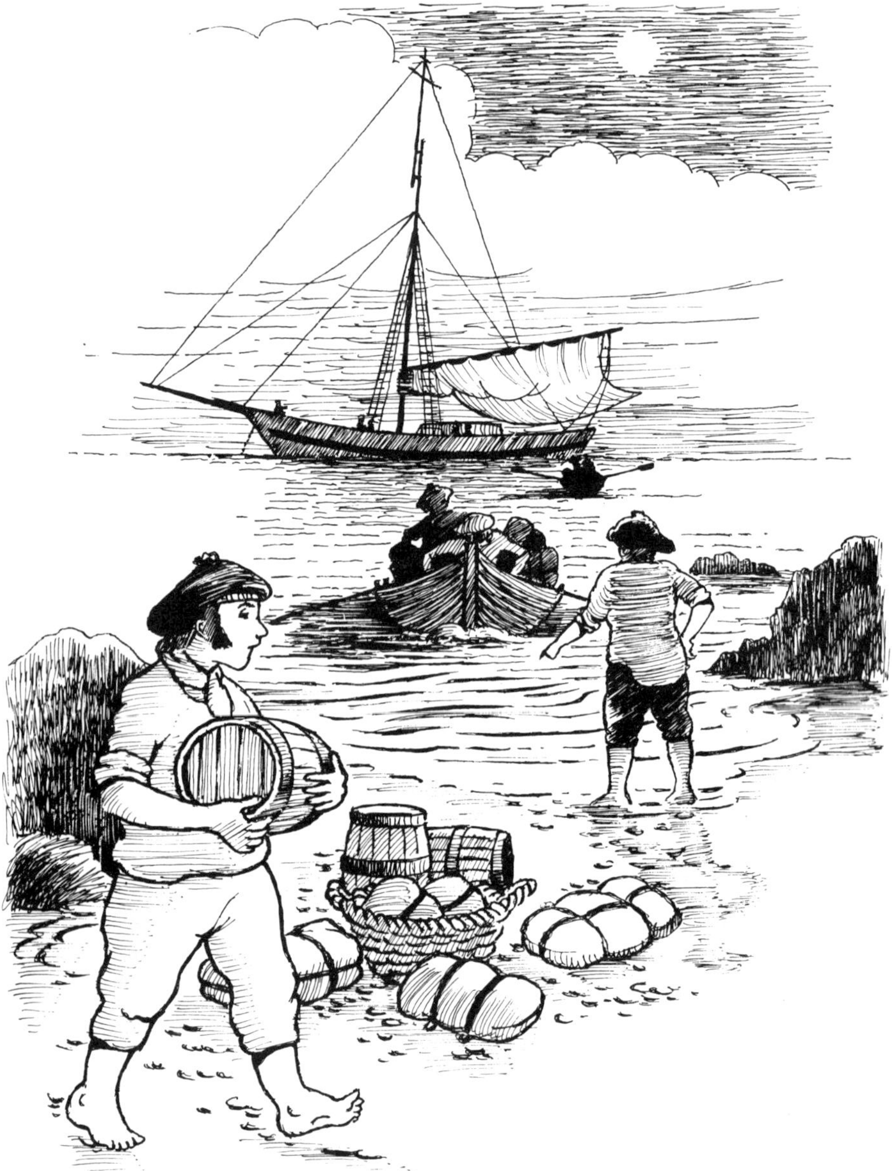

Miller; in the same month the Excise Board issued an order for instruction, requiring him to take six weeks' training in gauging and book-keeping, which he did with James Findlay, at Tarbolton. He entered Ellisland at Whitsun; a month later his commission as an exciseman was issued. He was not yet allocated to any post, but the officer for the district in which Ellisland was situated was transferred to another position, to leave it open for Burns, who commenced duty in October 1789. Clearly his interests were being well served by Graham's patronage. This initial post in the Dumfries First Itinerary involved some two hundred miles on circuit each week, at a remuneration of £50 per annum, plus a proportion of fines. Within two years, he was promoted in December 1791 to the Dumfries Third Division and moved from Ellisland into town, now earning £70 per annum plus the probability of another twenty or thirty pounds in fines. Just a year later he was transferred to the Dumfries First (Port) Division, the best assignment in the area because of its prize-money from confiscated contraband. His income was now in the three-figure range. His work was proving satisfactory; complaints about subversive political opinions were set aside; in December 1794 when his superior officer, Alexander Findlater, fell ill, it was Burns who served as Acting Supervisor of Customs for Dumfries for the four-month period. Had he lived longer, he would through seniority have reached a Supervisor's post by 1797, with a basic £90 and supplements bringing it up to near £200 per year. He could have become a Collector (basic salary £120), then an Assistant Commissioner (basic £200). That other famous Scot, Adam Smith, author of *The Wealth of Nations*, had in fact been a Commissioner of Excise from 1778 till 1790 at a salary of £800.

CHAPTER 5

# THE LOWER ORDERS

The lower orders were subordinate. They were socially inferior to people of the middle rank.

*The rank is but the guinea's stamp . . .*
*A man's a man for a' that.* CW 535

A noble sentiment, but poets (like other people) do not always practise what they preach. Burns may sometimes mention them, but his contacts were limited and he never numbered among his associates humbler folk such as cotters or colliers.

'The Cotter's Saturday Night' is an idealised picture based more on sentiment than on fact. A cotter – otherwise cottager or coteman – was a minor tenant or sub-tenant who paid his rent in labour; from another point of view he could be described as a labourer, usually married, who received in lieu of wages a house and yard, grazing for a cow, an acre of so of land, and perhaps some meal and fuel – this 'benefit' amounting in all to less than £15 in value per annum. In fact, only in Carrick did cotters survive in any numbers till the end of the 18th century. Throughout most of the country they were a disappearing breed. The cot-houses, often a single apartment attached to the end of a farmhouse were described as 'wretched... about 12 or 13 feet square, the floor damp, had neither partitions, inner doors, nor smoke funnels... generally inhabited by people in extreme indigence.' Burns rightly wondered:

*An what poor cot-folk pit their painch in,*
*I own it's past my comprehension.* CW 141

On an improved farm, unmarried farm workers were more economic to employ. As Aiton reported: 'The strong hardy race . . . not meeting with due encouragement in the country, and tempted with higher

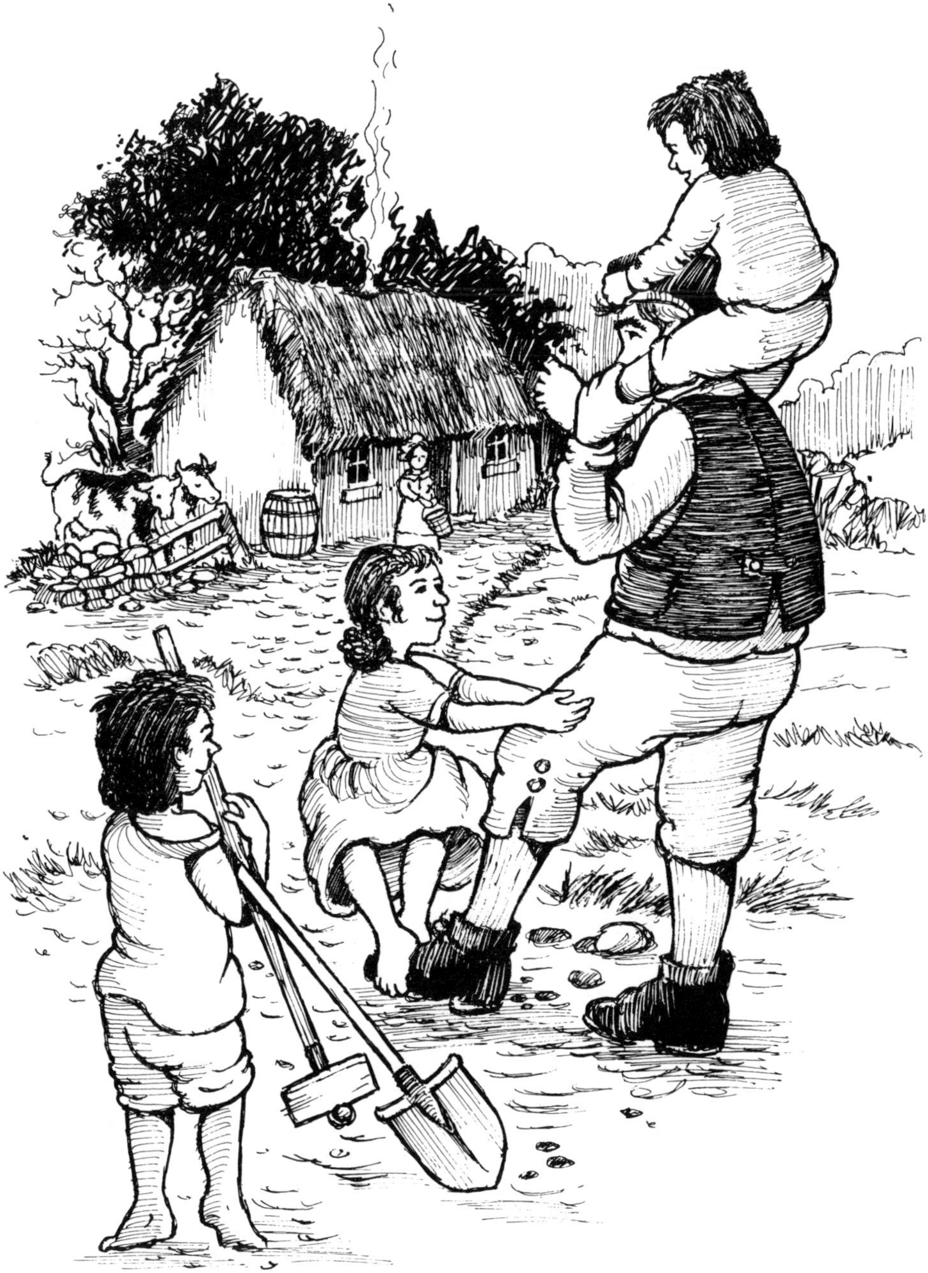

*The cotter comes home*

wages from the cotton or other manufactories, have deserted their rural habitations, and frugal and virtuous habits, and have taken up their abodes in towns.'

For those wishing to remain on the land, there was a positive disincentive to marriage, for so great was the demand for labour on the improved farms that wages for hired hands were easily keeping pace with inflation. Work was certainly hard. Day labourers and those employed at jobbing work worked a ten hour day, from six till six, with an hour off for breakfast and another for dinner. Servants hired by the half-year had no fixed hours, and might work even longer hours overall but they had the perquisite of free bed and board, which was a valuable portion of their income. A good ploughman's annual wage rose between 1760 and 1800 from £5 to £18, plus bed and board; and inferior ploughman from £3 to £12. Best dairy or servant maids rose similarly from £2 to £6, others from £1.60 to £4. Herds, who were needed till the hedges on the improved farms rendered them unnecessary, could get £1.20 rising to £3. Common labourers, employed by the day without food - less than 4p per day in 1760, 7p in 1800, for men; 2½p rising to 5p for women–could rise to £25 or £15 respectively, though only if working regularly throughout the year, which was not always possible. Skilled workers, like mowers, thatchers, carpenters, shoemakers, and tailors who went round the farms plying their trades for the farmers or their families, were paid on a day-rate just a little less than labourers, but they were provided with their food.

Opportunities were better in the towns and villages of course. Skilled craftsmen were earning from £15 to £30 a year and keeping pace with the rising cost of living. Journeymen masons, shoemakers and weavers with ambition could set themselves up as their own masters and might then do even better. Those who forsook the customary weaving or otherwise became involved with cotton from about 1785 onwards had good prospects. Cotton handloom weavers could expect from £30 to £35 a year; their numbers multiplied rapidly; and despite times when trade was slack, they would by the early 19th century become the aristocrats of the labour force. Until the end of the 18th century there were only a few factory workers - 'manufacturers' as they were entitled. But at a place like Catrine Cotton Works there was a wide range of occupations. In 1796 the twist mill employed over 400, carding, roving, spinning, including some picking cotton in their own homes, plus overseer, clerks, smiths, mill-wrights, and other mechanics. The jeanie factory employed another 200 in similar jobs. Children were employed from the age of nine. There was an undoubted attraction in a place where several members of the family could find employment and there was scope for developing skills – and at Catrine the comfort of a new house and a benevolent employer. Fullarton complained that 'the demand for cotton workers was so great that farmers could hardly engage men or women servants to remain at country work.' He reported that a good worker in one of the cotton houses could earn from 10p to 15p daily; women from 5p to 10p daily; and children from 7p to 15p weekly. The wage bill for Catrine in 1796 suggests that these figures were (perhaps temporarily) inflated. It might be a fair guess to suggest an average adult could earn somewhere around £30 a year, with more when trade was brisk.

The Colliers formed another group which was growing in numbers in the 18th century. There was a tradition of social inferiority attached to this occupation. Colliers and salters had, in previous generations, been recruited from the ranks of vagrants and criminals who were bound to the mines. They and their families were legally serfs. An Act of 1774 made provision for their emancipation and another in 1799 made them finally free. In fact, as the minister of Stevenston reported in 1791: 'Long before the late act of Parliament, the coal-hewers and their children in this district, were set free from their ancient servitude by a voluntary deed of their master; and this much more effectually than that act of Parliament did. They are here quite on the same footing with all other workmen.' Indeed, with the rapid expansion of mining and the demand for experienced men, wages rose till they were the equal of skilled craftsmen. In Stevenston in 1791 they earned from 12p to 15p a day and worked a five-day week. In Sorn they could earn up to 12p a day. In the Stevenston area when things were booming, a miner might earn £35 a year, or more towards the end of the century. But, said the parish minister: 'The high wages of the miners, earned by disagreeable and severe labour, are too often immediately dissipated; little laid up for the maintenance of their families, whose education is too much neglected.' While some miners were doing relatively well, and there were opportunities for promotion to overseeing jobs at the larger collieries, wages of the salters were consistently lower than those of the coal miners with whom they were associated. In 1800, colliers at Stevenston were earning over £1 for a six-day week; blowermen at the saltworks were getting only 30p; saltwork grieves, only £1.

All along the Ayrshire coast were small communities of fishermen who eked out a bare existence. Early in the 18th century they had been kept busy with the herring fishing. In West Kilbride parish there were then over thirty herring boats ('busses') and about 150 men involved. But by the 1770s the herring shoals had gone, and fishing virtually came to an end in the West Kilbride, Ardrossan, Irvine area. White fish became the main catch. Largs was kept busy supplying Paisley; Ayr and Newton supplied Kilmarnock, Irvine, and Glasgow. But along the Carrick coast there was only the local supply to the countryfolk; though here especially fishing could be for a time profitably combined with the 'free trade' of smuggling. How prices varied can be gauged by the example of salmon, which fetched only ½p a pound at Ballantrae while at Ayr the price rose to 1p or more. While herring and white fish were caught by the fishermen and sold by their wives, the salmon fishery on the Doon was owned by the Earl of Cassillis and at the mouth of the Ayr had been purchased by a combine of lawyers. Only a score were employed, with 3 boats ('cobles') on the Ayr and 4 on the Doon.

There was room for surplus fishermen and sailors in the navy, and for footloose landsmen in the army. The 18th century was an era of wars. When Burns was born at Alloway the Seven Years War had four more years to run. The American War of Independence lasted the eight years of his residence at Lochlea. And he died, as he was born, in wartime, in the third year of the French Revolutionary War. A short life of 37 years, 15 of them with Britain at war. John Galt in *The Annals of the Parish* notices the visit of recruiting parties, and in *The Provost* tells how Irvine suffered 'the pressgang, headed by their officers, with cutlasses by their side, and great club-sticks in their hands.' With their miserable pay and hard life, soldiers and navymen were held in low esteem.

Lowest on the social scale were the paupers and vagrants. Persons who by reason of age or infirmity were unable to maintain themselves and were without relatives to come to their aid were cared for by the kirk session of their native parish. In Mauchline in 1771 there were 21 on the roll. Some were casual poor like 'Bastard Child the father unknown' or 'able to work but has three small children' and these were awarded what was regarded as appropriate relief in money and kind. Three were quite unable to work or provide for themselves and were granted 7/6d a month (37½p), giving a maximum of £4.50 a year, which may be regarded as the basic subsistence for that period. Other parishes, particularly in south Ayrshire, could not afford even this and had to authorise begging. In north Ayrshire, Stewarton kirk session in 1788 'ordered the Kirk Treasurer to get Twenty Four Badges of Hard Tin made bearing the name of the Parish and all regularly numbered That the Poor of the Parish who are allowed to beg may be supplied with one each. And the Meeting further ordered the Kirk Treasurer to pay out of the Parish funds any sum not exceeding one shilling Sterling to the Person who shall take up a Vagrant and Lodge such vagrant in safe custody.' The following year one person applied for a badge and also 'two silly creatures.'

While the kirk sessions struggled to support the deserving poor, they found it impossible to cope with the vagrant poor. Aiton in 1811 had to report: 'Begging from door to door is still practised all over the county of Ayr. The streets of the towns and villages, and public and private roads, in all parts of Ayrshire, are occasionally infested with vagrant beggars, and sometimes with tinkers and gypsies, who sorn and thieve, and pilfer and extort alms, from the weak and timid, to the disgrace of the police, the terror of the inhabitants, and discredit of humanity. In several of the towns and villages, houses are open at all times, for the reception of these vagrant beggars, where these depraved and wretched creatures spend their sinister gettings in the grossest riot and debauch. In the day time, they prowl through the towns, or roam in the country, begging, stealing, or swindling, as opportunity may offer. At night, they return to their miserable haunts to consume their spoils, in feasting, drinking, swearing, and carousing at the expense of the simple, whom they have duped, or the timid whom they have terrified; and insulting and disturbing the virtuous inhabitants.' In what was primarily a *View of the Agriculture of the County of Ayr*, Aiton made one of his numerous digressions and on this occasion was impelled to quote – as an extended footnote – the whole of Burns' poem, 'The Jolly Beggars' which he praises as 'a just and well drawn picture of the subject.' The 'gangrel bodies' who assembled in Poosie Nansie's howff in Mauchline were typical. There was the old soldier who 'must beg, with a wooden arm and leg'; the 'martial chuck' who was a camp whore reduced to beggary; a 'raucle carlin' who subsisted by picking pockets, 'for mony a pursie she had hooked'; a 'pigmy scraper' who played his fiddle at weddings and fairs; and 'a sturdy caird' who was a wandering tinker. It may seem odd that Burns who has in general so little to remark about those below him on the social scale should

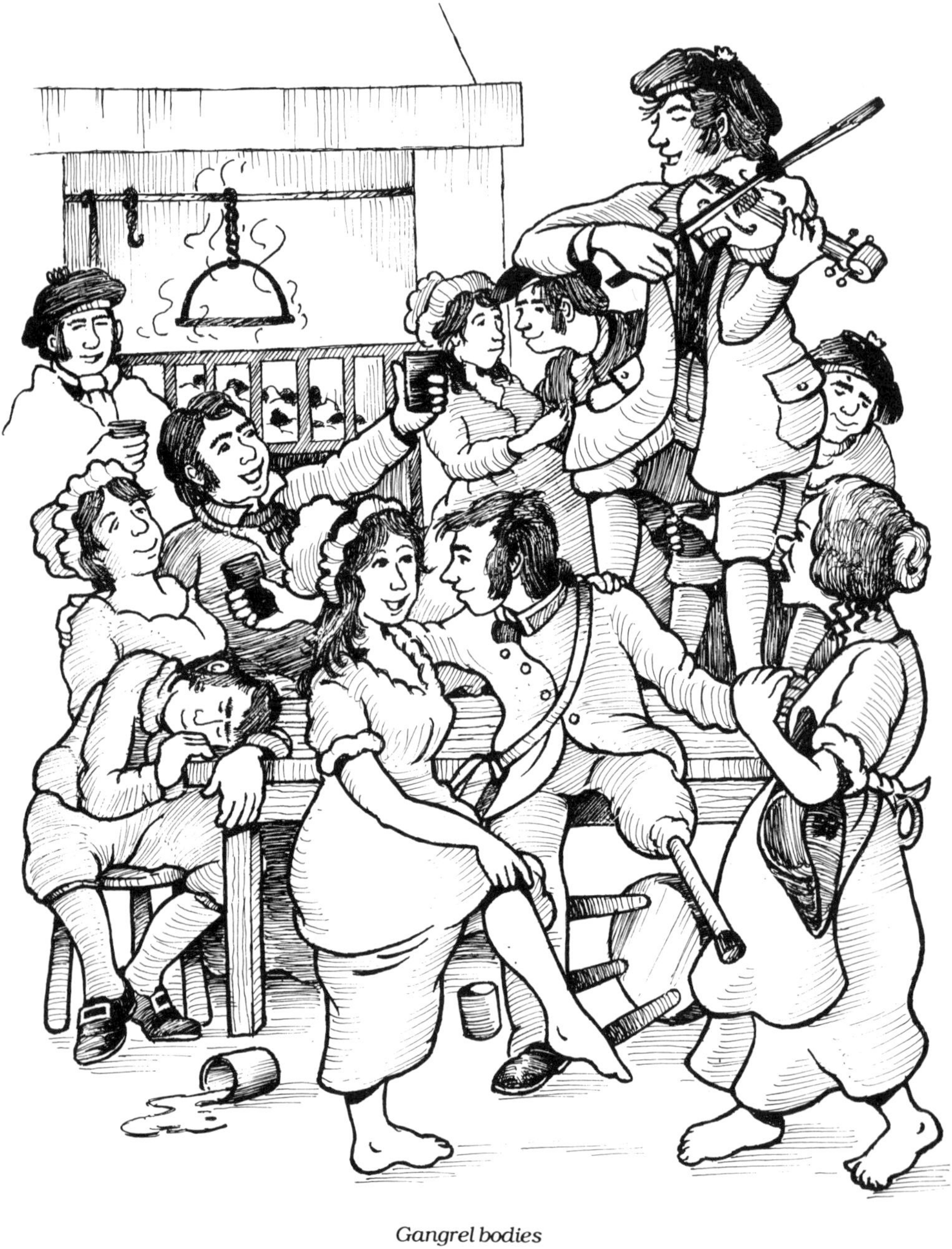

*Gangrel bodies*

choose to devote his muse to these, the lowest of the low. But he entitled his poem 'Love and Liberty' as a romantic disquisition on philosophic anarchism. He was advised against publishing it; later he apologetically wrote, 'I have forgot the Cantata you allude to, as I kept no copy'; and I appeared only posthumously, with the original manuscript passing to the Azores and returning via Nova Scotia and Ireland.

The lower orders must have suffered the most severely from the social dislocations which were inevitable in a period of increasing labour mobility. This mobility was both involuntary and voluntary: some persons were finding it difficult to survive in their old occupations and were forced to move; others were attracted to new occupations which were offering better prospects. Even within the same trades, there were local differences which must have stimulated movement. Farm servants who could only get from £6 to £7 a year in parishes like Dalrymple would be tempted to go elsewhere, when in Sorn the rates were from £10 to £12. Wherever manufacturing was expanding and there was a demand for labour, wages generally went up in that area. Thus areas like Ayr, Stevenston, Kilmarnock, and even Catrine and Muirkirk exercised a strong pull on all types of labour. Those areas which remained purely rural, and where demands for farm labour were declining due to elimination of small holdings, suffered depopulation. Though Webster's parish population figures for 1755 are in some respects suspect, and those in the Statistical Account of the 1790s are themselves approximations, there is no reason to doubt the decline in numbers in some 15 of the 45 Ayrshire parishes over this period. Even in the other parishes it seems likely that there was a drift from rural into village or town occupations.

In mid-century 75% of the population lived in the countryside. By the 1790s the increased population was swollen by natural growth and some immigration from Ireland and the Highlands, and most of them were now working and living in towns and villages.

CHAPTER 6

# AGRICULTURE

The agricultural revolution of the late 18th century transformed what was a basically-subsistence economy into modern commercial farming. It was, said the blind minister of Kirkoswald, 'a total and happy revolution.' So satisfactory was the progress that commentators at the end of the century could find little to commend in what had been superseded, and Colonel Fullarton in his *View of Agriculture* in 1793 was particularly critical about what he called the 'antient system.'

Yet the old forms of farming had maintained the population for countless generations since the Scottish lowlands were first settled. Like all primitive economies, it had its temporary difficulties. As Fullarton noted: 'The people having hardly any substitute for oatmeal were entirely at the mercy of the season. If the seedtime were unfavourable, the summer bad, or the autumn late or stormy, a dearth or famine unavoidably ensued. The price of meal fluctuated, therefore, between extremes, which are never known in countries better cultivated; or where the means of subsistence are so varied, as to render the failure of one species suppliable by some other. At the beginning of this century, and the end of the last, there was a succession of bad seasons which lasted several years, and reduced the county of Ayr and other provinces adjacent to the lowest gradation of want; obliging hundreds of families to fly for subsistence to the north of Ireland, where their descendants still remain.'

The unit of farming was not the modern isolated farm, but the 'toun' – a cluster of several cottages, each the home of a family, and the several families had originally combined in the cooperative cultivation of the adjacent land. Beside each cottage was a small patch of ground enclosed by a dry-stane dyke – the kailyard or vegetable garden. The best land, often nearby, formed the croft or infield, open and unenclosed. This had originally been held in runrig by the several tenants, each having several of the riggs or strips into which the field was divided. By the 18th century each had his own recognised riggs, though they might well cooperate in ploughing; and the infield received all the dung from the middens and was cropped year in, year out, with seldom any intermission. The poorer land formed the outfield, also unenclosed. The only manure the outfield received was the droppings of cattle which might be folded there after the harvest. Patches were cultivated till exhaustion, then left fallow to recover. In the better lowland areas, the ferm-touns were close together and much of the land under cultivation. Over the rest of the country most of the land between the ferm-touns was rough pasture for the lean black cattle, the sheep and the fowls, which wandered about in the care of herds, or tethered, to keep them from straying onto the unenclosed arable patches.

The farms produced oats as the main crop, supplemented by 'bigg' (a coarse barley) and peas, and sometimes some hay from a natural meadow. The pressure of a growing population resulted in overcropping, producing the deficiencies which were remembered by Fullarton and his contemporaries.

'The land over-run with weeds and rushes, gathered into very high, broad, serpentine ridges, interrupted with large baulks . . . The little soil there was, collected on the top of the ridge, and the furrow drowned with water. No fallows, no green crops, no sown grass, no carts or waggons, no straw yards; hardly a potato, or any other esculent root, and, indeed, no garden vegetables; unless a few Scotch kail, which, with milk and oatmeal, formed the diet of the people; with little straw, and no hay, except a scanty portion of the coarsest quality collected from the bogs. The quantity of dung produced was of small avail; and that portion, little as it was, the farmers dragged on cars or sledges, or on what were called tumbler-wheels, which turned with the axletree, and supported the wretched vehicle, hardly able to draw 5 cwt. The ground was scourged with a succession of oats after oats, so long as they would pay for seed and labour, and afford a small surplus for the family; and then remained in a state of absolute sterility, or over-run with thistles, till rest enabled it again to reproduce a scanty crop.'

So wrote Fullarton, and the minister of Kilwinning repeated the complaints. 'In the year 1742 . . . the parish was then wholly uninclosed, excepting an inclosure or two about Eglintoune Castle. The farmers plowed with four, and sometimes six horses, and three men. The business of the third man, it was pretended, would keep the plough steady, and prevent its starting aside, or going out of the straight line. The ridges were excessively broad, and raised very high in the middle. Nearly two-thirds of every ridge were left, in a great measure, without any of the soil, and even the very little that remained being, during the winter, almost covered with water, was soured, and consequently in a state that produced very little, either of grass or grain.'

The various innovations in husbandry before the 18th century were piecemeal, limited in scope, and in many respects superficial. But in the 18th century, slowly at first but with increasing momentum, the great landlords, followed by the lesser gentry, were stimulated to extensive and far-reaching improvements on their estates. There were several contributing factors. The landlords were no longer content to subsist on the traditional meagre rents in meal, labour, and fixed money dues in a period of inflation. The expansion of the traditional Scottish manufactures of linen, woollens, and leather goods meant good money could be made supplying more of their raw materials from the farms, and increasingly also supplying foodstuffs for the growing numbers of manufacturers. And the successes of improving landlords in England and the Lothians were models to be followed. Commercial

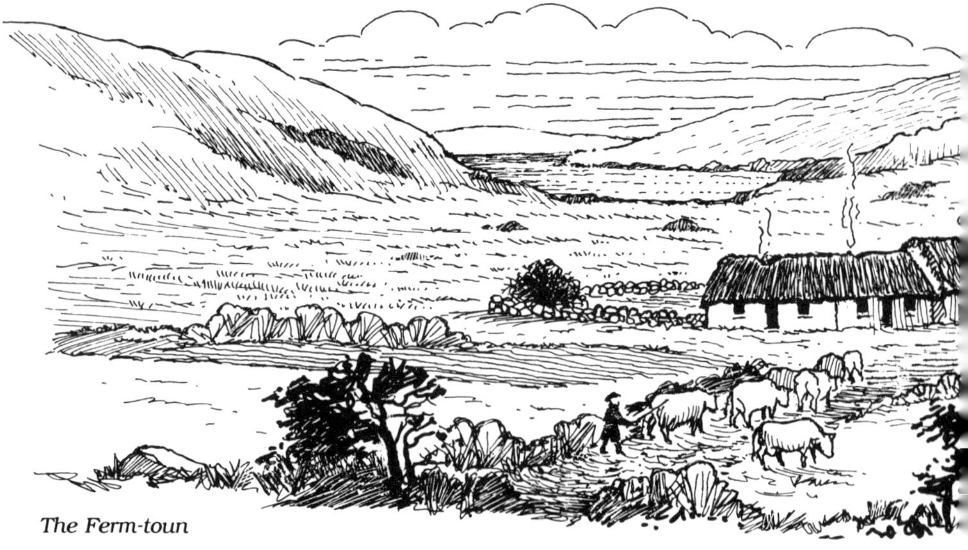

*The Ferm-toun*

farming had become a profitable and practicable proposition.

Alexander, 10th Earl of Eglinton, succeeded to that title in 1729 at the age of six. About mid-century, while in his twenties, he began at Eglinton in Kilwinning parish those schemes of agrarian improvement which earned him Fullarton's description as 'the reviver of agriculture in Ayrshire.' Though young and inexperienced, with no proven examples to follow, he started off with several advantages. His father had cleared the estate of a load of debt; the Eglinton policies included over 3,000 acres of the most fertile soil in the district; and £7,800 compensation paid for the abolition of heritable jurisdictions in 1747 provided ready capital. The Earl had the opportunity to study improved farming techniques in England, the resources to hire experts, and the enthusiasm to plan and superintend personally the work of improvement. John Service, a local historian of a later date, dramatised the transformation scene:

'I have lang been of the notion and the idee that not only Eglintoun but also the haill boun's of Ayrshire and the Gallowa's are muckle in Earl Sanners' debt. Before he cam hame the kintra side was in a very wild and unsettled condition. He found it a moss and a wilderness and he left it smiling and blooming like a rose . . . Coming hame aboot the '48, he brocht wi' him, frae various pairts of England and the Lothians,

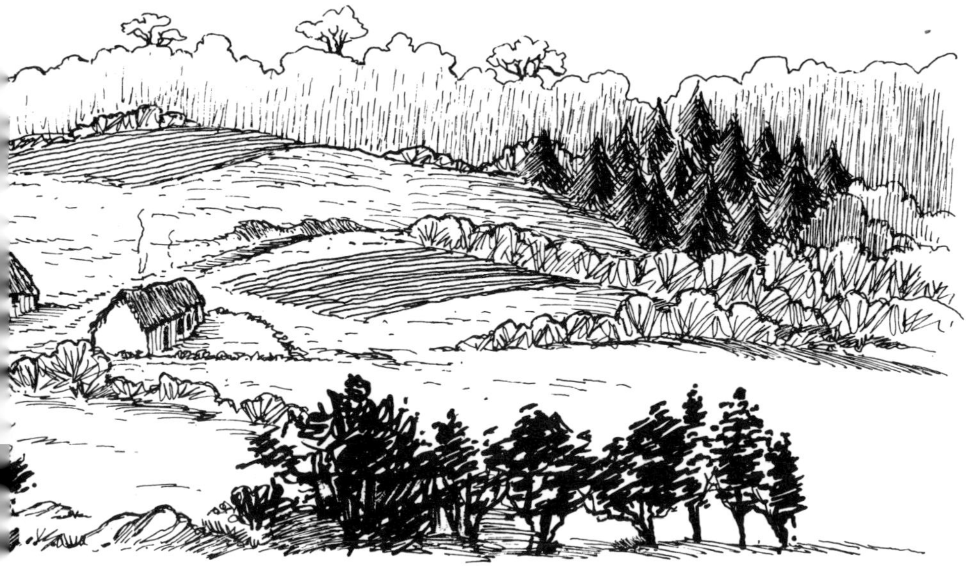

ploughmen and folk who kent a' aboot the dairy and drilling and fallowing, the setting o neeps and the rotation o' the craps. And, like the wee Pecks, they fell to their wark and wrocht ferlies in a blink. A great deal was dune, too, in the way o' mending the breed of horses and kye, till noo an Ayrshire is far kent and noted as baith the bonniest coo and the best o' milkers. Nor was it lang till the vera face o' the kintra, runkled and soor-leukin' as the auld maid's lang negleckit, put on the rosy bloom and happy smile of the expectant wife. Miles of fences were made and the bare parks and hill-sides were baith sheltered and adorned by a cleiding of m'unts and belts of trees; thorn dykes were set, and mony a sweet-smelling flower and southern bush made the dark woods of Eglintoun look gay. The Earl was here, there and everywhere on his farms, arranging the marches and the dykes, breaking up auld muirland grun', or laying aff the roads and plantin's, and opening up stane quarries, or felling here and there a tree that hid some noble view. And not only was he of this eydent, throughal turn, but he was affable and condescending to a degree. He would crack to the cottars and the farmers aboot their weans or their craps as if he were ane o' themsel's, and he gaed oot and in amang them, clippin' his beard a' the time wi' a wee pair o' shears, or roosin; here a chicken-cavie or there a braw wee lassock's cheeks, till he was the idol and delight of a' the mithers o' the kintra-side.'

About the same time and not very far away, similar renovations were being carried out by John, 4th Earl of Loudoun. He succeeded in 1731, aged 26, and followed a military career, serving against the Jacobites, and later holding commands in America and Portugal. Yet even when abroad he was frequently sending home specimens of trees to grace the plantations he had established around the castle, which in a generation's time moved Robert Tannahill to praise as 'Loudoun's bonnie wood and braes.' With his retirement from active service in 1763 the Earl was able to devote closer attention to his 10,000 acre estate, mainly in Loudoun parish, but extending into Kyle (and including Mauchline Castle and Mossgiel farm). Aiton remembered how 'His Lordship frequently collected his tenants together at Loudoun Castle, conversed with them on rural affairs, set his own lands, laid off roads, and attended to every improvement.' The minister of Loudoun in the Statistical Account commended his patron: 'He had both a great taste and great quickness of parts. He prudently began with making roads through the parish as early as the year 1733; and an excellent bridge was, by his influence, built over Irvine water; and the road from thence, and from his house to Newmilns, was the first made road in the shire of Ayr, which was done by the statute work . . . At the same time Earl John began to plant and inclose; he is said to have planted above one million of trees . . . They were all planted from the year 1733, progressively to the year 1775. The number of farms planted and inclosed are about fifty, inclosed and sub-divided into small farms, from 20 to 30 acres each; in all about 6,000 acres. Add to this about 1,570 acres; the whole of which is inclosed, and amounts to 7,570 acres, including 95 acres of natural wood, and 250 acres of planted ground. About 1,000 acres in sheep farms are not yet inclosed . . . The late John, Earl of Loudoun . . . deserves the name of the father of agriculture in this part of the shire'.

The two earls were members of the Society of Improvers in the Knowledge of Agriculture in Scotland which had been formed in 1725 and which was succeeded in 1784 with what became the Royal Highland and Agricultural Society. Locally in Ayrshire, the Earl of Eglinton formed about mid-century a Society for improving of agriculture and manufactures in the Shire of Ayr. A Kilmarnock Agricultural Society was instituted in 1786, a Carrick Farmers' Society in 1797, and parish associations were also formed. Tarbolton in the 1790s had a Farmer Club (for agricultural improvement) and a Farmer Society (for charitable self-help). This is a measure of the keen interest in and enthusiasm for agricultural improvement which, after the pioneering work of the two Earls, became widespread in north Ayrshire from the 1770s and spread to central and south Ayrshire generally in the 1780s.

In north Ayrshire, in the vicinity of the Irvine water, large-scale renovations were made by lairds like William Fullarton who succeeded to the estate of Fullarton in Dundonald parish in 1759 at the age of five. Though becoming a soldier and politician he found time to extend improvements his father had initiated and to write a *General View of the Agriculture of the County of Ayr* which has been quoted so extensively in this chapter.

A neighbour of Fullarton's and a distant connection by marriage was Alexander Fairlie of Fairlie House. Burns's father had worked on this estate when first he came to Ayrshire before moving to Alloway. Burns himself stayed briefly on it, with a half-sister of his mother's called Jean Allan, at Old Rome, in 1786, to escape the warrant for his arrest put out by Jean Armour's father. Fairlie himself took four copies of Burns' Edinburgh edition. Among his estate workers was one Josey Smith, a ditcher who was fond both of versifying and whisky drinking. 'Go and sing ballads and by damned to you,' Fairlie told him. Josey obliged with the first part of his request and composed a song about his master:

*On the green banks of Irvine lives Fairlie of Fairlie,*
*Who oft speaks of good things, and does them but rarely.*
*Lord Eglinton's tenants they walk very barely,*
*Being robbed of their riches by Fairlie of Fairlie.*
*It's in the low regions, oh! how he will fret,*
*When there is no farming or farms for to set.*
*The devil and him they will scold it right sairly,*
*And Hell will resound with the shrieks of auld Fairlie.*

Managing not only his own estate, he acted after 1769 as factor for Earl Archibald, and on the Eglinton estates he found full scope for his ideas. 'Persevering with uncommon firmness in combating the prejudices of old tenants, dividing the lands and making restrictions suitable to the soil and situation, he has rendered the farmers, in general, more wealthy and respectable, and the lands more valuable.' Aiton recalled hearing him criticising a tenant for over-ploughing. The farmer insisted on blaming the weather for the failurc of the crop. Mr. Fairlie, provoked by his obstinacy, after hastily taking a pinch of snuff, replied with some warmth, 'If you will only comply to my improved plan of plowing one-fourth of your farm, you will have the *best* of crops *in spite of a season.*'

From the banks of the Irvine water the examples set by these improving lairds spread north to other parts of Cuninghame, and southwards throughout Kyle. In remote Carrick, Sir Thomas Kennedy, afterwards 9th Earl of Cassillis, 'took the lead in this improved mode of agriculture'.

The improvements involved new approaches to treatment of the soil, crops, implements, stock and farm management.

As land is the basis of farming, a good deal of attention had to be devoted to the soil and its welfare. The old hump-backed riggs were flattened and the land renovated by fallowing, reploughing, trenching, liming and manuring. The old distinction between infield and outfield was abandoned and areas of what had been moss or rough pasture were reclaimed. To counteract the acidity of the Ayrshire soils, lime had been used in the 17th century if not before, but now it became the 'staple manure'. Various drainage schemes were devised but none was particularly effective till tile-draining was introduced by the Duke of Portland on his Ayrshire estates after 1825. Proper rotations were introduced on the improved fields, to make best use of the land and prevent overcropping, which was a constant temptation to the less far-sighted farmers. The most popular course was one introduced at Eglinton, developed by Fairlie of Fairlie, and spread through the county as the Fairlie Rotation. The sequence of crops was as follows: (1) Oats; (2) Oats, or latterly a root or green crop; (3) Oats or barley; (4) Hay; (5)–(9) Pasture. The Fairlie Rotation became something of a fetish, but in the first stages of improving the land it proved sound policy for the landlord to insist that only a third of the land should be in tillage any one year.

As far as the actual crops were concerned, oats remained, as always, the 'great staple of provisions in the county' and its output greatly increased. Wheat, though more frequently sown, remained a difficult and occasional crop. Barley or bere–and especially the hardier variety called bigg–remained common, though its cultivation fell off as a result of the malt tax. Other grain crops like rye and rape were seldom grown. Better strains were being supplied by seedsmen like Tam Samson of Kilmarnock. The introduction of root crops was an important innovation, and potatoes had become a principal farm crop by the last decades of the 18th century. Carrots, parsnips, and turnips were also tried, but even in the 1790s not more than a score of farms in the county were growing these last. 'Turnips have been tried, but with no great success, the soil being too wet, and the servants have an aversion to them, as they are thereby exposed to much cold dirty work', said the Kirkmichael minister. Among the green crops, peas lost in popularity to beans which after 1770 were more widely grown, alone or along with oats as mashlum. Kail was grown as a field crop, and cabbages tried. Among the innovations, many of the farmers had to be persuaded of the value of the new sown grasses. Ryegrass was introduced about 1760 and after a decade became common, and along with clovers and other grass mixtures clothed the fields with the rich green sward that was to become such an essential element in a dairy economy. The remaining crops of flax and hemp were still grown in small quantities, but were rather frowned on as tending to exhaust the soil, and in any case the demand for flax was diminishing as the new imported cotton was coming into its own.

New implements were being tried, but the first experiments had limited success. The old wooden Scotch plough was still as good as any of the new types imported from England, except on the lightest soils, and it was only in the 1790s that cheaper iron made possible the abandonment of the traditional plough. Seed was still sowed broadcast. Harvesting was done by sickles; and the grain, after being stooked in sheaves till dried, was then stacked and winnowed either by flails or by the new threshing machines. For transport about the farm, cars or sledges were superseded by carts. John, Earl of Loudoun, remembered, according to the Statistical Account, 'when there was neither cart nor waggon in the parish, but his father's, Earl Hugh's, and his factor's. Now there are above 250 in the parish.' Even in the remote parish of Colmonell, 'thirty years ago, there were only two in the parish, but now there is scarcely a farmer who has not one, two, three or some even more in his possession.' Even so, the ordinary farm cart at the end of the century could carry only from 10 to 12 cwt.

In the early 18th century and before the cattle in Ayrshire were small in stature, usually black or dark brown, sometimes rigged with white, and with crooked irregular horns, presumably belonging to the indigenous Scottish breed of Kylo cattle. Both for beef and for milk they were of poor quality by later standards. But in one corner of the county a better type was known. Since the early 17th century the parishes of Dunlop and Stewarton had been noted for their dairy produce, and Fullarton confirmed that there 'a breed of cattle has for more than a century been established, remarkable for the quantity and quality of their milk in proportion to their size. They have long been denominated the Dunlop breed.' During the 18th century several landlords brought from England cattle of various types and introduced them to their local herds. Crosses with the older Dunlop breed presumably produced the brown and white dairy cattle known by the 1790s as 'the Cunningham kind' and the ancestors of the modern Ayrshire breed. The Tarbolton minister recognised them as 'of a race famous for the abundance of their milk'. Robert Burns had some sent to him at Ellisland in Dumfriesshire, beginning what would eventually become the massive export of Ayrshire cattle. The 'black cattle' of the older types were not however immediately superseded, but continued, especially on the poorer upland pastures of Kyle and Carrick. There too the indigenous blackfaced sheep maintained their sway, though sometimes improved by crossbreeding with imported types. On the lowland farms there was a prejudice against keeping sheep in enclosed fields, though often a few specimens of imported breed were kept as 'pet sheep' to supply the farmers' wives with their own wool. There was a limited interest in horse breeding, but horses of the new Clydesdale breed were latterly imported from neighbouring Lanarkshire. It was typical of course that various landlords made experiments with other types of stock – oxen, mules, asses, rabbits and pigs. Only the last was significant. Finding that hogs – as they were called – could be largely maintained on the whey by-product of cheesemaking, the traditional superstition against swine was overcome and by the end of the century farmers were beginning to keep and fatten pigs for pork and latterly bacon.

'Nine out of ten of the arable farms in the county of Ayr, and many of those devoted to pasture, may be considered as new farms,' said Aiton in 1811. The new farms were created as part of the enclosure

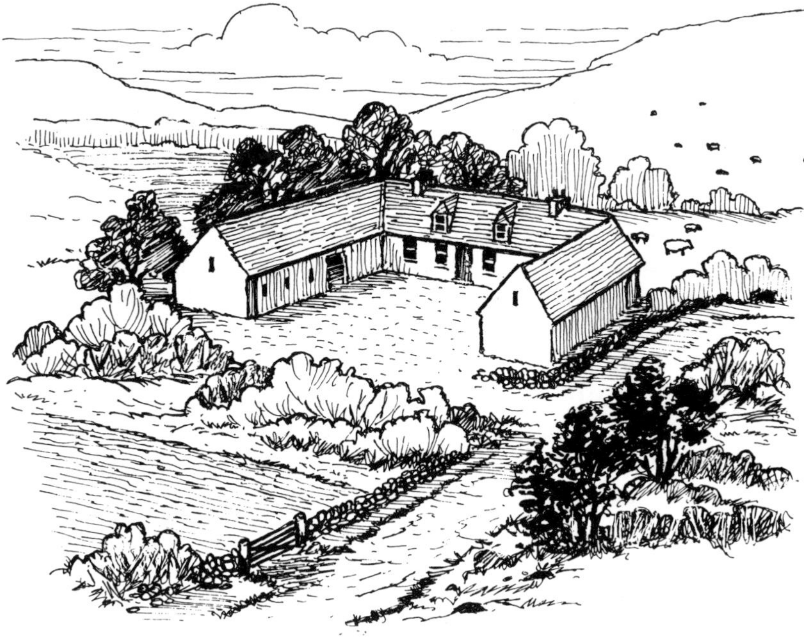

*A new farm*

movement. On the great estates the proprietors with the help of surveyors completely replanned and laid out their property with geometric symmetry, creating farms with fields levelled, amply furnished with hedges, trees, roads; and the new farm steadings were conveniently located–built often on a new site, with fields all around and a farm road leading down to a parish road. Typically, the new farmhouse comprised a dwelling of several rooms fronting a courtyard, flanked by byre, stable, dairy, and other out-houses. On the smaller estates where capital was lacking the landscape was modified rather than replanned. The field systems were based on the older land divisions, the fields were less adequately levelled, there was less planting and roadmaking, and the old farmsteadings survived - inconveniently situated, sometimes two or three of them close together, on the side of a parish road. Efforts of lesser lairds were usually 'feeble, desultory and unavailing' and many small properties were not enclosed till the 19th century.

Contemporary observers (and often the historians who rely on them) tend to notice only successes and ignore the failures. The problems involved in agrarian improvement were many and difficult. Techniques which had been successful in other parts of the country sometimes proved quite unsuitable in Ayrshire. Some landlords attempted schemes which were beyond their resources — and suffered when the Ayr Bank collapsed in 1772. Both proprietors and tenants had to overcome prejudices. Aiton recalled: 'I am old enough to remember, nearly, the commencement of enclosing the land, and the introduction of ryegrass, as a crop, into the parish of Kilmarnock. The popular prejudice and extraordinary clamour among the tenantry against these innovations were very strong. Restricting the tillage to one-third of the possession was remonstrated against, as an encroachment on the liberties of the people. The conversion of the Statute Labour, cutting the land with new roads and the erection of Toll-bars, were considered such dreadful inroads into their rights, that many suffered themselves to be poinded for non-payment of the former, and to be severely fined for shunning or pulling down the latter. The tenants were disposed to consider every improvement that they were required to make on their possession, as tending only to augment their labour and increase the rent rolls of the proprietor . . . They prognosticated great evils and pronounced loud anathemas on all who attempted to introduce improvements or to make the least deviation from the good old way. I remember to have heard many woes prognosticated against John Orr of Barrowfield, Esq., and Bruce Campbell, Esq., his factor, when they began their improvement on the estate of Grougar; and when Alexander, Earl of Eglinton, fell by the hands of Mungo Campbell, the general outcry among the lower orders was that it was a punishment inflicted by heaven on the Earl for introducing innovations in agriculture, and raising the rents of his lands. Selling of meal by weight instead of measure was, when first introduced, equally unpopular; and the introduction of winnowing machines was testified against, from some of the pulpits, under the denomination of *Deil's wind.*'

While many fell by the wayside, both proprietors and tenants, by the last years of the 18th century the new farming had ousted the old. The parishes of Ayrshire which beforehand were producing enough only for their own needs, or even requiring to import it, were supplying wool, flax and hides for the manufacturers and a growing supply of foodstuffs for the towns of Ayrshire and beyond. Grain, meal, and potatoes; mutton, beef, veal, pork and bacon; even rabbit meat from estate warrens; dairy produce; bullocks, cattle and other livestock to supply the farmers and merchants of neighbouring areas.

By the end of the century there was a growing concentration on dairy farming. This was the most profitable form of enterprise on the damp clay lands of Ayrshire, with a short growing season, and the new Ayrshire cattle feeding on grass with oats, hay, and turnips for winter feed. Dunlop cheese became the principal dairy product. This sweetmilk cheese was introduced into that parish by Barbara Gilmour at the end of the 17th century. It became popular as the 18th century advanced and in the 19th and early 20th century became the chief product of the Ayrshire farms. Liquid milk could be sold in nearby towns, but it was impossible easily to transport, or preserve, save by converting it into cheese. That it was already the common practice in the late 18th century was noted by John Galt. In the fictitious parish of Dalmailing, the Rev. Micah Balwhidder found that his new second wife had been bitten by the craze. In the *Annals of the Parish* we read: 'Then we had milk cows and the calves to bring up, and a kirning of butter and a making of cheese; in short I was almost by myself with the jangle and din. The second Mrs. Balwhidder sent her butter on the market days to Irville, and the cheese from time to time to Glasgow – and they were both so well made that our dairy was just a coining of money, and after the first year we had the whole tot of my stipend to put untouched into the bank.'

A contemporary (George Robertson) summed up what the change from a subsistence economy to market production meant in some of its human implications: 'The milk, the cheese, the cream, the butter, were reserved by the thrifty housewife from the family with jealous care, that they might be converted into cash – even the butter milk, and the whey, were sent to market, and as for a taste of the curds, this was placed under a most rigorous interdict. In vain did the younglings at times look with greedy eyes or watering mouth to the large vessel in which it was placed, or implore a little of its sweet and desirable contents – all was peremptorily prohibited – the law was absolute and universal. The milk was carefully skimmed that the butter might be more abundant, the return in cash larger and more boastful. Even the master and mistress of the family shared very scantily of those delicious viands with which they were daily versant . . . they starved in the midst of plenty.'

## CHAPTER 7

# INDUSTRY

Ayrshire when Burns was born in 1759 was as yet hardly affected by the stirrings of industrial growth; his early years saw some beginnings; and as he reached manhood significant developments were taking place. In the year 1781 Burns went to Irvine to learn flax dressing. Robert and Gilbert had done experimental flax-growing at Lochlea, and had some plans to specialise in that crop. But Robert's stay in Irvine was cut short by the burning down of the flax-shop and the failure of the business – symbolic, because the local linen trade was in decline. The call of duty took Burns back to Lochlea and his sick and impoverished father early in 1782. He was moved to declare just a year later that 'this country has been, and still is decaying very fast.' In fact in the 1780s the well-established coal industry in the Stevenston area was enjoying a period of expansion; the new and important cotton industry was introduced in 1785; in the year after the Kilmarnock edition, the great Catrine Cotton Works were established and also the Muirkirk Iron Works; Kilmarnock was booming with an extended range of manufactures; all over north Ayrshire weavers were setting up handlooms to produce muslins with the cotton that was becoming the new staple of Scotland; more and more people were moving into towns and villages to find their livelihood from industry. To Burns and his contemporaries, however, these seemed novelties and industrial changes were overshadowed by the great changes which were at the same time transforming agriculture and the countryside.

The undoubted authority on the history of Ayrshire industry, Dr. C.A. Whately, has indicated: 'It is probably true to say that the extent and diversity of Ayrshire trade and industry has been underestimated to date. It is wrong to say that only domestic and craft manufactures existed in Ayrshire in 1750'. But most enterprises were of this type, and even by the end of the century there were few firms employing more than a handful of workers.

In the early part of the 18th century in the royal burgh of Ayr there were the nine incorporated trades of weavers, dyers, tailors, skinners, shoemakers, hammermen, coopers, fleshers and squaremen (including masons, wrights, slaters and glaziers). In the other royal burgh of Irvine there were six incorporated trades. But the growth of the two royal burghs in the 18th century was modest. The vested interests of the old trades did not favour expansion. Most developments at Ayr occurred in Newton outwith the confines of the royal burgh, and similarly at Fullarton outwith Irvine. Both royal burghs were easily outstripped by Kilmarnock, a burgh of barony with weavers, bonnetmakers, glovers, tailors, skinners and shoemakers, whose council and merchants sought unfettered growth. Elsewhere in the county industrial growth was sponsored by landowners who extended mineral exploitation, established manufacturing enterprises, built up existing villages or created new communities, some of which remained quite small like Sorn and Straiton, though others became new towns like Catrine, Wallacetown, Darvel and – in the early 19th century – Troon and Ardrossan. The stimulus to industrial expansion came with the opening-up of world markets in the 18th century. It was some time after the Union of the Parliaments in 1707 before the expansion of the Clyde-American trade made its influence felt in Ayrshire. The settlement of the country after the suppression of the Jacobite menace in 1746 was an important factor; the defeat of the French in the Seven Years War gave Britain a dominant position in world affairs after 1763, with the American War from 1775 to 1783 only a temporary setback to Atlantic trade. In fact, the widening opportunities that stimulated the most far-reaching agrarian changes in the last two decades of the 18th century were producing at precisely the same time the beginnings of major industrial development in Ayrshire.

Initially the traditional branches of the textile industry enjoyed expansion. Ayrshire shared in the expansion of the Scottish linen manufacture in the early 18th century, reaching a peak in 1770-1 with near 190,000 yards stamped. But this was less than two per cent of the Scottish total, and while the Scottish output continued to grow, Ayrshire's production declined and became concentrated in the north, in the Garnock valley, where Beith by 1811 had seventy thread-spinning mills, each employing from 8-10 workers. More important locally was the manufacture of woollens. In Kilmarnock in 1747 a group of local merchants set afoot a novel and successful experiment in mass production by establishing a weaving shed producing blankets, carpets and other coarse woollen goods. Other small companies and individuals followed this lead in extending production and turning over from the older serges. To meet increased demands for yarn the original company installed carding and spinning machinery powered by a water mill, though the actual weaving was done by handloom. Stocking manufacture began too at Kilmarnock, knitted on needles by women who were 'so expert at the business, that many of them could knit three stockings of the largest size, every day.' Bonnet-making continued at Kilmarnock and Stewarton, and though fashions changed and local demand waned, there was a considerable export trade, especially for the American market. Mills for spinning wool were set up in Maybole, Dalmellington, Cumnock and Newmilns, and throughout the county spinning and weaving were carried on domestically. In Maybole parish in 1793 there were 80 looms for wool in town and country, employing 300 persons. In the neighbouring parishes of Dailly and Kirkoswald, coarse woollen cloth, blanketing and plaiding were manufactured in farmhouses and cottages from raw material imported from Galloway and Argyll. Tailors travelled from one farm to the next, making clothes for each family from the bundle of the homespun. But woollen manufacture had expanded beyond this primitive beginning to cater for the wider market, with agents of commercial firms managing the domestic producers.

The first exotic fibre introduced was silk and from about 1770 many customary weavers turned to this new line. For a short period silk indeed became the principal type of weaving in Kilmarnock, Ayr Kilwinning and Saltcoats. But by 1790 it had been generally superseded by cotton.

After 1783 there was an increasing flow of cotton across the Atlantic, and in 1785 some handloom weavers in Ayrshire began to turn to cotton. In 1779 the first cotton factory in Scotland had been established at Rothesay followed by others at Neilston, Johnstone, East Kilbride, Deanston, New Lanark and (in 1787) at Catrine. These mills were devoted to yarn spinning, with water wheels providing power to operate the 'frames', 'jeanies' and 'mules'. From these and smaller establishments yarn was supplied to the thousands of handloom weavers who set up looms in their but-and-bens in towns and villages throughout the west of Scotland and carried on this weaving process

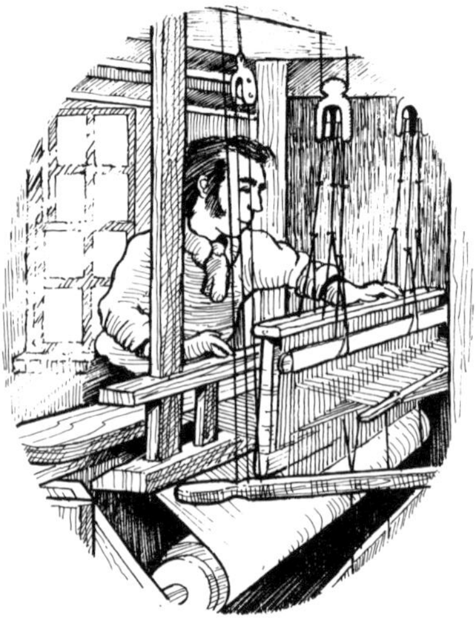

*Handloom Weaving*

domestically as contrasted with the factory spinning system. By the end of the century cotton had become the principal manufacture of Scotland in general and Ayrshire in particular.

Cotton spinning in Ayrshire began in 1787 with the founding of the Catrine Cotton Works by Claud Alexander and David Dale. The former came from Newton-upon-Ayr, had a successful and profitable career in India in the service of the East India Company, and returned to his native Ayrshire. He purchased the estate of Ballochmyle on the banks of the Ayr, only a few miles from Mossgiel where Burns was farming. The previous owners were 'the amiable and excellent family of Whitefoord' but, said the poet, 'Sir John's misfortunes obliged him to sell his estates.' The new proprietor took possession of Ballochmyle in 1786; not yet married, he was accompanied by his 31-year-old spinster sister Wilhelmina, whom Burns addressed as 'the bonie lass of Ballochmyle.' Alexander's partner, David Dale, was born in Stewarton in 1739, became a herd boy, then a handloom weaver, then a dealer in linen yarn, and entered the cotton trade in 1783 by building the New Lanark Mill in association with Richard Arkwright, the English inventor. Other enterprises followed with Dale becoming a 'captain of industry' and amassing a considerable fortune, part of which he liberally devoted to charitable and religious purposes. In Glasgow it was said of him that 'David Dale gives his money by shovelfuls, but God Almighty shovels it back again.'

Work began in 1787 in building the works and the attached township called Catrine, on the banks of the River Ayr where water power was available. Spinning had begun by November 1789. The twist mill was a considerable building of five storeys plus garrets, containing 5,240 spindles and employing 318 persons. In 1790 a jennie factory was added, with 76 spinning jennies, employing a further 200 persons. Another 280 persons were employed at home, picking cotton. This was then and for long after the largest factory establishment in Ayrshire. The new town of Catrine contained in 1793 a population of 1601, and for their welfare Alexander provided a church and school, a brewery, allotments and his personal benevolent patronage. In addition to Catrine, cotton spinning was carried on in much smaller 'cotton houses' in north and west of Ayrshire. These were set up about 1790 in Beith, Dalry, Kilwinning (2), Irvine (3), Kilmarnock (several), Dundonald and Monkton. These, reported Fullarton, 'were filled with spinning-jennies, and moved by horses where water could not be procured.' The largest, in Irvine, had 80 employees, and altogether fewer than 400 persons were involved compared with Catrine's total labour force of 800. Like the Catrine Works they supplied cotton yarn almost exclusively to merchants in Glasgow and Paisley, whose agents distributed it to handloom weavers.

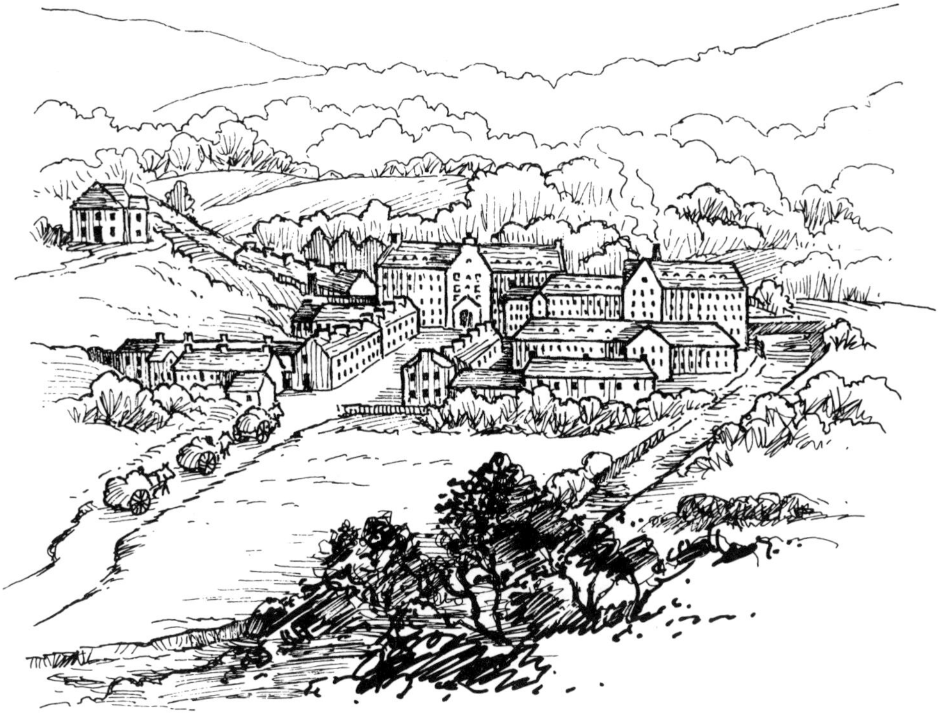

*Catrine new town*

The writers of the Statistical Account in the 1790s report weaving in almost every parish throughout Ayrshire. Linen was still being worked for the market in the Garnock Valley area; silk was occasionally being woven; woollens were being produced everywhere. But they were all outstripped by the new muslin weaving. Between the 1790s and 1810 numbers grew in Beith from 70 to 205, in Kilwinning from 146 to 333, in Newmilns and Darvel from 344 to 640, and in Kilmarnock from 200 to over 1,000. Others further south took up muslins but never to the same extent. In central Ayrshire it became popular at Catrine in the shadow of the spinning works, in and around Ayr, but hardly beyond that. Curiously Carrick became more enthusiastic than Kyle. In Maybole, Kirkmichael, and even remote Straiton, cotton was worked as much as wool, while Girvan with 500 weavers in 1810 had become one of the principal muslin towns of Ayrshire. Altogether by that year nearly 6,000 muslin weavers were at work in the county, about 4,000 of them in Cuninghame, north of the River Irvine.

By that time, too, an associated branch of the cotton industry was growing up–that of tambouring or 'flowering'. It was introduced into Irvine in 1790 with a works employing 70 girls, and spread to Ayr, Kilmarnock, and other smaller places, to employ several hundreds. Young girls were introduced to this work 'as soon as they can wind pirns, handle the tambouring needle, or clip off the excrescencies of raised work.' Though one writer wrote of the 'many female children happily engaged in the tambouring business' another complained that by doing they failed to learn even to 'cook their own victuals, wash their clothes, or manage ordinary domestic business. Their health is by no means promoted by these sedentary employments; and I am sorry to say that their virtue is often but slender.' When we visualise the dimness of the cottage rooms where they stitched, often by the flicker of candlelight, we cannot but marvel at the intricacies of their needlework, and the even more delicate

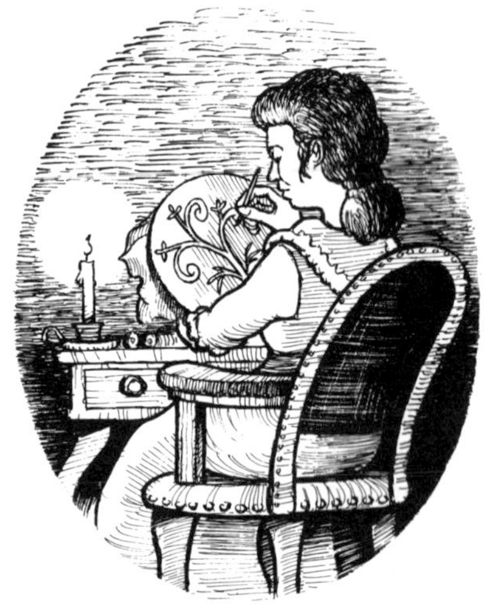

*Tambouring*

Ayrshire embroidery that reached its peak of popularity in the 1830s and 1840s before the collapse of the cotton industry in general.

While the expansion of the textile trades was the outstanding manufacturing development of the later 18th century, there was some modest expansion of other local trades. The making of boots and shoes and saddlery work was expanded, especially in Kilmarnock, where over 400 were thus employed by 1790. By 1810 coarse pottery was being made at Cumnock, Coylton, Sorn, and Stevenston, providing utensils for domestic use. Breweries were established at Ayr, Irvine, Catrine and Stewarton. Salt was evaporated from sea-water at Shalloch, Turnberry, Ayr, Newton, Prestwick, Troon, Saltcoats, Ardrossan and Hunterston. There were some small distinctive enterprises - snuff boxes from Cumnock, millstones from West Kilbride, whetstones from Stair, knives from Kilmaurs, coarse paper from Galston, coaltar and lamp black from Muirkirk and also from Tarholm near Enterkin and from Ayr harbour, sugar refined at Ayr, tobacco and snuff from Kilmarnock, soap from three manufactories at Ayr; small ships were built at Newton-on-Ayr, Saltcoats and Irvine; and minerals were being worked.

During the 18th century the output of coal in Ayrshire grew from probably less than 25,000 tons in 1700 to around 240,000 tons in 1800, a tenfold increase mostly accomplished in the last two decades of the country. For long before 1780 coal had been worked over the greater part of Ayrshire, intermittently and in small quantities, quarried from outcrops through 'coal heughs', mined from 'ingaunees' entered from sloping shafts, occasionally from bell pits. The voracious demand for lime to improve the fields moved landlords to build limekilns and produce a vastly-increased output of coal for limeburning. It was also after 1780 that towns and villages had grown sufficiently for the domestic market to become important and wherever coal was accessible it succeeded peat as domestic fuel in this period. And it was only after 1780 that there was an important demand for coal for industrial purposes.

The main centre for coal mining in Ayrshire in the early 18th century was the Stevenston area. Here alone was there mining enterprise on a large scale. In 1678 Robert Cuninghame, an Edinburgh surgeon and father of seventeen children, inherited the Auchenharvie estate, sank several shafts, including 'the deep shank' which was possibly the first deep coal pit in Scotland, drained by two pumps operated by horse power and water wheel. He erected a harbour at Saltcoats, exported coal to Ireland, and built four salt pans using the small coals to evaporate salt on a larger scale than had previously been possible by the 'poor people who lived in cots on the shore.' In 1701, 5,700 tons of coal were exported through Saltcoats harbour, forming perhaps a quarter of the total county output of coal from all sources. Though Robert Cuninghame's heavy capital investment led him into financial difficulties, production at Auchenharvie and throughout the Stevenston area expanded. Newcomer steam engines to drain pits at Stevenston were installed. By mid-century, over 10,000 tons were being exported annually from Saltcoats. In 1770 Robert Reid Cuninghame succeeded to the diminished estate of Auchenharvie, entered into partnership with Patrick Warner of Ardeer, and — inheriting his great-grandfather's enterprise – began a new period of expansion. He sank no fewer than 25 pits, installed at least four steam engines, increased the number of saltpans to five, rebuilt Saltcoats harbour, and built in 1772 a 2¼ mile canal to convey his coals down to the harbour. By 1793 he was employing over 200 men (not counting boys) and 23,000 tons of coal were being raised annually, most of it for export to Ireland.

The success of the Auchenharvie export trade encouraged imitation wherever transport to the coast was feasible. In Irvine, Kilwinning and Dreghorn parishes half-a-dozen pits employing possibly 200 miners altogether began to produce coal for export through Irvine harbour. Further south, Ayr harbour was handling loads from the half-dozen pits of Ayr, Newton and St. Quivox. Here too deep workings were made possible by the installation of steam pumps, while in the same era two waggon-ways were constructed to lead coal down to the harbour.

Inland, enterprising landowners were exploiting coal for lime-burning, sinking sometimes deep shafts drained by 'fire engines' (as the steam pumps were designated), hoping to dispose of a share of their augmented output by transporting it to the coastal ports. The most ambitious developments were at Riccarton, south of Kilmarnock, where Sir William Cunningham of Caprington had by the 1790s about 120 miners producing over 3,000 tons annually, some of which was conveyed by ponies to Irvine for export. Colonel Fullarton and others projected a canal from Kilmarnock to the coast; but it was not till 1809 that the Marquis of Titchfield constructed a railway from his mines around Kilmarnock to his new port at Troon. In south Ayrshire, the small isolated field at Dailly was worked – about 1700 a coal seam went on fire and is still burning! – but it could be used only locally 'due to the expense of land carriage to the coast and the want of a good harbour at Girvan.' And in remote Muirkirk, the vast unexploited resources of coal could be utilised locally after the opening of the ironworks in 1787, with some 50,000 tons being thus used by 1810.

Throughout the 18th century hopeful landowners were prospecting for minerals other than coal. As early as 1718 efforts were being made to work copper near Culzean, and soon afterwards lead on a small scale at Kirkmichael and Straiton. At the end of the century lead was also being worked by a group of Quakers at Dalleagles near New Cumnock, and nearby at Craigman graphite was worked by the earl of Dumfries. A similar smallscale development of iron was initiated by Lord Cathcart about 1730. At Terreoch in Sorn parish on the banks of the Ayr local iron ore was smelted using charred peat, and some of the ore was even later transported to the coast to be conveyed to the ironworks at Bonawe in Argyll. Such charcoal furnaces were being superseded by new ironworks based on the lowland coalfields, the first and most famous being that set up at Carron near Falkirk in 1759; and eventually the one at Muirkirk in 1787. In the year that the latter was started, Robert Burns paid a visit to the former. He was not admitted, since it was a Sunday, but he left behind some uncomplimentary lines descriptive of such new establishments:

*We cam na here to view your warks*
*In hopes to be mair wise,*
*But only, lest we gang to Hell,*
*It may be nae surprise.*
*But when we tirl'd at your door*
*Your porter dought na bear us:*
*Sae may, should we to Hell's yetts come,*
*Your billy Satan sair us.* CW 286

During the 1780s several of the leading figures of the growing Scottish iron industry had been prospecting in Ayrshire and Muirkirk was thought a likely site. One of the promoters explained: 'Nothing can induce us to go into such a Desert and Inland Place as Muirkirk but the absolute Certainty of having the coal and ironstone and limestone very cheap.' Representatives of various iron companies formed a consortium to develop Muirkirk, which would be able to supply their various works with bar iron. Thomas Eddington further explained: 'My original idea of the business was that we should erect cheap works to smelt the materials while they were got cheap, and to abandon them whenever the Stone and Coal became dear and carry our machinery to some other situation.' In fact, Muirkirk proved to be a worthwhile venture which continued in operation till 1923. Work started in 1787; two years were spent opening up pits and building furnaces; the first furnace was blown in 1789. There were three furnaces for making pig iron, a forge for making bar iron, and a foundry. By 1810 between 300 and 400 men were employed. And from 1796 a more short-lived separate company was operating a furnace at nearby Glenbuck. From Muirkirk pig iron was being supplied to foundries in Kilmarnock, Ayr, Paisley, Carlisle and Ireland. Malleable iron was sold to a wide market. And various iron products were being manufactured at the iron works.

All of these several industrial developments were beginning to make a major transformation of Ayrshire society, whose significance could hardly be realised by Burns and his contemporaries.

CHAPTER 8

# COMMERCE

Until the 18th century most buying and selling was carried on at the weekly markets and periodic fairs of the burghs. Besides the two royal burghs of Ayr and Irvine there were fourteen lesser burghs of barony. The royal burghs by their charters had a monopoly of foreign trade, but they were unable to check competition from Kilmarnock. Commerce was progressing despite, and in defiance of feudal restrictions. New markets and fairs were being instituted whenever and wherever the necessity was felt, till by 1811 according to Aiton: 'There are some fairs held at every town, and at every parish church in the county of Ayr. There are five or six in Ayr, five in Irvine, three great, and several small ones in Kilmarnock, four in Maybole, five in Newmilns, five or six in Cumnock, and no less than twelve in Mauchline every year!' There were altogether more than two hundred fairs in the county annually, with perhaps an average of a thousand persons attending each. The initial impulse for these meetings was economic – though by the end of the 18th century the fairs had become principally and in some cases exclusively popular social assemblies. 'In former times, these fairs were attended by a vast number of merchants, with cloths of all kinds, hard-wares, and all sorts of merchandise. Mechanics and manufacturers carried thither the various articles of their several crafts. The shoemaker exhibited his shoes; the carpenter his rakes, flails, cars and harrows; the turner his plates, ladles, and caps; the cooper his bickers, boyns and cogs. Wool, flax, yarn, etc., were sold at every country fair. Every travelling merchant, and even those who kept shops in town, exhibited their goods and wares, at the country fairs, for many miles round their residences.' But in the course of the century the markets and fairs were being superseded and losing their commercial importance, 'Since all the towns and villages have been supplied with shops containing every species of goods, and the number of chapmen greatly curtailed, horses and cows form the chief articles of traffic or show; except at the fairs of Ayr and Maybole, where the home manufactured plaidings are sold, to a great extent . . . Every farmer can now sell his cattle, cheese, butter, grain, and other produce of his farm at his own door, to greater advantage, and at higher prices, than he can obtain by carrying them to fairs. And nine-tenth parts of them are sold by the farmers at home.' Obviously too for the sale of many of the new products, local markets were an anachronism. The new economy required new methods of exchange.

The establishment of banks which could supply credit was an essential prerequisite of widespread improvement. The first bank in Ayrshire was that established in the county town by John McAdam & Co. in 1763. This was followed and swallowed up by the ill-fated Ayr Bank of Douglas, Heron, & Co. Formed in 1769 by a co-partnery of a hundred and forty nobles, gentry, merchants, and lawyers from various parts of Scotland, and with its headquarters in Edinburgh, this banking company began business with 'a limited capital of £95,000 and an unlimited confidence in itself.' The circulation of its banknotes was far in excess of its funds, and it lent to the Ayrshire landowners and others seeking capital virtually anything that was asked, just at the time when enthusiasm for estate improvement was in full flood. A London speculator was the villain of the piece; his firm went bankrupt and various associated undertakings were involved. The Ayr Bank, one of these, crashed spectacularly, with liabilities of over a million pounds sterling. 12th June 1772 was known as 'Black Monday'; hundreds of people in Ayrshire were ruined. A good many Ayrshire estates changed hands, with landlords forced to sell off to repay loans from the Bank. But though proprietors as individuals might be ruined, the improvements wrought by the borrowed funds remained intact, and from an impersonal point of view the Ayr Bank did 'an immense deal of good.' Following the dissolution of the firm of Douglas, Heron & Co., in 1774 another Ayr Bank was formed by Messrs. Hunter & Co., with offices in Ayr, Maybole, and Irvine. In 1775 the Bank of Scotland opened branches in Ayr and Kilmarnock, and the Paisley Bank had an office in Irvine. These conducted their business on a more sober footing, and played an essential part in the further development of commerce.

In the new economy, improved facilities for the transport of produce and people were essential. The new enterprises, both agrarian and industrial, involved the receipt of raw materials and fuels, and the despatch of products, on a regular basis. The thoroughfares which had been sufficient for the casual and limited traffic of earlier days were no longer adequate. It is difficult for us to imagine our land without made roads, yet that was precisely the state of affairs in Ayrshire till after the middle of the 18th century. Before that time such travellers as there were had to make do with rude tracks, which were suitable enough for horsemen, occasional pack animals, and droves of cattle. They were, said Aiton, 'formed by accident in barbarous times, by far too numerous, crooked and ill-constructed.' They twisted and turned to avoid traversing arable land, following the irregular march lines between properties. Sometimes lairds encroached by inches, then feet, upon the thoroughfare, and to quote Aiton again – 'when the ground on the opposite side of the road, happens to belong to two of these kinds of earth-worms, I have seen a public road, in the vicinity of a market town, reduced to eight or nine feet, in width.' The coast road followed the shore over a fair part of its distance and remained in use till after 1776 when Armstrong on his map warned: 'There is a dangerous quick-sand on the Road at the Foot of Powburn–to avoid it keep as near the Sea as the Tide will allow.' A similar warning was given in the Statistical Account, which remarked that 'some persons have been burried alive at this spot.' Rivers were more often than not crossed by fords. Roy's manuscript map of 1755 shows twenty four bridges in Ayrshire. Some of these were recent, but others had been in existence long before. Two well-known examples of these still survive – the Auld Brig O' Doon, over which Tam O' Shanter escaped from the witches, and the Auld Brig at Ayr 'where two wheelbarrows tremble when they meet.' Their narrow causeways were designed in an era before wheeled vehicles were in common use.

Wheeled vehicles were rare. According to Aiton, 'the first carts, that were used in Ayrshire, were in laying down the materials, of which the bridge over the water of Irvine, between Kilmarnock and Riccarton, was built in 1726.' Fullarton reported that about the middle of the century 'the late Lord Cathcart, being extremely desirous of improving his estates, ordered a number of carts to be made, and given gratis to his tenants. But they were at that time so little accustomed to these machines, and the roads were so bad, that very few accepted of his Lordship's present.' Farmers continued to use cars or sledges, while loads of coal, lime, grain and other produce were carried in creels or sacks on horseback.

There was a system of statute labour whereby 'tenants, cottars, and other labouring men' could be required to work six days a year on road repair, but at best it was practicable only to 'mend holes in roads that had never been made.' In earlier generations, Aiton opined, 'The road towards heaven was too much talked of, to admit of any thing being done to those leading to market towns.' Only with the increased traffic in the second half of the 18th century, and an actual deterioration in conditions, did demands for improvement become clamant.

John Galt in the *Annals of the Parish,* under the year 1767, graphically depicts the state of affairs: 'The king's highway, as I have related in the foregoing, ran through the Vennel, which was a narrow and crooked street, with many big stones here and there, and every now and then, both in the spring and the fall, a gathering of middens for the fields; insomuch that the coal-carts from the Douray moor were often reested in the middle of the causey, and on more than one occasion some of them laired altogether in the middens, and others of them broke down. Great complaint was made by the carters anent these difficulties, and there was, for many a day, a talk and sound of an alteration and amendment; but nothing was fulfilled in the matter till the month of March in this year, when the Lord Eaglesham was coming from London to see the new lands that he had bought in our parish. His Lordship was a man of a genteel spirit, and very fond of his horses, which were the most beautiful creatures of their kind that had been seen in the countryside. Coming, as I was noting, to see his new lands, he was obliged to pass through the clachan one day, when all the middens were gathering out, reeking and sappy, in the middle of the causey. Just as his Lordship was driving in with his prancing steeds, like a Jehu, at one end of the vennel, a long string of loaded coal-carts came in at the other, and there was hardly room for my lord to pass them. What was to be done? His Lordship could not turn back and the coal-carts were in no less perplexity. Everybody was out of doors to see and to help; when, in trying to get his Lordship's carriage over the top of a midden the horses gave a sudden loup, and couped the coach, and threw my lord, head foremost, into the very scent-bottle of the whole commodity, which made him go perfect mad, and he swore like a trooper that he would get an act of parliament to put down the nuisance–the which now ripened in the course of this year into the undertaking of the trust road.'

In 1767 'An Act for repairing and widening several Roads in the County of Ayr' was passed, to improve a score of main thoroughfares in north and central Ayrshire which 'were much frequented by travellers, but . . . impassable in winter for wheel carriages and horses.' This measure was typical of a series of local acts which were taken out for different parts of Scotland from 1751 onwards. Local and piecemeal efforts at improvement by landlords like the 4th Earl of Loudoun had proved ineffective. The nominated roads were placed under the supervision of a County Board of Trustees who arranged for the levy of tolls at suitable points and applied the proceeds to reconstruction and maintenance work. The statute labour was commuted to a money payment to be applied to parish roads. There was opposition to the turnpike system. Some landowners objected to encroachments on their properties. Travellers resented and sometimes evaded tolls. Those for whom the casual demands of statute labour had been a slight imposition found the regular levy of a money rate a burden. It was, said the minister of Irvine, 'a very hard and oppressive tax.' Seven years later in 1774 a second Turnpike Act was obtained to extend the system of trust roads and include south Ayrshire. An important provision, the Trustees were now allowed to borrow money for roadmaking, repaying the loan from the road rate and the rents made from letting out their tolls. The work of improvement was accelerated by this Act and by the election to the Turnpike Trustees some ten years later of one particular landowner – John Loudon McAdam.

The McAdams were a Kirkcudbrightshire family, one of whom, James McAdam, helped to found the first Ayr Bank. His son, the roadmaker-to-be, was born in Ayr in 1756. Some of John's early years were spent at Blairquhan near Straiton. While there he attended Maybole school, and is reputed to have constructed in his leisure hours a model for a new road between Maybole and Kirkoswald. When he was fourteen his father died and he was sent to America to be under the care of an uncle, who was a prosperous New York merchant. As McAdam reached manhood he set up in business himself and made a fortunate marriage; despite financial reverses in the War of Independence, he was a fairly wealthy man when he returned to his native Ayrshire in 1783. He purchased the estate of Sauchrie, between Ayr and Maybole, and for the next thirteen years interested himself largely in road improvements, carrying out experimental methods of road construction at his own expense near Sauchrie, pushing through schemes for highway development as a member of the Ayrshire Turnpike Trustees, and earning recognition as a Deputy Lieutenant for the county. When he left Ayrshire he had formulated the ideas that won him eventual fame, and he left behind him a legacy of good roads in many parts of Ayrshire.

'Few counties, on the whole, are so well accommodated,' wrote Fullarton in 1793. Aiton re-iterated this in 1811: 'There are probably few districts in Scotland, where so many excellent roads have been made, within so short a period, and at so much expense.' Traffic rapidly multiplied. Farmers provided themselves with carts, usually single-horse vehicles with two wheels of 48 to 54 inches diameter, carrying 10 to 12 cwt, latterly more than a ton. Besides the everyday farm traffic, the transport of coal and lime increased. Carriers' businesses were established with carts plying as far as Edinburgh. Passenger

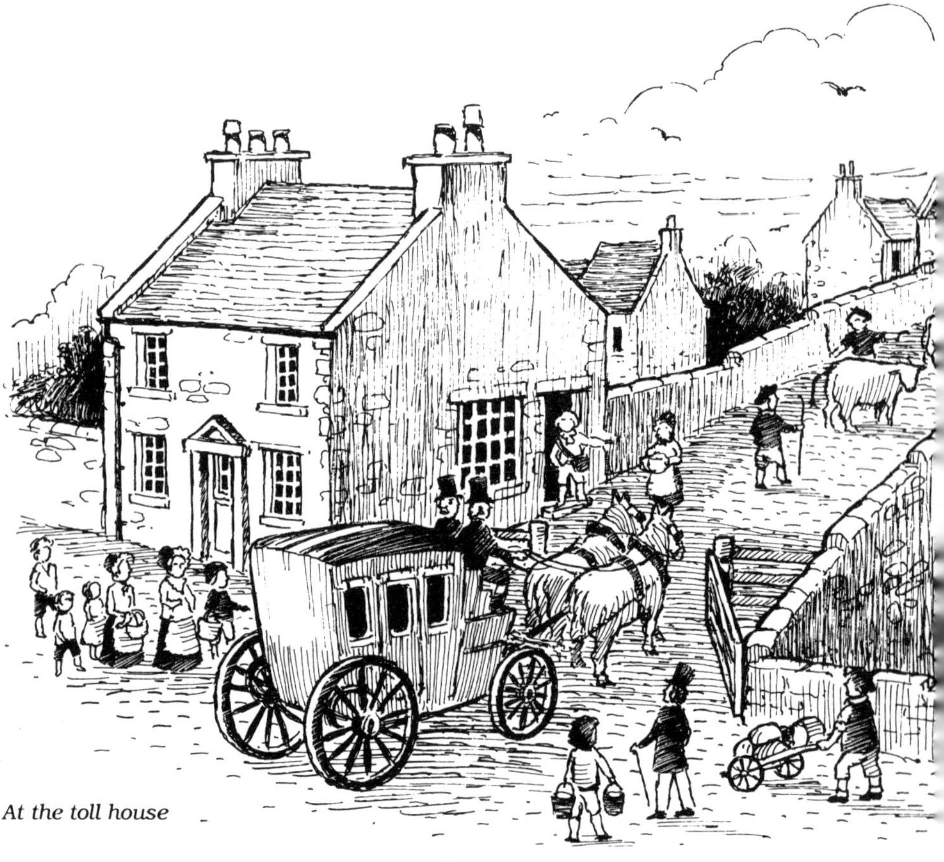

*At the toll house*

traffic was augmented too, and beside the private vehicles of the gentry, public coaches appeared on the roads. By the 1790s there was a thrice-weekly service from Glasgow via Kilwinning and Irvine to Ayr and on to Portpatrick. On the more direct Glasgow–Kilmarnock–Ayr route there was a daily mail coach. And the 'Camperdown' coach followed the same route from Glasgow to Kilmarnock and on through Mauchline to Dumfries for Carlisle and the south. Later, direct communication was also established with Edinburgh.

But even the new roads were not able to stand up very well to constant passage of heavy coal traffic. Novel methods were considered. The Saltcoats canal was such an experiment. 2¼ miles long, 12 feet wide, and 4 feet deep, for conveying Auchenharvie coals down to Saltcoats harbour, it was opened in 1772 and thus shares with the Monkland canal the honour of 'first in Scotland'. It was followed by two other short canals in the same locality to take coals to the Garnock river for transportation down to Irvine. Their utility suggested the possibility of a longer canal whereby Kilmarnock coalmasters could transport their coals to the sea at Troon. A survey of the route was made by John Goldie, and a bill promoted by Colonel Fullarton – both acquaintances of Burns. 'This undertaking,' said Fullarton, 'would certainly render Kilmarnock the most eligible and flourishing manufacturing town in the west of Scotland . . . Perhaps the canal, instead of stopping at Kilmarnock, ought to be extended to Glasgow, which is only 21

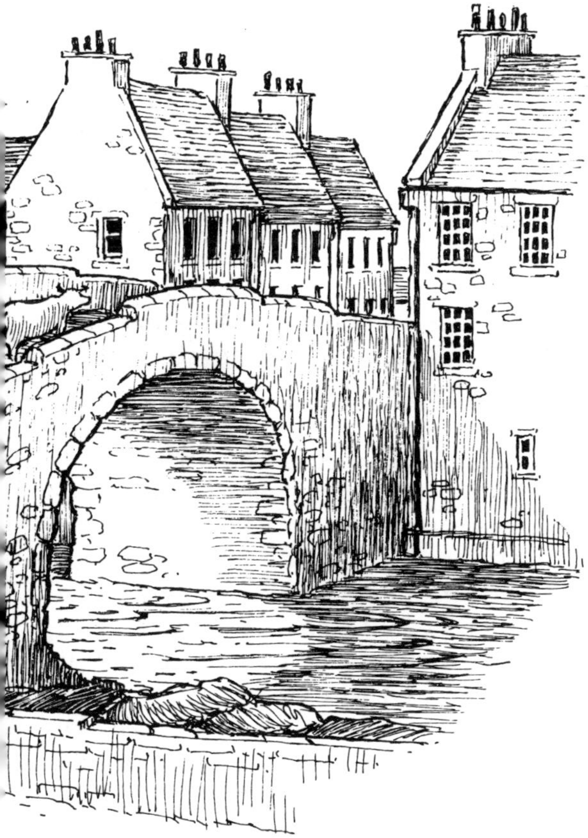

miles farther.' But this project, like the later and more grandiose one for a ship-canal from Glasgow to Ardrossan, came to nothing. Similarly a proposal to extend another short canal at Muirkirk iron works towards Ayr some 25 miles west did not get beyond the talking stage. An alternative to canal transport, and ultimately a more successful one, began with the construction of wagon ways, specially constructed rail tracks along which horses could tow coal wagons. On Armstrong's map of 1775 two 'coal waggon ways' are shown at Newton-upon-Ayr; later, Richard Oswald of Auchincruive laid a longer line; while at Muirkirk the iron company also had one. A more ambitious line between Kilmarnock and Troon, which was begun a generation later in 1808 is claimed as the first real railway in Scotland. The Marquis of Titchfield, who in 1809 succeeded as 4th Duke of Portland, had purchased lands around Kilmarnock and also the Fullarton estate at Troon. An act of parliament–the first such for Scotland–was necessary to allow a 9½ mile wagonway which would traverse several properties. A double track of four feet gauge was laid. Cast iron flanged rails (made in Glenbuck) were laid on stone blocks, and the intervening track filled with road metal. The line crossed Shewalton Moss; a four-arch bridge carried it over the River Irvine; and the enterprise took four years to complete at a cost of over £50,000 sterling. Later (in 1816) an early Stephenson steam locomotive was tried, unsuccessfully, on this line. Normally coal and other merchandise in wagon-loads up to 12 tons were hauled by horses. Passengers were occasionally carried - from Kilmarnock down to the shore at Barassie - and in 1844 the line was re-laid and incorporated into the 19th century railway system.

The spectacular advances in land transport were accompanied by an improvement in facilities along the Ayrshire coast for the growing volume of shipping. Before 1700 the only harbours were those of the royal burghs of Ayr and Irvine, joined by Cuninghame's small new harbour at Saltcoats. All were busier as the 18th century advanced with coastal, Irish, and even some transatlantic trade. Saltcoats dealt almost entirely in the coal trade, and in the 1790s had 41 ships with a total capacity of 4,200 tons manned by 320 men, though a dozen of the larger vessels 'do not frequent their own incommodious port, but find employment in the carrying trade.' Ayr with 33 vessels of 2,500 tons and 190 sailors was reviving. In 1772 an Act empowered the council to undertake large-scale improvements. In 1790 a lighthouse was erected on the north side by the coalmasters of Newton. Irvine earlier in the century had seemed the most promising prospect, for Glasgow merchants were making considerable use of it. In the 1790s Irvine had 51 vessels of 3,682 tons with 305 sailors. But here as at Ayr and Saltcoats there was no scope for large-scale extension of the port facilities. Fullarton rightly observed that the three Ayrshire harbours were 'too defective to admit of trade sufficient to produce a direct influence on the character of Ayrshire husbandry'–or, we might add, on Ayrshire industry either. Aiton explained that there was 'not a harbour between Liverpool and Greenock that a ship over 250 tons can enter.' The expansion of Greenock and Port Glasgow, and the deepening of the Clyde in 1773 making Glasgow itself a seaport, meant that the great volume of shipping on the Firth – and all the larger vessels – by-passed the Ayrshire harbours. Glasgow became the entrepot even for the greatest share of Ayrshire commerce.

Only at the very end of the century, when the economic developments were rapidly accelerating, were efforts made to provide vastly-augmented port facilities. The change in outlook can be seen at Troon. In 1707 William Fullarton had obtained a charter erecting his lands into a burgh of barony and constituting Troon a free port. But nothing was done to improve what was simply a creek. About 1740 the merchants of Glasgow proposed to feu the lands of Troon and proceed with the construction of a harbour, but the offer was rejected by another William Fullarton 'lest a rise should be occasioned in the price of butter and eggs.' By the 1790s his son, Colonel William Fullarton, was considering the possibility of a harbour at Troon, linked to Kilmarnock by canal. He himself had not the resources to carry the scheme to fruition. He sold out to the Marquis of Titchfield, who in 1808 began work on Troon harbour. £100,000 was spent constructing this new port. And further up the coast, on another rocky promontory, a second new port was constructed at Ardrossan by the 12th Earl of Eglinton, the 'Sodger Hugh' of Burns's 'Earnest Cry and Prayer'. Work on Ardrossan harbour began in 1806 and £100,000 was spent on it before Earl Hugh's death in 1819. Work also began on a sea canal between Glasgow and Ardrossan. From Glasgow (Port Eglinton) it extended through Paisley but never got further than Johnstone. Yet the Ardrossan harbour became Ayrshire's major port in the 19th century, and the Duke of Portland's Troon harbour similarly the chief coal-exporting port. Ayr and Irvine remained small, and Saltcoats harbour dwindled into insignificance.

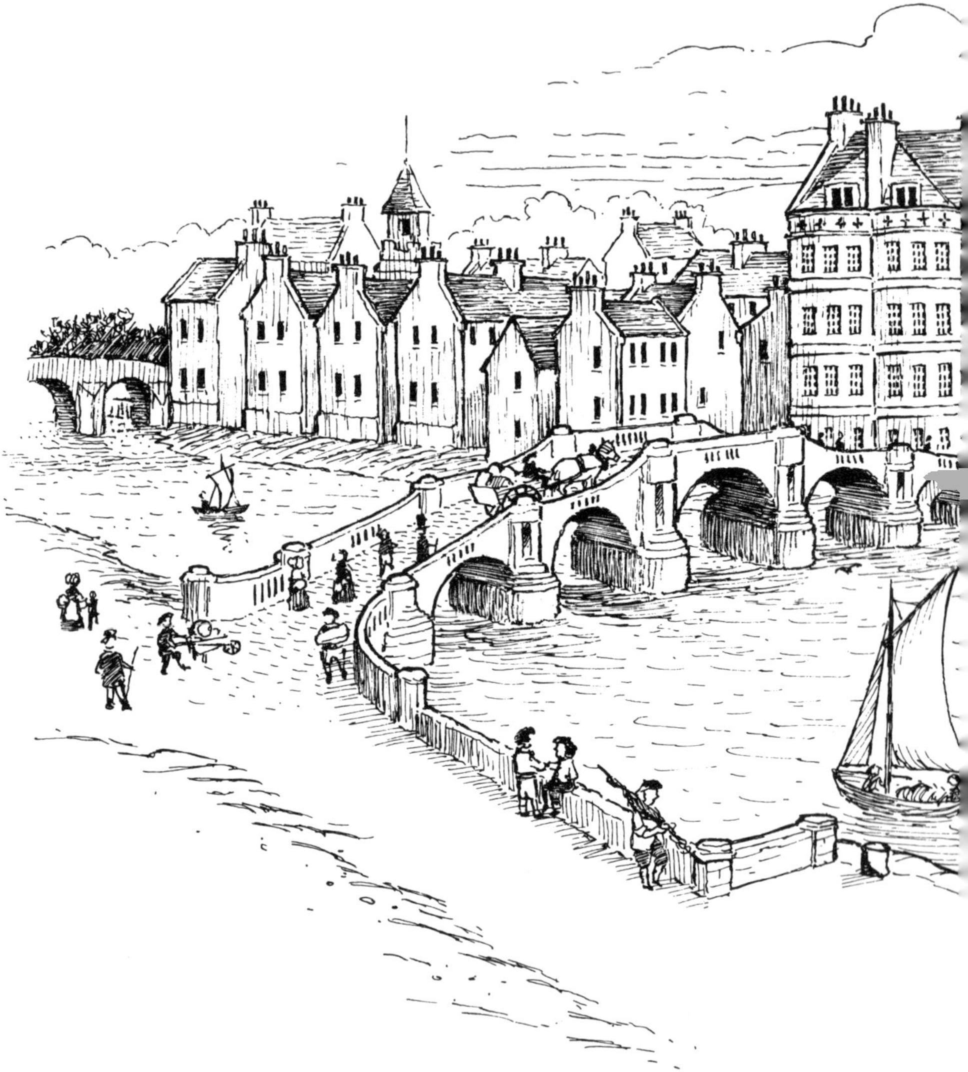

*Ayr and the Twa brigs*

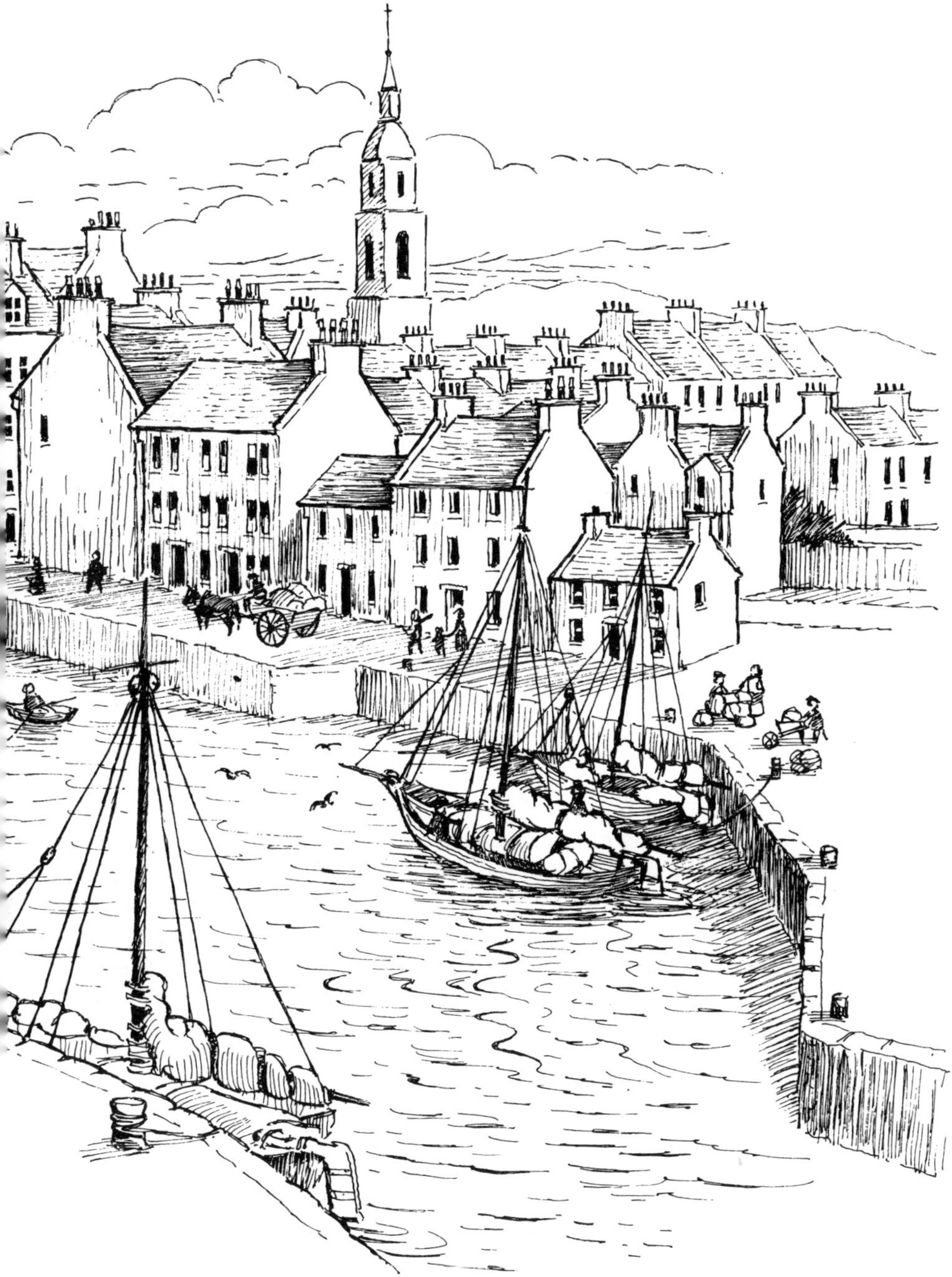

The very limited extent of Ayrshire shipping trade by the end of the 18th century can be gauged from the customs house registers of shipping. Imports were almost entirely of foodstuffs and raw materials. As far as foodstuffs were concerned, most were for trans-shipment to Paisley and Glasgow. Grain came from Ireland and Galloway to Ayr, Irvine, and occasionally Saltcoats, while some was brought from America through Irvine. Dairy products from Ireland also passed on their way through the county via Irvine. From America and the West Indies came from time to time cargoes of sugar, tobacco, and other produce, to Irvine or Ayr. Raw materials which arrived were nearly all for use in the county. All three ports kept up a steady trade in timber from the Baltic, while Irvine and later Ardrossan supplemented their requirements with cargoes from America, and ship-timber came from Wales for the ship-building yards. The Baltic also supplied iron and hemp. Hides were brought from Ireland and Galloway. From Ireland also were imported lime, linen yarn, and some manufactured linen cloth. The principal export of all three ports was coal, shipped mainly to Ireland in colliers which returned in ballast; some went from Irvine to America. Coal was also handled by coastal vessels, as was farm produce, some salt, and miscellaneous merchandise for Arran, Kintyre, and Galloway. Exports of manufactured goods were chiefly handled by Irvine: textiles and leather products to Ireland and America, including silks and cottons from Paisley for Ireland.

The greatest proportion of Ayrshire's manufactures, however, went by way of the Clyde. This was particularly so in the case of cotton, which was in the hands of Glasgow merchants. By 1800 the roads of north Ayrshire were busy with loads of raw cotton and manufactured products, coming from and going towards the warehouses of the city, and loads of farm produce going to feed the city population. And when Robert Burns planned to emigrate, it was from Greenock that he intended to depart.

One experiment in 1788 led eventually to a revolution in shipping. Its inspiration came from Patrick Miller of Dalswinton. In 1785 he engaged James Taylor from Leadhills as tutor. Miller was experimenting with paddle-boats driven by hand; Taylor suggested the use of a steam engine, and with the assistance of William Symington, another native of Leadhills, a steam-driven paddle boat was constructed. On 14th October 1788 it was driven at five miles an hour on Dalswinton Loch in Dumfriesshire – the first successful venture in steam navigation.

Among those present was possibly Robert Burns, who by now tenanted Miller's farm of Ellisland nearby. In 1802 Symington's *Charlotte Dundas* was steaming on the Forth-Clyde Canal, and ten years later Bell's *Comet* began regular steamer services on the Clyde.

CHAPTER 9

# THE KIRK

The Church of Scotland in the 18th century was constitutionally based on an Act of the Scottish parliament of 1690 whereby William and Mary did 'establish, ratify and confirm the presbyterian church government and discipline, that is to say the government of this church by kirke sessions, presbyteries, provinciall synods and generall assemblies . . . to be the only government of Christs Church within this kingdome.' This was confirmed in 1707 when Queen Anne and the new United Kingdom parliament made an Act for securing the Protestant Religion and Presbyterian Church Government in Scotland. Before these, since the Reformation of 1560, there had been a long and tangled conflict about control of the kirk, punctuated by the National Covenant of 1638, the Solemn League and Covenant of 1643, and the final period between 1660 and 1690 when the Covenanters of Ayrshire and Galloway had raised three rebellions and suffered in the Killing Times in defence of their principles.

The presbyterian system was now recognised. The presbyteries, reconstituted in 1690, were centred on royal burghs. The presbytery of Irvine had oversight of all the 16 Cuninghame parishes north of the River Irvine, save Largs. The presbytery of Ayr comprised all 19 parishes of Kyle, plus the parish of Newton-upon-Ayr newly created in 1779; and 7 of the 9 Carrick parishes, excluding Ballantrae and Colmonell – 27 in all. The presbyteries met monthly, composed of all the parish ministers and one elder from each parish. But the oversight the presbyteries could exercise was remote and limited. The effective unit was the parish. Parish ministers, though elected during brief periods, from 1649 till 1660 and from 1690 till 1712, were thereafter appointed by a patron, normally the principal landowner of the parish. Each parish had also its kirk session. Kirk sessions were bodies which had been in continuous existence since the time of the Reformation, exercising always an influential oversight of varied aspects of parochial life. Members were the elders of the congregation, a small self-elective group who by nature of that fact were always conservative in matters of religion. The parish minister was one of their number, the 'preaching elder' nominally of equal status. But he owed his appointment to a patron, he was responsible in matters of doctrine to the presbytery, and as moderator of the session he had the powers of their chairman.

The parishes of Ayrshire is the mid-18th century averaged a congregation of around a thousand souls. The places of worship could accommodate only a fraction of these numbers. Most indeed were old pre-reformation buildings adapted for protestant services. The church in Ayr where William Burnes and his family worshipped was built in the 17th century. But Mauchline was a typical church, variously described as 'a tabernacle pleasing to the eye' and 'as ugly a lump of consecrated stone as ever cumbered the earth.' It was a long narrow low-walled structure with a high steep roof and a bell tower above the east gable. Because of subsidence the floor was several feet below ground level, and from the main door in the south wall there were steps leading down into the interior. Just left of the entrance, against the south wall was the pulpit, to the right was the small Barskimming loft to provide seating for that landowner and his retainers. Opposite on the north wall was the Loudoun loft and the Ballochmyle loft. To the east the old chancel was partitioned off to form a school room and above it was the East loft with ten pews leased to lesser lairds. To the west was the Auchinleck loft and below it the repentance seat. A stone floor was laid over the area in 1774 and a dozen pews provided for public annual auction, but most of the congregation stood, or squatted on stools. In the middle of the area were the long communion tables.

Within the old damp and dark cramped kirk, lit by half-a-dozen small windows, sometimes supplemented by candles, Rev. William Auld conducted the church services. There were usually two diets of worship each Sunday, with sometimes a week-night meeting which might involve worship, instruction, or catechising. The parish minister was responsible for the conduct of the services, in which the central feature was the sermon. This exposition was expected to occupy at least an hour (as measured by a sandglass) and one passage of scripture was analysed in a series of sermons. In Sorn eight verses of Psalm 19 provided material for a series which commenced in April 1704 and continued for the next nineteen months. Praise involved the unaccompanied singing of psalms, led by the precentor, usually the parish schoolmaster who also acted as session clerk. The congregation sat while singing but stood during prayer. In the course of the regular service, one or more miscreants might be publicly rebuked, either while standing at their usual place, or at the Repentance Seat – the so-called 'cutty stool' – in the most serious cases dressed in sackcloth.

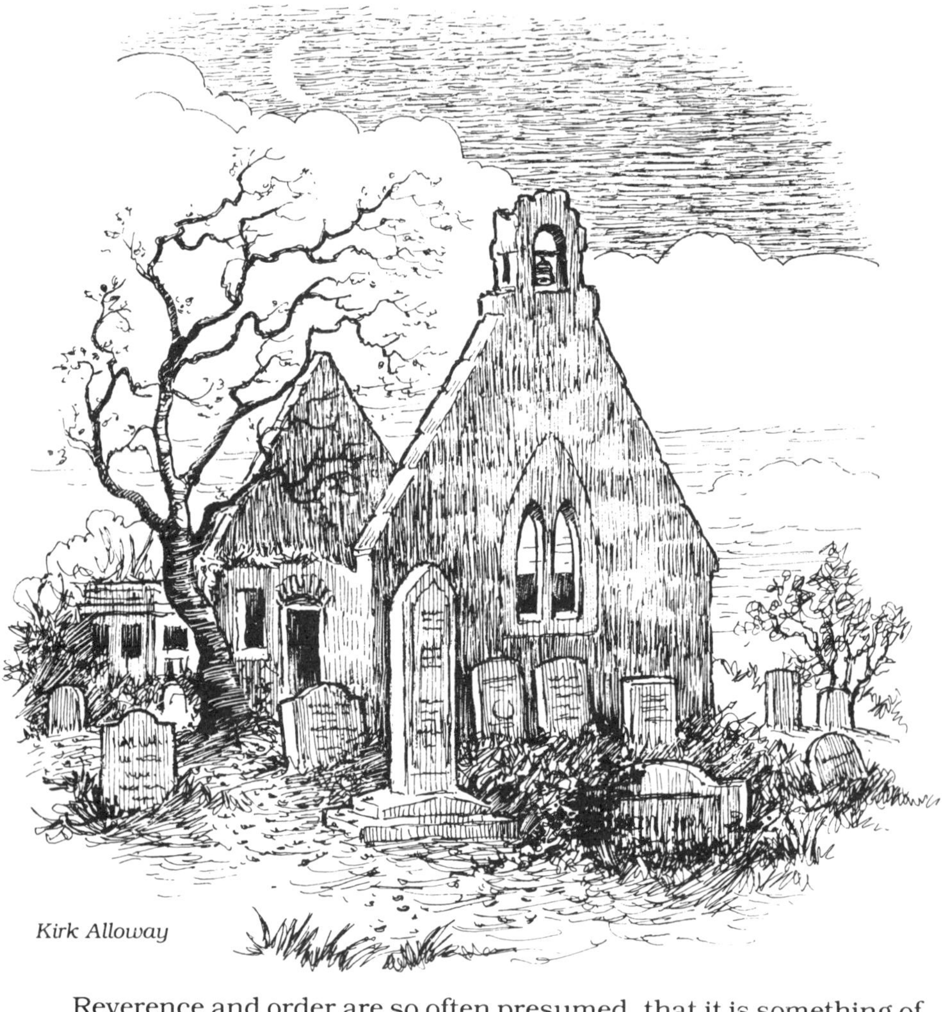

*Kirk Alloway*

Reverence and order are so often presumed, that it is something of a shock to read Aiton's description of an 18th century church service in Ayrshire: 'The people seldom take their seats in the church, in proper time, and in a composed and becoming manner. When the weather permits, they stand in groups, round the church, retailing the news of the day, or conversing on their ordinary business, till the minister is about to enter the pulpit, when they rush into the church, in a tumultuous and irregular manner; and sometimes a large portion of the congregation, enter the church after the service is begun. The doors are allowed to remain open, and dogs, cats, hens, chickens, &c. enter and disturb the worship. It is not uncommon, for the dogs to fight several battles, among themselves in the church, in the time of divine service; and there are instances of the owners of these dogs coming to blows in the church, in support of favourite tykes. The people are frequently during the service, and even during the most solemn parts of it, gazing round them at the audience, or making signs or gestures to their friends. If any person enters, or retires during the service, every eye in the church is fixed on them, and nothing from the pulpit is attended to for a time. As the Psalms, at the close of the service, draw near a period; and during the most solemn act of pronouncing the blessing, the congregation are employed in putting up their bibles, and hymn-books, collecting their staves, hats, &c. and the females in tucking up their coats, and preparing for the road. No attention is paid to that most solemn part of the service. The people are throng while the minister is pronouncing it, and whenever it is finished, the congregation start as if it were a race.' The environs of the church were treated in an equally irreverent manner. The kirk session of Mauchline as their records report, were vexed by cattle straying into the kirkyard which had become 'a Sort of Dunghill and common office house for the whole town, a receptacle for all filthiness so that one can scarce walk to Church with clean feet' and also 'a place of randevous for all sorts of idle and disorderly persons, who break the windows of the Church, break the tombs & gravestones and deface the engravings thereon.'

In addition to the usual regular church services it was considered desirable to provide communion services to celebrate the Sacrament. Twice annually was the norm, though there were sometimes long periods when it was found impossible to arrange communion services. When they were held there were important preliminaries – examination and purging of the roll, distribution of the lead communion tokens, a fasting day and preparatory service, the setting up of tables in the kirk, the provision of claret wine by the patron. In earlier times when communion services were held only irregularly in many parishes, communicants tended to flock from the whole surrounding district, and this custom survived. Regular church services were abandoned in a number of neighbouring parishes as parishioners and ministers assembled to attend such a 'Holy Fair.' The popularity of Mauchline reached its peak in the 1780s. Numbers taking communion there, on the second Sunday in August, rose from 578 (1750), 850 (1771), 1000 (1779) to 1300 (1780), 1350 (1784), 1242 (1785), about 1400 (1786), over 1300 (1787), about 1400 (1788), then dropped to 700 (1793), 600 (1794), 500 (1805), 400 (1819). Mauchline was thronged with visitors for the whole weekend, as is reflected in the church offerings. In the year 1785 – when Burns described the scene of 'The Holy Fair' – the collections were: 'Fast day: 19/10; Saturday: £1/11/11; Sacramental sabbath: £4/1/2½; Monday £1/14/2'. The total of less than £9 brought less than 1p average from the 1242 communicants. On these occasions two elders attended the collection plate set in the open just outside the main entrance gate opposite the Cowgate. A wooden preaching tent was set up where visiting ministers addressed the crowds waiting in the east end of the kirkyard, around the old ash tree where latterly the church bell was hung. At the west end were tents where food and drink could be purchased and itinerant hucksters supplied inappropriate entertainments. The communicants entered the church in groups of eighty, so that in 1785 there must have been fifteen or sixteen 'tables' or services going on throughout the whole Sunday.

Throughout the year the kirk session concerned itself with the spiritual welfare of the parishioners. The minister himself was responsible for regular visitation of all households to catechise adults and children, and ensure that family worship was being performed. The elders were allocated districts and were responsible for reporting any misdemeanours. In Ayr there were 20 elders. In Mauchline there were nominally fifteen. Landlords and merchants were sometimes elders, but most were persons of the middle rank – craftsmen and in the country, tenant farmers. Such were most zealous, and half-a-dozen or fewer formed the nucleus of what Burns vilified as 'the houghmagandie pack' of Mauchline.

The 18th century kirk session was a sort of omnicompetent agency of community welfare. In default of any effective civil authority it concerned itself with theft, embezzlement, assault, murder, riot, vandalism, vagrancy, as well as matters like sabbath-breaking. In fact, all that it could effectively do was to issue a rebuke, and refer the issue to the Justices of the Peace or the sheriff. The same was true in cases of immorality – which by their lights concerned only one of the seven deadly sins! The session was effective as a court only when it was pursuing those parishioners who were guilty of sexual lapses and who were prepared to submit to the session's authority. Persons cited to appear before the session sometimes failed to compear, and others who were found guilty sometimes did not appear in church for the public rebukes and final admonishment. In a growing population and a rapidly changing society the kirk sessions were losing their control. The session records are filled with reports of sexual misdemeanours and have conveyed the impression of a period of gross immortality. A close analysis of the years from 1783 till 1788 in Mauchline reveals two cases of adultery, five of ante-nuptial fornication, four of fornication outwith marriage, and the one sizeable figure of thirty-three cases of fornication leading to illegitimate births. The numbers for successive years were 5, 6, 3, 6, 7, 6. The total number of baptisms in Mauchline kirk was 72 (1786) and 59 (1787). The illegitimacy rate was therefore about 10% which is no higher than in many places in southwest Scotland in the 20th century; indeed in 1976 the figure for the Cumnock and Doon Valley District (which includes Mauchline) was 12.1%, and the Scottish average 9.3%. For those who submitted to the authority of the session for whatever offence, the penalties included fines, exclusion from communion of those who remained impenitent, three appearances before the congregation for fornication, five or more for adultery. Public penance was abandoned in Mauchline in 1809, just as fixing miscreants by the neck to the 'jougs' outwith the church seems to have been given up by the 18th century. And testimonials from the session for persons moving from one parish to another could now be easily done without in a society where the power of the sessions was being flouted by more and more people.

Three case studies will reveal how various were the responses to charges presented by Mauchline kirk session.

In 1773 George Gibson, tailor and innkeeper, his wife Agnes Ronald ('Poosie Nansie') and their daughter Janet Gibson ('Racer Jess') were accused of re-setting stolen goods. They were summoned on 3rd January, but did not compear. Witnesses were examined, the case continued, and on 22nd April the session decided that 'George Gibson keeps a very irregular house, that his wife and daughter are guilty of resetting of Stollen Goods.' They were summoned for rebuke, but none appeared. At the next meeting on 29th April it was further stated that 'Agnes Ronald, wife of George Gibson is habitually drunk, troublesome to her neighbours, and frequently disturbs the sober passengers.' To answer this further summons Poosie Nansie eventually compeared on 6th May but only to announce to them 'that she is resolved to continue in her disorderly way, declares her resolution to continue in the Sin of Drunkenness.'

The second case extended from 1777 till 1787, involving a long running feud between the session and Gavin Hamilton, the lawyer friend of Burns. For seven years from 1777 the session unsuccessfully attempted to obtain from him moneys to which they believed they were entitled, being arrears of the poor rate for whose collection he had been responsible. In July 1784 as a result of what Hamilton called 'private pique and ill nature' they included his name on a list of those who 'habitually neglect to attend upon God's Ordinances' and the Clerk was ordered to advise them in a 'private and friendly manner' about more regular attendance at church. Skilled in the minutiae of the law, Hamilton took the case to the presbytery, and after protracted argument the session was forced on 17th July 1785 to declare Gavin Hamilton 'free from public scandal or ground of Church Censure.' Two years later the session again tackled Hamilton, this time for ordering his servant Robert Bryan to dig potatoes on the 'last Lord's day' of July 1787. Once again the lawyer, after a five month contest, forced the session to drop the charge against him, and the case concluded on 13th January 1788 with Robert Bryan acknowledging 'his sin in breach of Sabbath' and being rebuked by the session.

The third case concerns a young couple who conventionally submitted to the session's authority - Robert Burns and Jean Armour. On 2nd April 1786 the session noted that Jean Armour, an unmarried woman, is said to be with child, and has gone to reside elsewhere. Two elders, James Lamie and William Fisher, were appointed to speak to the parents. On 19th April Lamie reported that he had spoken to Mary Smith, Jean's mother. She declared she did not suspect anything, that Jean had gone to Paisley to visit friends and would return soon. On 11th June 'The Session being informed that Jean Armour is with child order their officer to summon her to attend upon Sabbath first.' On 18th June she compeared not, but sent a letter to the minister, acknowledging that she was with child and naming as the father

Robert Burns in Mossgiel. Robert Burns was summoned, compeared at the next meeting on 25th June, and signed an acknowledgement that he was the father of Jean Armour's children – the twins who would be born on 3rd September, Robert who would be taken to Mossgiel, Jean who would live with the Armours but survived only fourteen months. On two Sundays in July, just before the publication of the Kilmarnock edition of his poems, and finally on 6th August, Robert and Jean had to appear before the congregation, standing in their own places. 'August 6th 1786. – Robert Burns, John Smith, Mary Lindsay, Jean Armour, and Agnes Auld appeared before the Congregation professing their repentance for the sin of fornication, and they having each appeared two several Sabbaths formerly, were this day rebuked and absolved from the scandal.' The following year Burns made his 'eclatant return' to Mauchline from Edinburgh and Jean was 'in for it again.' He departed once more, before the death of little Jean in October. The mother, pregnant again, was once more summoned before the session on 2nd December 1787; but she sent an excuse on the 9th. Burns returned to Mauchline on 23rd February 1788 to find that Jean had left the Armour home and taken refuge in Tarbolton. 'Jean I found banished like a martyr, and I have taken her a room' in the Back Causeway in Mauchline. He left her for a short visit to Ellisland. Just after his return, on 3rd March Jean gave birth to twin girls. On 10th March one died. On 13th March the session summoned her to appear before them on the 23rd. About the 13th, Burns went off again to Edinburgh. The second girl died on the 22nd. There is no record of the session having met on the 23rd. In April Burns returned and acknowledged Jean Armour as his wife in a legal ceremony. This is said to have been in the writing office of Gavin Hamilton's house, with John Farquhar of Gilmilnscroft present as a justice of the peace. In the session records for July they are listed among the 'Persons under Scandal' as 'their recent affair not settled.' On 5th August final settlement was made: 'Compeared Robert Burns with Jean Armour his Alledged Spouse. They both acknowledge their irregular marriage and their sorrow for that irregularity and desiring that the Session will take such steps as may seem to them proper in order for the Solemn confirmation of the said marriage. The Session taking this affair under their Consideration Agree that they both be rebuked for this Acknowledged irregularity and that they be taken solemnly engaged to adhere faithfully to One another as husband and wife all the days of their life. In regard the Session have a title in Law to some fine for behoof of the poor They agree to refer Mr. Burns to his own generosity. The above sentence was accordingly executed and the Session absolved the said parties from any scandal on this Account. Sgd. William Auld, Moderator, Robert Burns, Jean Armour. Mr. Burns gave a Guinea note for behoof of the poor.'

Discipline was one only of the duties of the kirk sessions, though the one that has attracted most notice. The relief of the poor and the provision of education were also the concern of the sessions and the assiduity with which these objects were pursued, often in the face of difficulties, should arouse nothing but admiration. Care for those in distress was a responsibility of the medieval church which was honourably inherited by its protestant successor. Knox in his *First Book of Discipline* indicated that each parish should look after its own poor, and a series of acts of parliament in the 16th and 17th centuries made this a mandatory duty. The income of the kirk session - church collections supplemented by fees for burials (mortcloth money) and private baptisms, fines for misdemeanour, some rents, and occasional donations - was almost entirely devoted to the relief of the deserving poor. Such were natives of the parish who by reason of age or infirmity were unable to maintain themselves and were without relatives to come to their aid. But funds, always scarce, became even more limited in a century of rising population and social dislocation. An Act of 1692 had authorised the levying of a stent on landowners and tenants but the heritors (landowners) of most parishes were reluctant to meet and organise this. In practice poor relief was normally left to the kirk session. In Mauchline in 1771, with a paupers' list of 21 persons, an expenditure of £56 and an income of only £37, the heritors agreed to stent themselves by a poors rate of one penny on each pound Scots of valued rent, raising over £20 annually which covered any deficiency and built up a poors stock which was invested with the Tanyard Company of Kilmarnock, passing £100 by 1776. Around 1780 the annual stent was abandoned and the capital steadily eroded away. In 1791 Rev. William Auld complained that 'it is the poor in Scotland who maintain the poor.' In 1811 Aiton indicated that only in Ayr, Kilmarnock, and Loudoun were regular assessments made. By that time there were 1,132 paupers in 42 of the 46 Ayrshire parishes and numbers were increasing so fast that by 1845 government had to step in to form parochial boards and take over the poor relief duties which the kirk sessions had hitherto so valiantly undertaken. Similarly with education. The 1696 Education Act of the Scots Parliament made possible the establishment of a system of parish schools, but only because kirk session backed by presbyteries provided a constant incentive to coax the heritors into making provision, unsupported till a further Act of 1803 made it a mandatory responsibility.

With their concern for poor relief, education, and discipline in its widest sense, the kirk sessions were the central institutions in the 18th century parochial communities. Yet as that century advanced their position of power and influence was being steadily weakened, both by the external factors of a changing society and by internal dissensions within the kirk.

Burns grew up in a period when, as he said, 'Polemical divinity about this time was putting the country half-mad.' The traditional Calvinist theology of the Church of Scotland was still being vigorously propounded by many ministers, and firmly accepted by many elders and other parishioners in this part of Scotland where the Covenanting memories were green. But these Evangelicals or High-fliers or Auld Lichts were being increasingly challenged by the Moderates or Legal Men or New Lichts, and ministers of this persuasion, graduating from universities where the old theology faced criticism and appointed by patrons who were sometimes men of the Enlightenment, preached not on predestination but on practical morality. Robert Burns, whose father's 'Manual of Religious Belief' contained liberal sentiments, was from the beginning disposed towards the Moderates, and 'ambitious of shining in conversation parties on Sundays between sermons, funerals, &c. used in a few years more to puzzle Calvinism with so much heat and indiscretion that I raised a hue and cry of heresy against me.' John Goldie, the Kilmarnock merchant, published in 1780 *Essays on*

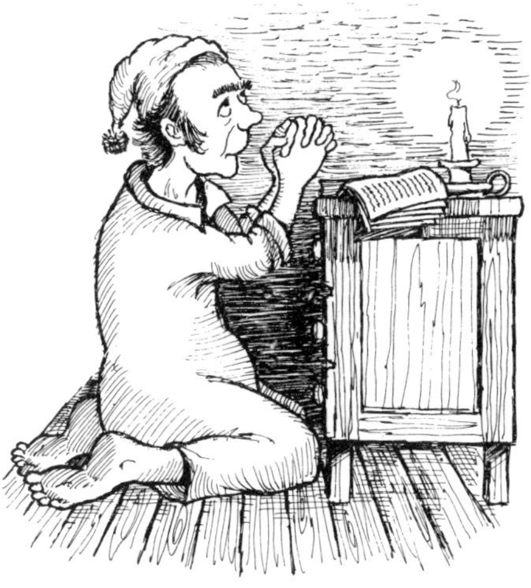

*Holy Willie*

*Various Important Subjects Moral and Divine.* A second edition in 1785 and a further work in the same year called *The Gospel Recovered* inspired Burns to write an 'Epistle to John Goldie' where he praises 'Gowdie's Bible' and its attack on 'sour bigotry'. This, followed by 'The Twa Herds' concerning a quarrel between two high-flier ministers over parish boundaries, and his 'Holy Willie's Prayer' did more than anything else to win Burns his local celebrity in Ayrshire. In 'Holy Willie's Prayer' where he satirised the hypocrisy of William Fisher, the Mauchline elder who had been bested by Gavin Hamilton, Burns brilliantly summarised the basis of Calvinism:

*O Thou that in the Heavens does dwell,*
*Wha, as it pleases best Thysel,*
*Sends ane to Heaven, an ten to Hell,*
*A' for Thy glory,*
*And no for onie guid or ill*
*They've done before Thee!* CW 93

In 'The Ordination', 'The Address to the Unco Guid, 'The Holy Fair' and other pieces he continued his satire. And when Dr. William McGill, one of the Ayr ministers, had published in 1786 *A Practical Essay on the Death of Jesus Christ* and he was charged with heresy, Burns returned to the attack in 'The Kirk's Alarm'. While Burns' personal religious beliefs were never completely committed to the Moderate point of view, and while as a poet he could view the ecclesiastical scene from the remoteness of Parnassus, the anti-Calvinist faction applauded him for the virulence of his verse:

*But I gae mad at their grimaces,*
*Their sighin, cantin, grace-proud faces,*
*Their three-mile prayers, an hauf-mile graces,*
*Their raxin conscience,*
*Whase greed, revenge, an pride disgraces*
*Waur nor their nonsense.* CW 129

Many had already deserted the Church of Scotland, and their numbers steadily increased throughout the 18th century. There were those who believed that the established kirk had betrayed its true Calvinist principles, and the introduction of lay patronage in 1712 seemed to confirm that it had lost its ecclesiastical independence. Very often the presentation of a new parish minister became the occasion for a local furore. John Galt began the *Annals of the Parish* with the placing of Rev. Micah Balwhidder who recalled that 'I was put in by the patron, and the people knew nothing whatsoever of me, and their hearts were stirred into strife on the occasion, and they did all that lay within the compass of their power to keep me out, insomuch, that there was obliged to be a guard of soldiers to protect the presbytery; and it was a thing that made my heart grieve when I heard the drum beating and the fife playing as we were going to the kirk. The people were really mad and vicious, and flung dirt upon us as we passed, and reviled us all, and held out the finger of scorn at me.' Galt's fiction was based on local fact. In 1764 when Rev. William Lindsay was presented by the Earl of Glencairn to the second charge in Kilmarnock, there was such a popular clamour and riot – in which the earl was struck on the face with a dead cat – that the church could not be reached and the induction took place in a public hostelry. In 1782 the ordination of Rev. William Boyd was similarly prevented by a mob at Fenwick and the ceremony had to be transferred to Irvine. Elsewhere bands of parishioners simply withdrew themselves when a new minister was presented, and formed their own separate church, as occurred in Mauchline following the death of Rev. William Auld in 1791.

Already at the beginning of the 18th century there were in Ayrshire small separate groups of followers of the extreme Covenanter, Richard Cameron, who complained that the Covenants had not been implemented in the settlement of 1690 and so remained outwith the Church of Scotland. These Cameronian praying societies survived, and in 1785 their largest congregation was able to build a Reformed Presbyterian church at Crookedholm by Kilmarnock. An actual Secession from the Church of Scotland in 1733 produced Ayrshire's first seceding congregation formed at Kilmaurs in 1740, with its own church built two years later. A schism in the secession church followed in 1747 as to whether members in burghs might validly swear the burgess oath. The General Associate Synod of Anti-burghers won converts in Ayrshire. The Kilmaurs church was joined by nine others in Ayrshire before the end of the century. The Associate Synod of Burghers also had ten. A separate break-away from the Church of Scotland in 1761 led to the formation of the Relief Kirk, represented locally by three congregations.

That the dissenters were themselves intensely disunited appeared in the first secession congregation at Kilmaurs. The congregation was in 1747 split between Burghers and Anti-burghers; Rev. David Smyton at first sided with the Burghers, then confessed his error and was re-instated. In 1782 he and the majority of the congregation insisted on his lifting the bread before blessing it despite a prohibition of the Synod, and the Lifters continued, with the Anti-Lifters leaving to form a separate congregation. Later in 1799 the whole General Associate Synod was split between Auld Licht Anti-burghers and New Licht Anti-burghers, while in 1806 a similar schism in the Associate Synod produced Auld Licht Burghers and New Licht Burghers.

Meanwhile the Relief Kirk in Irvine had been convulsed by its own peculiar schism. In 1783, just after Burns had left Irvine to return to Lochlea there came to the royal burgh one Mrs. Elspeth Buchan who became a member of the Relief congregation. Mrs. Buchan had a revelation, that she was the Third Person of the Godhead. Rev. Hugh White accepted her claims and was deposed. The Buchanites formed themselves into a community. Burns said that he had 'personally acquainted with most of them' and explained: 'Their tenets are a strange jumble of enthusiastic jargon, among others, she pretends to give them the Holy Ghost by breathing on them, which she does with postures & practices that are scandalously indecent; they have likewise disposed of all their effects & hold a community of goods, & live nearly an idle life, carrying on a great farce of pretended devotion in barns, & woods, where they lodge & lye all together, & hold likewise a community of women, as it is another of their tenets that they can commit no moral sin.' Mrs. Buchan was expelled from Irvine, her adherents followed her in the quest for the New Jerusalem. Their long trek took them past Mossgiel and through Mauchline. As they passed by Cumnock, Hugh Logan of Logan, the celebrated wit, remarked he was gey pleased to hear that Logan was on the road to Heaven. They went on to Dumfries and settled in Kirkcudbrightshire to await the imminent Second Coming. On the death of Mrs. Buchan in 1791 the community dispersed.

New congregations of a more orthodox sort were formed in the county by immigrant groups. In Ayr a congregation of Episcopalians was formed in 1743 and a church established in 1744, but partly because of the penal laws against Scottish episcopalians there was an intermittent ministry till well into the 19th century. Also to Ayr in 1765 came Moravian missionaries who became firmly settled, building a church in Mill Street which continued into the 20th century. And to Ayr came the Methodists in 1785, holding their first services in a stable, then becoming a recognised church. Finally, in the last decades of the 18th century, to Ayr and district there came trickling what would later become a flood of Irish immigrants. An occasional Roman Catholic priest made a visitation, and from 1803 till 1811 some pastoral work was done by the Abbé Nicholas who taught French at Ayr Academy. But it was not till 1827 that a chapel was built.

At the end of the 18th century the Church of Scotland still claimed parochial suzerainty. But many people were going elsewhere for spiritual solace. Others were now content to live unshepherded.

CHAPTER 10

# EDUCATION

Scotland is unique in its educational heritage. Before the Reformation, here as elsewhere some churches are known to have had schools where boys were taught singing and Latin to train them as choristers, and some were sent forward to university to prepare them for the priesthood. The only local example recorded is Ayr where a 'sang schule' was in existence in 1233. John Knox's *First Book of* Discipline proposed a national system of parish schools where all might learn to read – so to understand the Bible – and burgh schools where any lad o' pairts would be prepared for and encouraged to go to university to become a minister, a schoolmaster, or otherwise be of 'benefit to the commonwealth'. Though this ideal would be long in becoming reality, a series of acts of the Scots parliament from 1567 onwards provided a basis, and kirk sessions spurred on by the presbyteries tried to persuade heritors to provide parish schools and appoint schoolmasters. By 1642, twenty of the twenty seven parishes within the presbytery of Ayr were supplied with a school. Despite some setbacks in the difficult Covenanting times later in the century, the 1696 Education Act provided a new incentive. By the 1790s all Ayrshire parishes were supplied with a school save the small parish of Stair.

The first difficulty that the kirk sessions had to overcome was to persuade the heritors to undertake their statutory responsibility of providing a school building. At Dailly in 1741 it was decided to erect a new building 'thirty foot length, and fourteen foot wideness within the walls, with side walls six foot high, having four windows of two foot and a half by one foot and a half, of the form of close sash windows, with a hewnstone door, also two seats of fir dale for the scholars, running along both sides of the house from one gavill to the other, with a desk also of fir dale before one of the seats, of the same length, and a fire vent in each gavill.' Loudoun boasted that it had one of the best schools in the west of Scotland, with a slate roof and the master's dwelling in the upper storey, and the classroom 36 feet long, 16 feet wide, and 10 feet high. But elsewhere conditions were much less satisfactory. Maybole school was 'an old mean thatched house', West Kilbride 'an indifferent smoky inconvenient house', Stevenston 'old and inconvenient' and Ardrossan 'almost in ruin.' In some places like Mauchline the school was still held in the east end of the church – the former chancel which had been walled off.

The second difficulty of the kirk session was to persuade the heritors to stent themselves to provide a schoolmaster with an annual salary somewhere between one and two hundred merks – say from £5 to £10 a year. As the century advanced inflation made this less of a burden to heritors, who could leave the schoolmaster to augment this slim stipend from fees and other emoluments. But by the same token, inflation was making school-teaching a less attractive occupation. Schools sometimes had to close down because no candidate came forward to fill a vacant post and many of the candidates were poorly qualified. Parishes which wanted satisfactory teachers had to pay more than the minimum. Some gave a minimal increase by paying in pounds Scots (= 1/8 sterling) instead of merks (= 1/1½ sterling) and nearly half of the Ayrshire parishes went beyond this.

Burns attended a parish school in Dalrymple in 1772. Six years later when there was a vacancy there, all they could obtain was a young man 'inclining to be a schoolmaster'. By contrast, the parish school at Kirkoswald which he attended in 1775 was taught by Hugh Rodger and 'solely by his own industry and application he attained to such efficiency in mathematics and cognate subjects that while yet a young man he received the appointment of schoolmaster in Kirkoswald, and acquired in course of time an enviable degree of fame as a teacher of unusual gifts and accomplishments.' But the heritors paid him only 100 merks minimum plus the rent of a house. Similar parsimony afflicted another parish schoolmaster whose acquaintance Burns later made. John Wilson had to leave Craigie because he could not make ends meet on the minimum stipend. The great majority of the heritors felt he deserved better, but it was decided in a court case that the dissident minority could not be compelled to pay more. In Tarbolton Wilson fared no better, and to supplement his income he opened a grocery shop where he sold drugs and gave medical advice

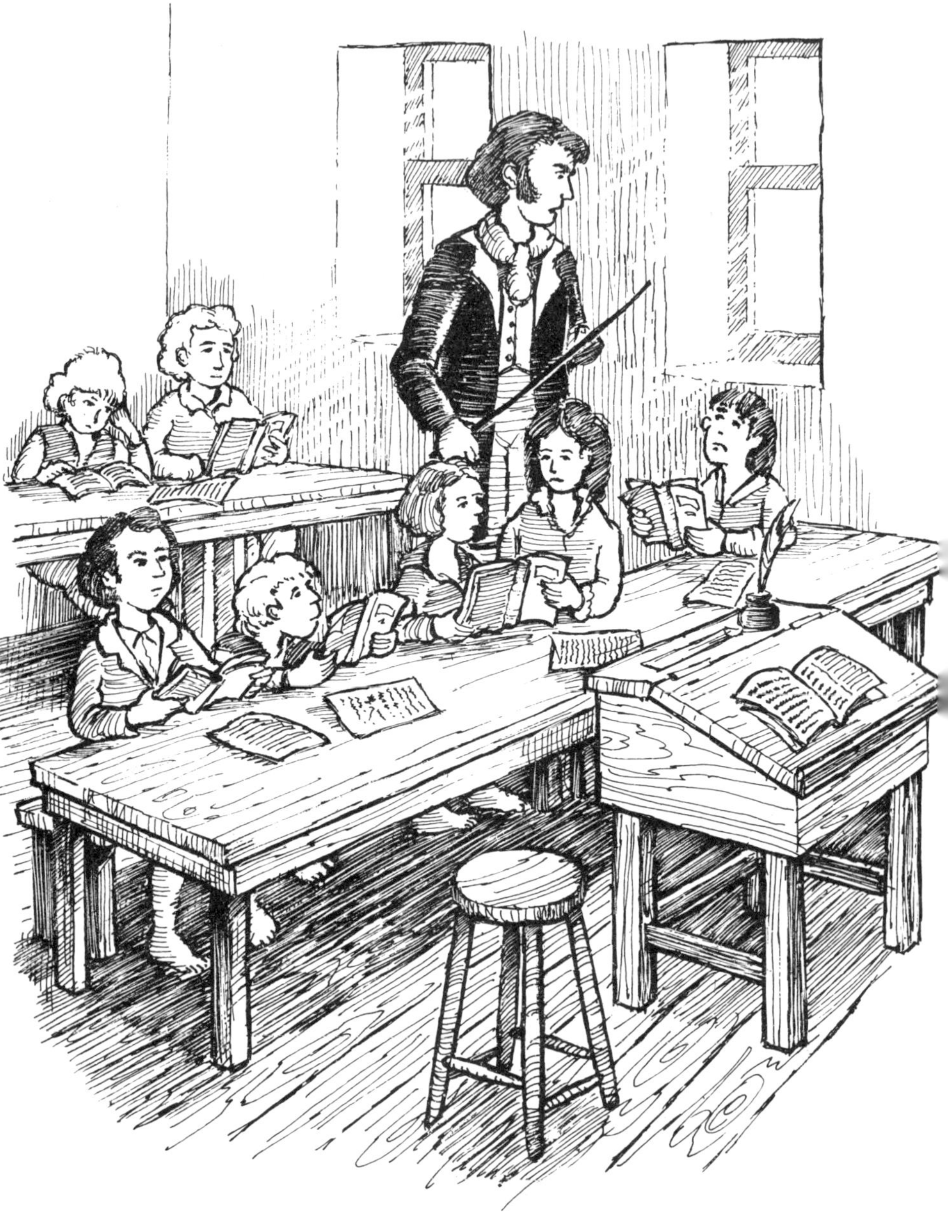

– which inspired Burns' satire on 'Death and Dr. Hornbook'. His neglect of the school forced dismissal in 1791, but he found employment as a schoolmaster in the Gorbals, where he appears to have done well enough. The parish schoolmaster of Mauchline, Andrew Noble, whom Burns must have known, was much more fortunate. He was appointed in 1763 at the age of seventeen when the salary was augmented to £120 Scots and the scale of fees also was increased. He remained in Mauchline as parish schoolmaster and session clerk for fifty-eight years till his death in 1821 at the age of seventy-five. A similarly lengthy career was that of William Simpson, the 'Winsome Willie' to whom Burns addressed one of his poetical epistles. Simpson was a graduate of Glasgow University who aspired to the ministry, but like so many others failed to obtain a charge and had to content himself with school-teaching. He taught for eight years in Ochiltree, then moved to Cumnock where he continued till his death in 1815. He had two brothers, Patrick and Andrew, also teachers. Patrick began teaching in Straiton, followed his brother in Ochiltree, completed fifty years there in 1833, and died in 1851.

The basic studies were reading and writing. Everyone who attended learned to read, but not all learned to write. A smaller group learned arithmetic – which was first introduced into Mauchline by Andrew Noble in 1763. In about a dozen schools Latin was also taught, to enable clever boys to go on direct to the university. Fees at Mauchline were typical: reading, 1/6 per quarter (7½p); writing, 1/6 (7½p); Latin, 2/6 (12½p); arithmetic 2/- (10p). Parents 'in low circumstances' were allowed reduced rates, and those 'upon the Public Charity' could have their children – whether boys or girls – taught gratis, with fees paid by the kirk session. Most children seem to have attended school for at least an occasional quarter, when work was light about the farm. Most of the pupils were boys, and few girls were enrolled for anything beyond reading.

In the course of the century some of the schools were attempting to widen their curriculum. A few schools were offering Greek and French. More were introducing practical subjects. Book-keeping was taught by the end of the century at Kilwinning, Beith, Stewarton, Muirkirk, Mauchline, Craigie, Ballantrae, and Dailly. Navigation was studied in Ardrossan and surveying in Kirkoswald and Loudoun. Similar and special developments were taking place in the three towns of Ayr, Irvine and Kilmarnock.

In the royal burghs of Ayr and Irvine the town councils had taken control of the burgh schools, and in Kilmarnock followed suit. In Ayr indeed the council had taken over from the church the responsibility for the appointment of a schoolmaster as early as 1554 and by the 17th century in all three towns were supplying not only the schoolmaster but an assistant master known as the 'doctor'. How significant were further developments is best seen in the case of Ayr. In 1746 when John Mair, who had been doctor since 1727, was appointed to take charge with the new title of rector, he turned the burgh school into what he called 'a sort of academy'. Of the three teachers, 'One of them is wholly to be taken up in teaching to read English, and that according to the newest and most approved method. The business of another is to teach Latin and Greek, and the province of the third is to teach Arithmetic, Bookeeping (*sic*), Geography, Navigation, Surveying, Euclid's Elements, Algebra, and other Mathematical Sciences and some parts of Natural Philosophy.' In 1761 John Mair went off to Perth to establish the first school in Scotland to describe itself as an academy. But the Ayr school was in effect, though not in name, the first academy in Scotland. With its modern studies it catered for the new needs of an expanding commercial economy and its pupils included not only the sons of the local burgesses but boys who were boarded in Ayr by well-off parents from the landward area and even from overseas. Fees were expensive, ranging from 10p per quarter for writing to more than £2 for a course in mathematics. This educational development in the burgh of Ayr culminated in the establishment of Ayr Academy in 1798. A bequest of £1000 from the estate of John Fergusson of Doonholm was supplemented by a flood of subscriptions – £50 made the donor a director of the academy – and under the guidance of Provost John Ballantine a royal charter was obtained. William Meikleham was appointed rector at a generous salary of £80, plus £20 for taking in boarders, plus fees; and the other four masters who were already among the best paid teachers in the county received appropriate augmentations. The academy started in the building of the old grammar school. The hours of attendance were: 7 a.m. (8 a.m. in winter) till 1 a.m., 2 p.m. till 4 p.m., 5 p.m. till 6 p.m., with astronomy in the evenings; on Saturday mornings the whole school met for awards of merit, reprimands, punishments, and fines. In 1800 demolition of the old school took place after rector, staff, and pupils moved into the grand new Academy built just behind the old school, with an initial roll of 269 pupils.

Similar though more modest developments occurred in the other two larger towns. At Kilmarnock the heritors and town council collaborated in establishing an Academy in 1811, while in Irvine the town council supported by subscribers set up an Academy in 1818. Thus there was being met an obvious demand by the wealthier burgesses for a modern education for their sons. Landlords were no longer content to send their sons to the local parish school. The wealthiest hired private tutors as a preliminary to a fashionable school in England. The lesser gentry sent their sons to board in one of the larger towns and attend the academy. Ayr and Irvine even took in pupils who had been sent home from overseas. In the towns private schools were also set up. Originally these were frowned upon as competing with the burgh or parish schools, but as the century advanced they were accepted as conveniently supplementing the limited public provision. In 1738 there were eight such schools in Ayr, seven of them run by women. In 1782 a boarding and public school for girls was set up in Ayr–'everything taught as complete as at Edinburgh.' Even in the villages the same sort of thing was taking place. In the fictional Dalmailing, Galt tells, 'Nanse learnt them reading and working stockings and how to sew the semplar for twalpennies a week . . . the lassies who had been at Nanse Bank's school were always well spoken of, for both their civility and the trigness of their houses when they were afterwards married.' These 'adventure schools' – that is, operated as a private venture – were common too in the country areas. At first prohibited by the sessions, they became tacitly accepted, and were even occasionally subsided, providing as they did for schooling in remoter corners of the larger parishes. David Sillar, member of Tarbolton Bachelors' Club, ran for a time such a school at Commonside. 'Poor uncle Robert', brother of William Burnes, worked in the lime quarries near Stewarton in the summer and kept a little school in the winter. In the Statistical Account examples are noted in Colmonell and Sorn similar to what was initiated at Alloway by William Burnes – a group of parents collaborating to hire a teacher for their children.

The enthusiasm which William Burnes devoted to the schooling of his family was perhaps exceptional, but not unique. Soon after he arrived in the Alloway area he made the close acquaintance of John Tennant, then occupying Laigh Corton farm, later at Glenconner as factor of the Countess of Glencairn's Ochiltree estate, — 'Guid Auld Glen.' Through him William Burnes made the acquaintance of his brother David Tennant, then English master at Ayr burgh school; and thus presumably Alexander Paterson, the Latin master, who had also come to Ayrshire from the north east. Even after Paterson's death in 1768, William Burnes and his wife continued to visit the widow frequently on a Sunday after attending Ayr church.

At Alloway a school had been held in the almost-ruinous kirk when David Tennant had been a child; by the 1760s it had been moved to Alloway Mill and there Robert was sent in his sixth year. But quite soon afterwards his teacher, Adam Campbell, was appointed master of the Ayr Poorshouse (which had been opened in 1756) and the school closed. Immediately William Burnes arranged with David Tennant to interview 18-year-old John Murdoch and in association with four other parents arranged a school in Alloway, boarding Murdoch in their homes and making up his fees to a stipulated sum. Robert and his younger brother Gilbert were pupils and even after the family moved to Mount Oliphant in 1766 the two boys continued to attend the school at Alloway. After two and a half years Murdoch moved off to teach in Dumfries, leaving William Burnes assisted by nine-year-old Robert to teach the younger members of the family. In 1772 Robert and Gilbert were sent week about for a summer quarter at Dalrymple parish school to improve their writing. In the same year John Murdoch returned to Ayr to succeed as English master David Tennant who had been promoted to Latin master. In the autumn of 1773 Robert spent three weeks - one before, two after the harvest - lodging with Murdoch in the Sandgate and attending Ayr burgh school, revising his English grammar, beginning French with Murdoch, and recommended to start Latin by William Robinson, the Writing master. Two years later in 1775, 16-year-old Robert was sent to stay with his mother's brother at Kirkoswald and spend a quarter at Hugh Rodger's parish school there, taking a course in mensuration and surveying. So he completed his formal education. His limited and irregular schooling was augmented by wide reading. Its extent is an index not only of his own enthusiasm but - just as significant - of the easy accessibility of books in 18th century Ayrshire. John Murdoch supplied not only school texts, but made available a range of literary works, including Shakespeare, Addison, Pope, and other English poets. William Burnes borrowed others from the widow of Alexander Paterson; had the loan of books on astronomy and natural history from the Ayr Library founded in 1762 of which David Tennant was a member; and had other acquaintances who were book-owners. From the gardener at Rozelle was obtained a volume on English history, from the blacksmith at Dalrymple Hamilton's History of William Wallace which made such a deep impression on young Robert. Purchases could also be made. William Burnes subscribed towards a history of the Bible; his brother-in-law Samuel Brown bought (in error) a collection of letters which provided Robert with models. Robert himself purchased a Latin grammar in Ayr and – more important – the poems of Robert Fergusson in Irvine. There were bookshops in Ayr, Irvine, Beith, and Kilmarnock. In Kilmarnock the bookseller John Wilson found it profitable to set up a printing press and between 1783 and 1790 (when he moved to Ayr) issued at least twenty-two publications. These were mainly sermons and religious works, but also Anson's *Voyage round the World*, Milton's *Paradise Lost*, an edition of John Mair's Latin grammar plus two texts in Latin; plus the Poems of Robert Burns in 1786 followed by those of George Campbell, John Lapraik, and David Sillar in each subsequent year, and a reprint of Allan Ramsay's *Tea-table Miscellany*. There was obviously both a demand for and a ready supply of books. And, wrote brother Gilbert, there were 'songs hawked about the country, in baskets, or exposed on stalls in streets.'

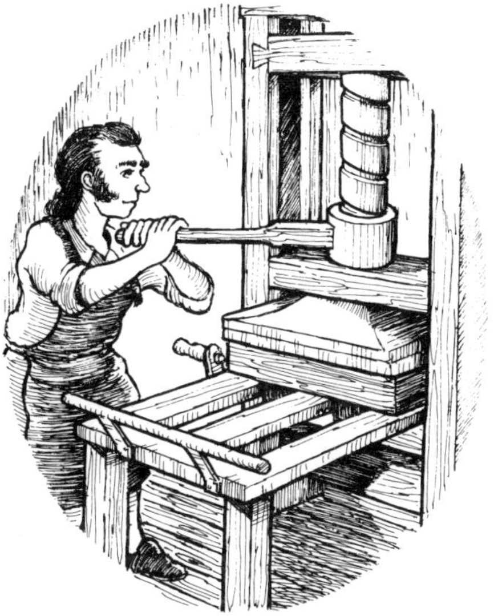

*Wilson the printer*

By the time he had reached his majority Burns had been able to acquire through reading some knowledge of religion and recent philosophy, geography, modern and classical history, agriculture and science in addition to an intimate acquaintance with English poetry, drama, essays and novels and such Scottish poetry and songs as were available in print. From Lochlea he could write to John Murdoch who had been dismissed from his Ayr post and gone to London: 'My favourite authors are of the sentimental kind, such as Shenstone, particularly his Elegies, Thomson, Man of Feeling, a book I prize next to the Bible, Man of the World, Sterne, especially his Sentimental Journey, Macpherson's Ossian, &c.'

He naturally became interested in libraries. Ayr Library founded in 1762 was followed by a Kilmarnock Library in 1797. But these catered for the more affluent members of society. When Burns left Tarbolton and its Bachelors' Club he was involved in forming a similar club in Mauchline called the Conversation Society, and fines for non-attendance were devoted to the purchase of books. When he moved to Dumfriesshire he found the same widespread passion for books. In the county town there was a Gentleman's Library dating from about 1745 and a Presbytery Library which had been formed in 1730. There was a library attached to the school at Lochmaben (1726) and the miners had formed their own reading societies at Leadhills (1741) and Wanlockhead (1756). In 1788 Burns collaborated with Robert Riddell in forming a circulating library which soon had 150 volumes. And in 1792 he also helped form Dumfries Public Library of which he was made an honourary member and to which he donated four volumes. In a letter to Sir John Sinclair and published in the Statistical Account, Robert Burns - with typical inverted snobbery signing himself 'A Peasant' - rather pompously describes the Dunscore Library: 'To store the minds of the lower classes with useful knowledge, is certainly of very great consequence, both to them as individuals, and to society at large. Giving them a turn for reading and reflection, is giving them a source of innocent and laudable amusement; and besides, raises them to a more dignified degree in the scale of rationality . . . A peasant who can read, and enjoy such books, is certainly a much superior being to his neighbours, who, perhaps, stalks beside his team, very little removed, except in shape, from the brutes he drives.'

CHAPTER 11

# POLITICS

Political power - like so many other things from patronage of literature and the arts to exploitation of minerals - was in the hands of the landowners. Nationally and locally, land was the basis of influence.

Ayrshire was represented in parliament both in the Lords and the Commons. Membership of the still-important House of Lords included sixteen Scottish peers, since 1707 elected at the beginning of each new parliament at an assembly of all Scottish peers held in Edinburgh. In the late 18th century the representative peers sometimes included as many as four from Ayrshire. The 4th Earl of Loudoun served for a long period (1734-1782) as did the 11th Earl of Eglinton (1776-1796); and the 10th Earl of Cassillis (1776-1792). In the House of Commons, which was growing in importance, there were two local constituencies.

There was one M.P. for the County of Ayr, elected by the more important landowners. Annually at Michaelmas a meeting was held in Ayr as the head burgh of the shire to draw up a roll of freeholders, who as occasion arose might meet to elect by public declaration the county member. Those enrolling were required to be adult male commoners, conforming protestants, and possessed of forty shilling land of old extent, or other land of four hundred pounds Scots valued rent. These numbered 97 in 1759 but here as elsewhere the roll was augmented by 'nominal and fictitious voters' as owners of large estates - including peers who as such could not vote in an election to the Commons - allocated suitable portions of land to lawyers or political friends. Thus by 1781 the roll had risen to a peak of 235 freeholders, but with other land changes it had dwindled to 110 by 1791. It is clear that the peers had sufficient influence to determine the outcome of an election, so much so that often the favoured candidate would be elected by acclamation without the formality of a contest. How effective were the peers in securing the election of their nominees to the Commons is most significantly indicated in the fact that four of Ayrshire's M.P.s in the second half of the 18th century were commoners who themselves later succeeded to peerages. Ayrshire was represented in the Commons by James Mure Campbell (1754-1761), later 5th Earl of Loudoun; Archibald Montgomerie (1761-1768), later 11th Earl of Eglinton; David Kennedy (1768-1774), later 10th Earl of Cassillis; Sir Adam Fergusson (1774-1784, 1790-1796); Hugh Montgomerie (1784-1789, 1796), later 12th Earl of Eglinton; William McDowall (1789-1790); William Fullarton (1796-1803).

As well as 30 county members, Scotland was represented at Westminster by a further 15 burgh members. The Ayr Burghs constituency comprised the royal burghs of Ayr, Irvine, Rothesay, Inveraray, and Campbeltown. The council of each burgh nominated a commissioner and the five men met, in Ayr or sometimes one of the other burghs, to select the M.P. Elections in the Scottish burgh seats were notoriously corrupt. The key to winning a seat was securing the nomination of appropriate commissioners, and John Galt in *The Provost* related the 'jookerie' involved in the choice by the councillors of their delegate. At this fictional election 'my lord's interest' was set aside and a candidate 'with the influence of the crown on his side' was successful. As so often, Galt's fiction is solidly based on local fact. In Ayr Burghs contests, 'my lord' Eglinton – despite his dominance in the county vote – was not even assured of winning Irvine. So long as the Campbells of Loudoun and Argyll agreed with the Stuart Earl of Bute, this was a safe seat for the Pitt-Dundas government side. Ayr Burghs M.P.s in the late 18th century were often lawyers or landowners from outwith the county seeking sure admission to the Commons; on two occasions it went to a son of an Earl of Bute.

Robert Burns, of course, never had a vote either in Ayrshire or Dumfries: 'I am too little a man to have any political attachments'. In 1788 when William McDowall, Col. Sir Andrew Cathcart, and James Boswell offered themselves as cadidates for the Ayrshire constituency, Burns guessed in 'The Fête Champetre':

*Or will ye send a man o law?*
*Or will ye send a sodger?*
*Or him wha led o'er Scotland a'*
*The meikle Ursa-Major?*
*Come, will you court a noble lord,*
*Or buy a score o lairds, man?* CW 326

Later, he became involved in the contests for the Dumfries Burghs seat in September 1789 and July 1790. 'I have just got a summons to attend with my men-servants . . . to escort Captain Miller from Dalswinton into Dumfries to be a Candidate for our Boroughs which chuse their Member that day.' This was a son of Burns's landlord and 'his Grace's creature' sponsored by the Duke of Queensbury. Rebelling against this so-typical aristocratic influence, Burns produced three election squibs where his versifying efforts supported Miller's Pittite Tory opponent, Sir James Johnstone. Five years later, he produced three election ballads in favour of the Whig candidate, Patrick Heron (whose Ayr Bank had foundered in 1772) against nominees of the Earl of Galloway, for the county seat of the Stewartry of Kirkcudbright. It is clear that as in Ayrshire, parliamentary elections were not between political parties but rather contests between rival landed interests.

As the affairs of the nation were managed by the great landowners, so were those at the county level. Until 1747 there were heritable jurisdictions, with Loudoun always sheriff of Ayr, and Eglinton and Cassillis responsible for the bailiery courts of Cuninghame and Carrick; and lesser landlords having their own baron courts. After the suppression of the Jacobite rebellion of 1745 such feudal jurisdictions were abolished not only in the Highlands, but throughout Scotland. The 4th Earl of Loudoun received £1500 compensation for the loss of the sheriffdom (plus around another £1000 for courts at Loudoun and Mauchline). Sheriffs thereafter were lawyers appointed by the Crown at a salary of £200 per annum. Three Ayrshire landowners reached high judicial office: Alexander Boswell of Auchinleck became Lord of Session, 1754, and Lord of Justiciary, 1755; Sir Thomas Miller of Barskimming was appointed Lord Justice Clerk, 1766, and Lord President of the Court of Session, 1788; his son became a Lord of Session in 1789.

The sheriff in addition to his civil and criminal jurisdiction had devolved upon him various administrative duties. The Justices of the Peace – also landowners – were concerned not only with the preservation of the peace, but also the suppression of begging, ensuring the provision of poor relief, and even roads and bridges. They were expected to have appointed for each parish two constables who would serve for six months' periods. The Freeholders at their annual Michaelmas Head Court meetings had to levy themselves for 'rogue money'–from 3/- to 6/- Scots on each £100 Scots of valued rent–for the apprehension and maintenance of criminals. The Commissioners of Supply whose numbers had grown from 13 in the 17th century to 70 comprised all the principal landowners and were responsible for the collection of the land tax. This was about £4 Scots on each £100 Scots valued rent, and was collected quarterly by the Collector of Cess. The ingathering of other taxes was added to their duties. Like the window tax on houses with more than twenty windows, such assessed taxes were troublesome, while producing an inconsiderable product. The Commissioners of Supply as the principal assembly of county landowners were from time to time assigned additional duties. They were responsible for repair of highways and bridges by forced or statute labour and might levy 'bridge money'. They were expected to co-operate with the Freeholders, the Justices of the Peace, and with the Road Trustees - another county body of landowners who were made specially responsible for the new turnpike roads. The Commissioners of Supply were also concerned with defence. In 1794 the office of Lord Lieutenant was resuscitated: Archibald, the Earl of Eglinton serving from 1794 till his death in 1796 when he was followed by Hugh, 12th Earl. On 10th April 1794 the Lord Lieutenant called a meeting of freeholders, justices of the peace, commissioners of supply, and heritors, when an assessment of 6d per £1 Scots of valued rent was agreed upon to raise two troops of cavalry for defence against the feared invasion. The West Lowland Fencibles were raised and commanded by Colonel Hugh Montgomerie of Coilsfield and Skelmorlie, later 12th Earl of Eglinton. The Ayrshire Fencible Cavalry was formed under Archibald, Lord Kennedy, later 12th Earl of Cassillis.

At the parochial level, the landowners were also dominant. All landowners were members of a heritors committee which was responsible for the maintenance of kirk and kirkyard, for the school, and for poor relief. The administration might be in the hands of the kirk session, but the heritors committee held the purse strings. The major local landowner was also the patron of the kirk who appointed the parish minister. Several landowners were also superiors of burghs of barony, often with powers of appointing bailies. Some new communities had been formed, created by landlords. Some remained small, like Sorn and Straiton. Some grew into considerable townships, like Wallacetown, Catrine, and Darvel, followed by Troon and Ardrossan a generation later. And until mid-18th century most people were tenants of landlords and as such dependent upon them for their livelihood.

There was little indeed that could be done in the county without the patronage or at least the tolerance of the landowners.

The dominance of the landlords was of course never absolute. The church retained always a measure of independence. The kirk sessions, though, tended to be subservient. When in 1784 a Mauchline lass named as the father of her child Mr. Thomas Montgomerie, brother of the laird of Coilsfield, the matter was delayed for over four months, a denial transmitted by the minister of Tarbolton was accepted, and the matter ended. More spirit was shown by the seceders, who often had to battle against landowners to find a site for a church and stone to build it. The ultimate challenge to the feudal social order came, however, from urbanisation. In the second half of the 18th century the agrarian changes involved consolidation of farms, elimination of cottagers, and rural depopulation. By the 1790s most Ayrshire folk were living in towns and villages. For a steadily increasing number, livelihood no longer depended on the personal whim of a landed superior, but rather on the impersonal fluctuations of trade. In the vigorously expanding Kilmarnock the council in 1771 successfully challenged in the Court of Session an attempt by the Earl of Glencairn to limit their independence. In Wallacetown, the superior discovered the impossibility of retaining even paternal control over an expanding urban manufacturing community and 'resides at a distance, and has little more connection with it than to collect the feu-duties.'

The towns provided two elements in the new movement for political reform. There were those of the middle rank – including lawyers and merchants – for whom municipal reform was as important as an extension of the parliamentary franchise. There were those of the lower orders, with a tradition of religious dissent, who focused economic grievances in a demand for universal suffrage. In Ayrshire's largest town in Kilmarnock where not one single person had a vote in parliamentary elections, reform feeling became particularly strong. A generation later, in the Kilmarnock reformers' demonstrations of 1819, among the flags borne was one which had been carried by the Covenanters at the battle of Drumclog – a symbol of how the tradition of religious independence was translated into political reform.

The need for municipal reform was most obvious in the royal burghs. In Ayr, each autumn before Michaelmas three election meetings were held. At the first the existing council of seventeen member selected seven new councillors (5 merchants, 2 craftsmen). At the second meeting the old and new councillors drew up leets for the offices of provost, bailies, dean of guild, and treasurer. At the third meeting the councillors, old and new, were joined by seven deacons of crafts and elected the five new magistrates, who with the five from the previous year, and the seven new councillors formed the town council for the ensuing year. The council was thus virtually self-elective, and the mass of the burgesses, far less the populace as a whole, had no share in the choice. What made matters worse was the chronic insolvency of the burghs, and the opportunities afforded for corruption. In Ayr, for example, the extensive lands of Alloway which belonged to the burgh were rouped in 1754, providing the burgh with £7,190 of ready cash and ten local merchants and landowners with estates at bargain prices. In *The Provost*, John Galt described municipal affairs in the burgh of Gudetown (Irvine).

But political feelings were not confined to the towns. In the countryside, improvements produced some conservative resistance from tenants and others. The Statistical Account reports instances of young trees and new hedges being uprooted in Stair and Kirkoswald in the 1740s, and Aiton recalled the same happening later around Kilmarnock, and also the breaking down of toll gates and refusals to pay a road tax in place of the statute labour. There was, he said, 'an extraordinary clamour.' There were still in places surviving irksome feudal duties like leading coals and crops for the landlord, and in four parishes by the 1790s multures still operated, with tenants thirled to the lord's mill. Grievances such as those were precisely what produced a spontaneous peasant revolt in France in the summer of 1789. That a similar jacquerie might affect Ayrshire must have been feared by some. Though no such crisis developed, the sentiments were there. Indeed, when the Kilmarnock edition appeared in 1786 it appealed not only to 'the

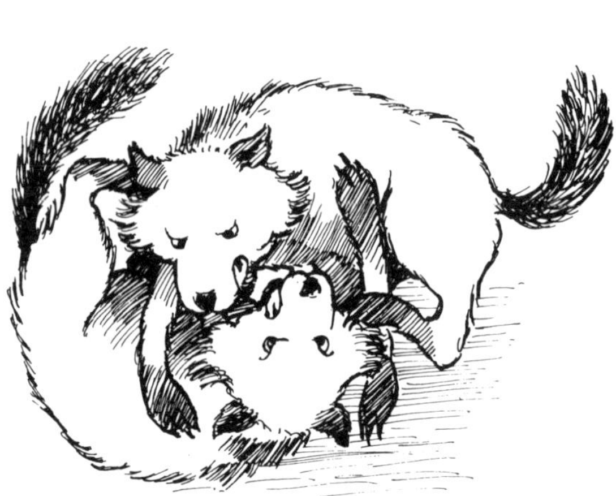

Learned and the Polite' but to a more popular audience who applauded the poet's praise of the peasant virtues in such items as 'The Twa Dogs' and 'The Cotter's Saturday Night'. In the apparently more frivolous 'Address to the Haggis' composed later that year there is just a hint of what a peasant rising might imply:

*But mark the Rustic, haggis-fed,*
*The trembling earth resounds his tread,*
*Clap in his walie nieve a blade,*
*He'll make it whissle;*
*An legs an arms, an heads will sned,*
*Like taps o thrissle.* CW 265

A desire for constitutional reform even pervaded the landed class. Various proposals for amendment of the franchise and the reformation of the burghs were debated in parliament. Many resented Henry Dundas who through power and expediency had since 1775 dominated the Scottish political scene until by 1790 he controlled 34 of Scotland's 45 seats. In 1786 Burns 'dinner'd wi' a Lord'. This first direct acquaintance with an aristocrat was with Lord Daer, son of the Earl of Selkirk, a noted reformer who would later help found the Society of the Friends of the People in Scotland. The meeting with Lord Daer was at Catrine House, the country home of Professor Dugald Stewart of Edinburgh University, and Burns was introduced by Dr. John Mackenzie of Mauchline, a fellow member of the Tarbolton (St. James) masonic lodge.

It is tempting to suggest some connection between the freemasons and the movement for political reform. Certainly there is no evidence to indicate any close political involvement of the sort as has been argued the freemasons in France had in the events of the Revolution there. But it is noteworthy that Burns's masonic connections admitted him to a fraternity of persons, many of whom were of a liberal persuasion. And the proliferation of masonic lodges is a most remarkable development in 18th century Ayrshire. The Mother Lodge Kilwinning (itself instituted 1599) chartered ten lodges in the county between 1734 and the end of the century; the Grand Lodge of Scotland (instituted 1736) chartered no fewer than 21 others. Tarbolton had two lodges - St. James formed in 1771 and St. David which had seceded from it in 1773. In 1781 there was a reunion and on 4th July of that

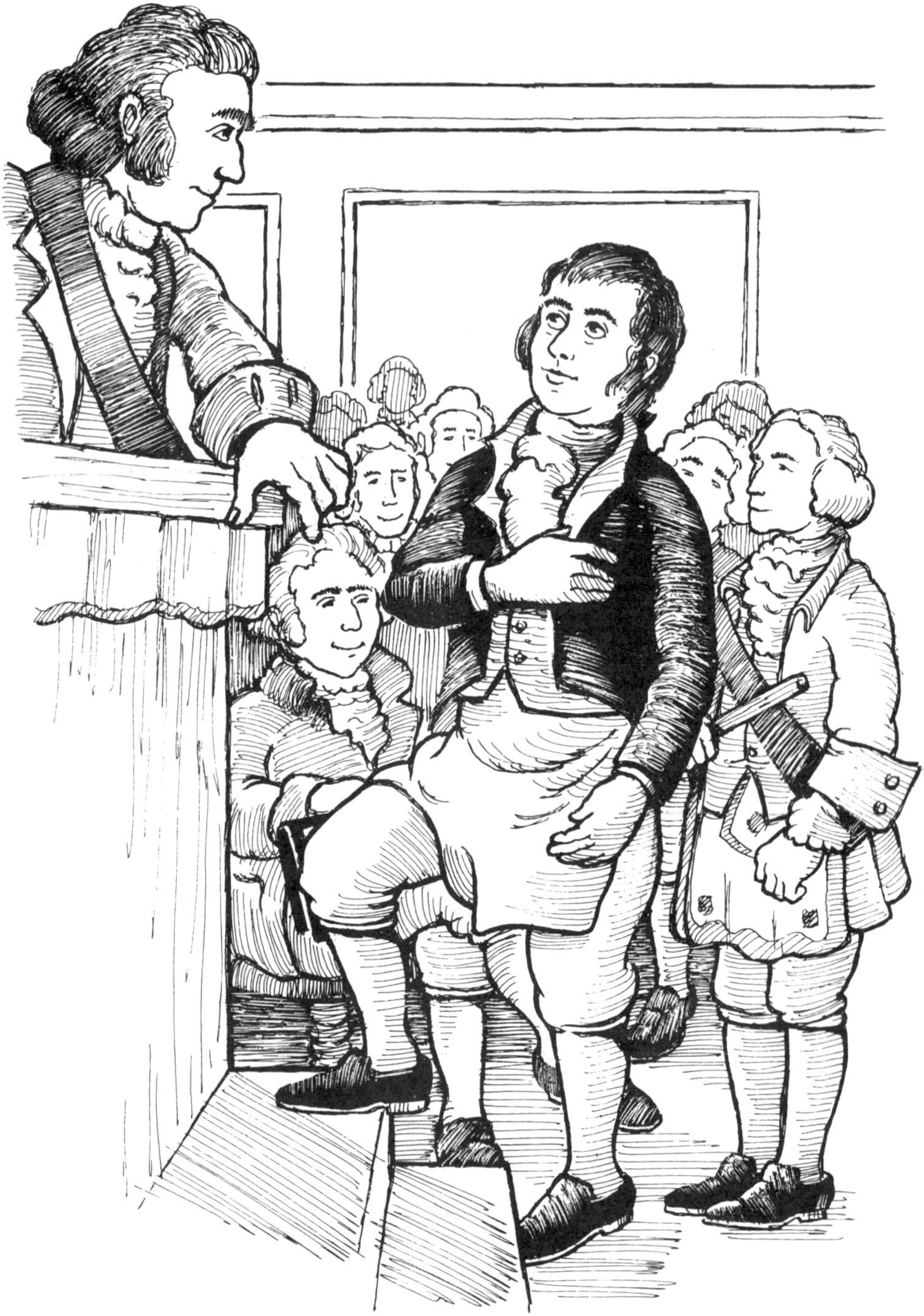

*Robert Burns, Freemason*

year twenty-two-year-old Robert Burns was admitted as apprentice to this united St. David Lodge. The following year there was a further schism, and Burns went with Captain James Montgomerie and others to form a re-constituted St. James Lodge, of which he became Depute Master in July 1784. Grand Masters of this lodge, apart from Captain Montgomerie, brother of 'sodger Hugh', were Gavin Hamilton who arranged for the lease of Mossgiel, and Sheriff-clerk James Dalrymple of Orangefield who was related to the Earl of Glencairn. Around the time of the publication of the Kilmarnock edition Burns visited several other Ayrshire lodges; he attended meetings in Edinburgh and on his tours; and in 1792 he was elevated to Senior Warden of Dumfries St. Andrews lodge. His masonic contacts certainly aided his material advance, and they opened up a wider world of ideas to one who was interested not only in literature but in public affairs.

'I suspect my political tenets, such as they are, may be rather heretical to some of my best friends,' admitted Burns in 1786. Such political pieces as he wrote before 1792 were few and characterised less by partisan content than by their satirical manner. In 'A Fragment' written in 1784 after the end of the American War of Independence, the generals and statesmen are treated with derision and disposed of with casual contempt, just like any high-flying parish minister or other local character. In 1785 'The Author's' Earnest Cry and Prayer to the Scotch Representatives in the House of Commons' similarly castigates these M.P.s for excise laws which threatened the drinking of whisky. A year later in the 'Address of Beelzebub' he singled out the Earl of Breadalbane for attack, and in 'A Dream' extended his satire to include members of the royal family. In the Dumfries Burghs elections of 1789 and 1790 the three pieces he contributed were in the same vein – and were not regarded by the persons involved as serious enough to cause political or personal offence. As he explained later in 1793, he wrote 'rather under the temptation of being witty than disaffected.'

What were the positive political beliefs of Burns it is not easy to delineate. Not everything in a poem should be taken as an expression of the author's personal beliefs, any more than statements made by a character in a play or a novel always represent their author's opinions. So many commentators have in fact done just this, that it is well to quote Thomas Crawford's observation that 'Burns has a natural gift for identifying himself with the men on both sides of a national struggle, and also for standing back and observing the warring factions quite impersonally, and from a distance.' Burns with a Wordsworthian 'willing suspension of disbelief' could project an attitude without necessarily accepting all its political implications. Thus he could pretend to a sentimental Jacobitism, without any desire to see the Stuarts restored to the throne. He could lament the loss of nationhood by the Act of Union, without considering seriously a return to Scottish independence. He could denounce aristocrats – unless and until he was personally acquainted with them. He favoured Equality, but was never egalitarian in his behaviour. Liberty to him meant different things on different occasions. None of the political ideas in his poems were original. But much of his appeal lay in his expression of 'what oft was thought, but ne'er so well expressed' – to use Pope's words.

Like other poets he was aroused by the excitement of the French Revolution. Only then, as his letters show, did he begin to concern himself seriously with political matters. Sympathy for the events of 1789 in France encouraged the movement for parliamentary reform in Britain, but Burke's *Reflections* in 1790, followed by Thomas Paine's *Rights of Man* in 1791, paralleled by developments in France, produced intense political differences throughout 1792. In November 1791 Burns had moved from Ellisland into Dumfries. In April 1792 he is reputed to have purchased four guns from the captured smugglers' brig *Rosamond* to send to the French revolutionaries. In fact it is later in the war before definite evidence appears of his political involvement. On 13th November 1792 he began subscribing to the new reformist paper, the *Edinburgh Gazetteer*. In a letter to the editor he urged him to 'Lay bare, with undaunted heart and steady hand, that horrid mass of corruption called Politics and State-craft'. He sent in several items including a poetical address on 'The Rights of Women' which he had written for the Dumfries theatre. He was accused of joining in the singing of the revolutionary song *Ca Ira* in that theatre, and being the 'head of a disaffected party.' On 6th December he wrote to Mrs. Dunlop of Dunlop that as well as the 'many alarms of the Reform, or rather the Republican spirit, of your part of the kingdom' there was 'a good deal of commotion' in Dumfries as well as in Ayrshire.

The Society of Friends of the People, which had been organised in Scotland earlier in 1792, in December arranged a Convention in Edinburgh, and another in March 1793. Thomas Muir, the radical Glasgow lawyer, was arrested in January, released on bail, but (after a trip to France) re-arrested in August, tried, and sentenced to fourteen years' transportation. Many moderates had become unhappy at the Convention's extremist demands for annual parliaments and universal suffrage; the outbreak of war in February 1793 rallied others behind Pitt's government; and the severe sentence on Muir was followed by a series of repressive measures which silenced opposition. In Ayr in 1793 it was noted that Thomas Paine's *Rights of Man* 'was found by the judicial power of the country to favour treasonable and seditious doctrines' so the Ayr Library at its annual business meeting decided that its copy should be 'burned in the presence of the committee.'

Burns was alarmed on 31st December 1792 on being notified of an inquiry by the Excise Board 'as a person disaffected to Government.' As a civil servant he ought not become involved in politics: 'I am a Placeman, you know, a very humble one indeed, Heaven knows, but still so much as to gag me from joining in the cry.' He was thus afraid of dismissal, 'being turned adrift, with my helpless family, to all the horrors of Want.' He wrote two explanatory letters to his patron in the excise, Robert Graham of Fintry, and was exonerated. His excuse was that 'As to France, I was her enthusiastic votary in the beginning of the business. When she came to shew her old avidity for conquest . . . I altered my sentiments.' Like so many others he had to learn to be discreet. In September 1793 – just after Muir's trial – he wrote 'Scots Wha Hae' as Bruce's address at Bannockburn but 'associated with the glowing ides of some other struggles of the same nature, *not quite so ancient*'. A year later in an 'Ode on General Washington's Birthday' he treated the American War of Independence in a similar allegorical fashion. In January 1795 in 'A Man's a Man for a' that' he enshrined the revolutionary doctrines of liberty, equality, and fraternity in a song which (says Kinsley) occupies a 'central place in the psalmody of radicalism.' In March 1795 Burns joined the Dumfries Volunteers and wrote for them the patriotic 'Does Haughty Gaul invasion threat.' It neatly concludes:

*But while we sing God Save the King,*
*We'll ne'er forget the people!* CW 538

He then produced the Heron ballads for the Kirkcudbrightshire election, having, like so many others, abandoned the dangerous radicalism of the time of 'commotion' for moderate Whig partisan politics.

The revolutionary movement had collapsed. The Convention of October 1793 disintegrated. The Pike Plot of 1794 came to nothing. In 1797 when a Militia Bill was introduced and parish schoolmasters had to draw up leets of able-bodied men there were riots, and trees of liberty were erected. But the Society of United Scotsmen formed in that year to continue the movement failed to win any real support and was eventually dissolved. The radical movement was resurrected only after the long wars ended in 1815, and not till 1832 was a first step taken towards parliamentary reform.

Universal suffrage would be a long time in coming. Yet already by the end of the 18th century more people were becoming acquainted with the principles of democratic participation. Voluntary associations were being established. In some of these the gentry were involved, such as agricultural societies, freemasons, some library societies. But in others the initiative came from people in the middle ranks or even the lower orders in the towns. The tradition had been established in 17th century Ayrshire with the Covenanters – the first real manifestation of popular initiative in Scottish history – and was continued by the 18th century seceders who formed their own congregations and organised their own churches. At the same time local societies of other kinds were being formed, of which the Tarbolton Bachelors' Club is a memorable example. 'Having heard that a debating club had been established in Ayr,' recorded Burns' first biographer, 'he resolved to try how such a meeting would succeed in the village of Tarbolton.' About the end of 1780 Robert and Gilbert Burns and five other young men formed the club, and drew up rules for weekly meetings, with a president elected by 'a majority of votes' and new members up to a maximum of sixteen admitted only by 'unanimous consent.' Democratic principles were by now obviously widely understood and accepted. As well as such clubs for social and educational purposes there were also the new friendly societies where those enjoying a reasonable standard of living arranged self-insurance to avoid the degradation of becoming a pauper dependent on the session's charity. About 1780 a Machlin Friendly Society was set up, with an entry fee of one guinea (£1.05) and funds ten years later standing at £300, allowing 10p weekly to members unable to work, and 15p to such as were confined to bed. Aiton reported that 'friendly or penny societies have been formed in many of the towns in Ayrshire, and promise to be antidotes against poverty. Masons, weavers, shoemakers, and other societies had been formed many years ago' but he complained that they wasted money on 'flags, swords, sponteens, gorgets, crowns, coats of mail, sceptres, robes, trains, and other fooleries, and in making fool-like parades.' Some of these friendly societies – including those of the miners – were by the end of the century exercising trade union functions until such combinations, like the mushrooming political associations for reform, were prohibited by Pitt's repressive legislation. The Society of Weavers in Fenwick, formed in 1761, developed another new function, when its twelve members on 9th November 1769 created – long before the Rochdale Pioneers in England! – the first consumers' co-operative society: 'It is agreed upon by the members of our Society to take what money we have in our Box and buy what Victwal may be thought Necessar to sell for the benefit of our society And the mannagers of our society may borrow what money They think Proper for that End and purpose.' Thus the foundations of the later labour movement had been laid in Ayrshire by the closing decades of the 18th century.

## CHAPTER 12

# THE WAY OF LIFE

Though society was changing in so many ways, nevertheless certain traditional features of everyday life changed slowly if at all: attitudes to birth, marriage, and death; the customary calendar of annual events.

Birth in the 18th century remained a chancy business. Modern historians can only guess at the birth rate, possible variations in this period, and alterations in life expectancy. All that is certain is that infantile mortality was extremely high, and some of those who survived childhood soon after expired. William Burnes was unusual in that all his seven children outlived him. He died aged 63. Of his sons, Robert died young at 37; William at 23, John as a boy of six. Gilbert lived till he was 67 and the three daughters had longer lives - Agnes, 74; Anabella, 68; Isabella, 84. Robert's family by Jean Armour was more typical - a large family of nine, most of whom died in childhood. The firstborn, Robert, lived till 71, but his twin sister died in her second year. The second set of twins were girls who died soon after birth. Francis died at 14. William lived till 81. Elizabeth died aged two. James lived till 71. Maxwell, born on the day of his father's funeral, survived only for three years.

Malnutrition and evil living conditions contributed to the high death rate. Disease made its toll on others. Smallpox was the main killer, and epidemics persisted right up till the end of the century. The minister of Kilwinning reported that 'It rages here, at times, with the utmost violence, and is often extremely fatal. In the summer and autumn of 1791, upwards of 90 children had the natural smallpox, and more than one half of them died.' Here as in some other parishes there was a prejudice against inoculation, though elsewhere, as in Mauchline - reported Rev. William Auld - 'Inoculation against the smallpox is practised with success.' It seems likely that inoculation and improved medical practices did in fact contribute to a reduced deathrate which was the prime reason for the growth of population in the late 18th century. Nevertheless, risks remained high. Midwives reared on traditional lore could not always be trusted. Parents ensured wherever possible an early baptism for the newly-born child. Thus Robert Burns was baptised by Rev. William Dalrymple of Ayr on 26th January 1759.

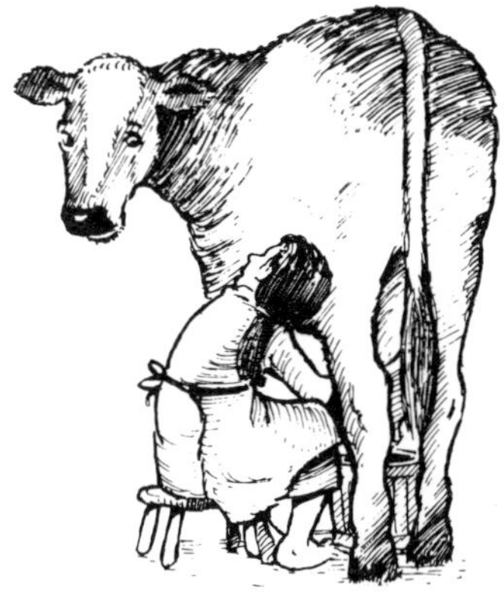

If infancy was dangerous, childhood was severe. On a farm, especially, girls were required to help their mothers from an early age in the housework and at the dairy, and boys to assist at the herding or in field work. Gilbert Burns later recalled that at Mount Oliphant, 'My brother, at the age of thirteen, assisted in threshing the crop of corn, and at fifteen was the principal labourer on the farm, for we had no hired servant, male or female.' Work took priority, and schooling was possible only in quiet periods about the farm. In one respect the Burns children were particularly unfortunate in the remoteness of Mount Oliphant. 'We rarely saw any body but the members of our own family,' said Gilbert. 'There were no boys of our own age, or near it, in the neighbourhood.' Generally, where children could assemble in their limited leisure hours, there were traditional children's pastimes, as Rev. John Mitchell noted in his 'Memories of Ayrshire about 1780'. 'The spinning of the peerie, the lashing of the top, the rolling of the hoop, the flying of the kite, and the skipping of the rope, the agility shown in the exercise of leap-frog, with the playing at ball, & the pitching of the quoit, took place as if by instinct, each at the appropriate season, as did the game *shinty*, in which two parties contended in close encounter which should drive a ball by clubs or bats beyond a certain limit, skating and curling when the thickness of the ice permitted these.' And there was the game called 'English & Scotch'. 'It seems to have

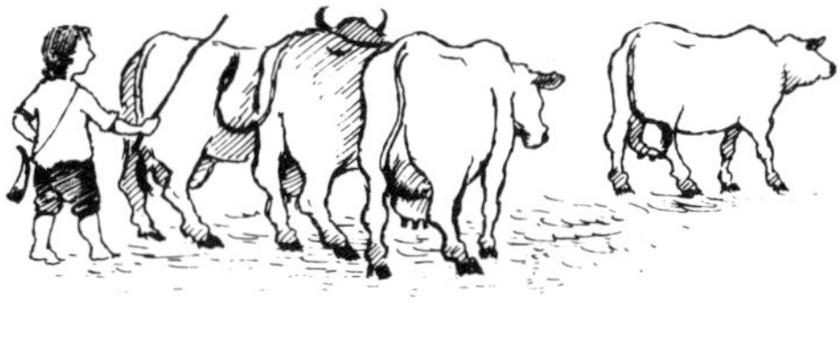

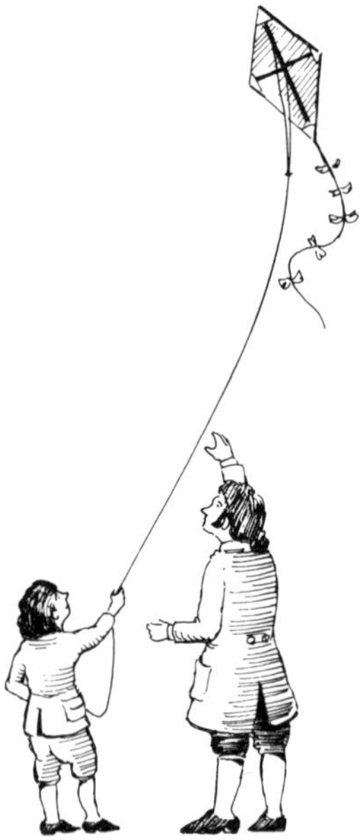

been borrowed from the Border Wars, and was played by boys alone. Having chosen a suitable field for the exercise, & having arranged themselves in two parallel rows closely fronting each other, with a line marked somehow between them, they set vigorously to work, each laid hold of his opponent just before him & the object to be gained was by main force to draw him over the line, and thus to take him as it were captive. In the end, and after the struggle had been finished, victory was held & declared to be in favour of that little army of juvenile warriors, who had either brought their antagonists entirely to submit, by crying out 'barley'; meaning we presume 'parlez'–that is, a cessation of hostilities, or who had captured the greatest number of their enemies.'

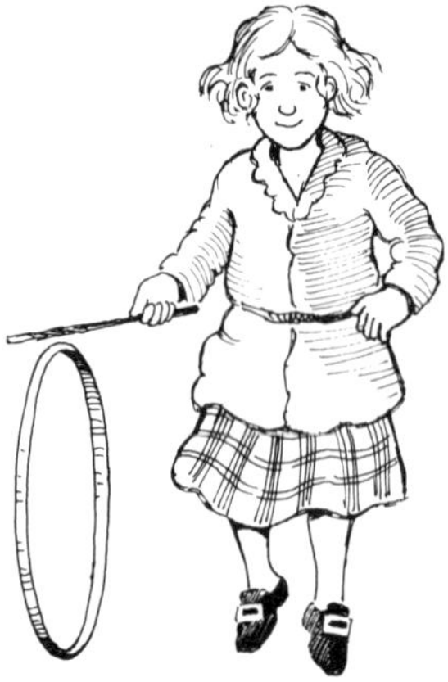

Adolescence brought more scope for extending social relations. When fourteen-year-old Robert went into Ayr to study French for three weeks, he 'formed several connexions with other younkers who possessed superior advantages.' Two years later he took the surveying course at Kirkoswald school, where, he said, 'I made a greater progress in the knowledge of mankind.' The move from Mount Oliphant to Lochlea in 1777 brought him into intimate contact with his peers in Tarbolton. In his twentieth year he went to a country dancing school there, 'in absolute defiance' of his father's commands. A year later he took the initiative in forming the Bachelors' Club. At the age of twenty-two he left home to serve as a flax-dresser in Irvine and from this, he said, 'I learned something of a town life.'

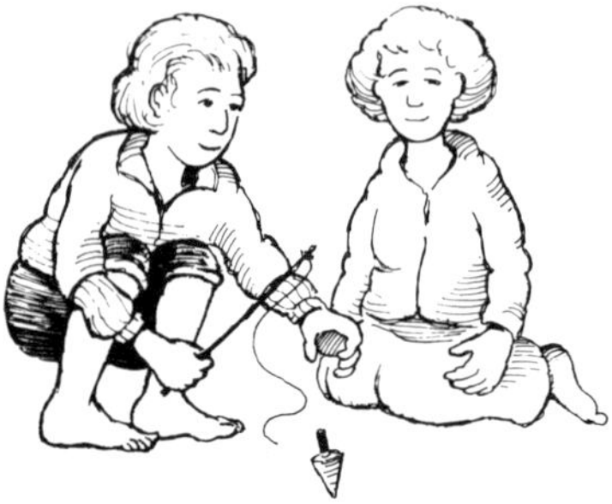

Adolescence also brought associations with the opposite sex. At Mount Oliphant,

Burns caught the 'contagion' of calflove with Nellie Kilpatrick, a 'bonie, sweet, sonsie lass' when they were 'Partners in the labours of Harvest' in his 'fifteenth autumn', and she 'just counted an autumn less.' His 'pulse beat such a furious ratann when I looked and fingered over her hand, to pick out the nettle-stings and thistles. Among her other love-inspiring qualifications, she sung sweetly; and 'twas her favourite reel to which I attempted to give an embodied vehicle in rhyme.' Thus, he said 'I first committed the sin of Rhyme', and 'thus with me began Love and Poesy.' The following summer at Kirkoswald while studying surveying, 'a charming Filette who lived next door to the school overset my Trigonometry, and set me off in a tangent from the sphere of my studies . . . and the two last nights of my stay on the country, had sleep been a mortal sin, I was innocent.' This association with Peggy Thomson seems to have continued or at least been briefly revived in 1784. Brother Gilbert remarked of Robert that 'when young, he was bashful and awkward in his intercourse with women'. But after the family moved to Lochlea, Robert admitted that 'far beyond all the other impulses of my heart was, *un penchant à l'adorable moiteé du genre humaine.* My heart was completely tinder, and was eternally lighted up by some Goddess or other.' He explained a courtship ritual: 'A country lad rarely carries on an amour without an assisting confident.' As such a confident – otherwise known as a 'second' or 'blackfoot' – enlisted to promote a crony's advances, Burns was 'in the secret of half the amours in the parish.' He himself paid his addresses to 'Nanie', a farmer's daughter called Agnes Fleming; 'Tibbie', identified as Isabella Steven, another neighbour; 'Annie', daughter of his close friend John Rankine; 'Eliza', possibly from Mauchline; Alison Begbie, a servant perhaps of Wallace of Carnell; 'Peggy', a servant at Coilsfield and his 'Deity for six or eight months'; and the mysterious 'Mary Morison'. At this period he may have become acquainted with 'Highland Mary', Mary Campbell, also a servant at Coilsfield and sometime nursemaid in Gavin Hamilton's household in Mauchline. When Burns went to Irvine in 1781, his sailor-friend Richard Brown introduced him to 'a certain fashionable failing . . . Here his friendship did me a mischief.' Here he must be referring to fornication, and the 'mischief' was that on his return to Lochlea and after his father's death he found that coitus interruptus, the only popular contraceptive, had failed him. Elizabeth Paton, servant lass at Lochlea, became pregnant, and on 22nd May 1785 presented him with a 'love-begotten daughter.' How persistent was this courtship pattern is indicated in the Third Statistical Account. Nearly two centuries after, in mid-twentieth century, an un-named writer (actually the Tarbolton parish minister) reported: 'The natural history of the sex relations begins with the meeting of groups of boys with groups of girls; goes on to a two-and-two relation, and finally reaches the one young man and the one young woman. In a great many cases the marriage is precipitated by the pregnancy of the woman.'

Opportunities for making acquaintances among the opposite sex occurred especially at markets and fairs. Aiton explained the procedure. 'The manner in which the unmarried people, of both sexes, conduct themselves at fairs and races, is far from being decorous, and calls loudly for reformation. Great numbers of lads and lasses are collected at the fair, in the course of the afternoon, where they continue till about midnight. The country girls travel to the fair, (unless in time of frost) without shoes or stockings, with their coats tucked up, and retire to the corner of some park, near the fair, where they put on their shoes and perform the labours of the toilette; after which, they saunter among the crowd, till their rustic admirers, who are also on the look-out, invite them to the change-house. This is done by tapping the fair one on the shoulder, treading on her foot, or by some pantomime gesture which she understands, and readily obeys, unless a swain, more to her mind, shall then make similar gestures. Nothing is so galling to the lasses, as to be allowed to stand long idle, in the market place, without being invited to the change-house by some young man. The place where groups of them stand, without being called upon, is termed 'the pitiful market.' A 'sturdy fallow' having made his signals, struts off to the ale-house, his 'clever hizzy' following at a short distance, proud of having gotten a 'chance', and envied by such as have had none.'

Aiton goes on to describe what was a widespread practice, spreading to America where it was known as 'bundling'. 'In the ale-house, the lad treats his lass, with ale, whisky, and sweet-meats, (called fairings), hugs her in his arms, tumbles her into a bed, if one can be found, though many persons be in the room, then, with one arm under her head, the other, and one of his legs over her, he enjoys a tete a tete conversation.' He continues: 'If she has many lovers, they press into the room, and even into the bed, where she is reclining; lay hold of her by the arm, leg, or any part of her dress which they can come at . . . She continues, for a time, in a sort of passive uncertainty, yielding to the greatest force, sometimes getting upright, at other times she is thrown upon the bed, until after enjoying several of these kind embraces, and hearing many supplications, one of the sturdiest of the chiels lays hold of her in his arms, whispers his prayer in her ear, and by main force, hurries her off . . . This is what they call 'holding the fair', and it is continued till about midnight, when the lads and lasses begin to pair off, and return to the fair one's home, where they generally spend an hour or two by themselves, in the barn, byre, or cart shade, talking over the events of the day.' Burns himself put it more explicitly in narrating the end of 'The Holy Fair':

*There's some are fou o love divine;*
*There's some are fou o brandy;*
*An monie jobs that day begin,*
*May end in houghmagandie*
*Some ither day.* CW 139

The ale-house sometimes played a further role as courtship advanced towards matrimony. In Galston, 'When a young man wishes to pay his addresses to his sweet-heart, instead of going to her father's, and professing his passion, he goes to a public house; and having let the land-lady into the secret of his attachment, the object of his wishes is immediately sent for, who never almost refuses to come. She is entertained with ale and whisky, or brandy; and the marriage is concluded on.' Unique for one of his class must have been Burns's five formal and stilted letters to Alison Begbie in 1781. It was almost certainly she who 'pledged her soul to meet me in the field of matrimony' but then 'jilted me with peculiar circumstances of mortification.'

Though the Kirk recognised only marriages to which the parish minister had given his blessing, irregular marriages were recognised in Scots law, where a couple publicly owned each other as husband and wife. In the spring of 1786 Burns gave Jean Armour some kind of written acknowledgment of marriage. In May of the same year he did the same sort of thing by an inscription in a Bible in two volumes presented to Highland Mary. And it has been alleged that Betty Campbell, a servant at Stair House, also received 'lines' from him, which she destroyed after a quarrel with him.

Jean Armour, daughter of James Armour and Mary Smith, was

born on 25th February, 1765. She was thus nineteen in 1784 when twenty-five-year-old Robert Burns came to Mossgiel in Mauchline parish. Their first encounters, at a dance and on the bleaching-green, may have occurred quite soon after. Later he was extolling the virtues of the 'Belles of Mauchline' with Jean as 'the jewel o' them a'.' In 1785 he was courting her, though the birth of Elizabeth Paton's illegitimate child to him in May must naturally have turned the Armours against him. By the end of the year Jean was made pregnant. Soon after he gave her his written acknowledgment of marriage. When her condition became known, James Armour arranged with Robert Aiken, the Ayr lawyer, to 'mutilate that unlucky paper' which was done in April. Burns obviously regarded the irregular marriage thus extinguished, and did his penance in the kirk of Mauchline on three Sundays in July and August to obtain, as he wrote, 'a certificate as a bachelor.' In a clandestine manner, he had meantime arranged an irregular marriage with Highland Mary, in May; but she died in Greenock in October. Burns was away from Mauchline from November till June 1787, when he resumed relations with Jean. Once again she became pregnant, left her parents' home, and in March 1788 gave birth to twin girls who soon after died. On brief return visits to Mauchline, Burns set up in house in the Back Causeway in February 1788; in April had a civil marriage ceremony arranged by Gavin Hamilton; and in August they were recognised as man and wife by the kirk session.

The tortuous and often harrowing nature of Burns' matrimonial career must have deprived him of much of the gaiety which accompanied weddings normally. These were, Aiton reported, normally celebrated on a Friday. The ceremony was followed by a 'penny wedding' where the expenses of a meal and the hire of a fiddler were borne by the guests and any balance was left as a wedding gift. In Cumnock there was a custom of 'riding the broose' where the young folk raced on horseback from the church to the home of the newly-wed couple, receiving there from the mother of the bridegroom a bottle of wine or whisky which was carried back by the winner to drink the health of the newly-weds. In Galston, the second day after the wedding there was a creeling. The young wedded pair with their friends prepared a small creel or basket. This was carried around by each of the men who were relieved of it by their partners, who were rewarded by kisses; and eventually the new husband, neglected by all the other maidens, was rescued by his wife. Burns, sadly, has little to say about weddings. His 'Mauchline

Wedding' is disappointingly brief. One song he rescued commemorates the custom of ceremonially and sometimes drunkenly putting the bride and groom to bed on their wedding night:

*O, ken ye how Meg o the Mill was bedded?*
*An ken ye how Meg o the Mill was bedded?*
*The groom gat sae fu he fell awald beside it,*
*And that's how Meg o the Mill was bedded!* CW 489

Marriage, whether regular or otherwise, brought responsibilities. Sex outwith the marriage bed was abhorred by the kirk, and adulterous relations leading to the birth of an illegitimate child most severely censured, in Mauchline at least. In strict legality Burns sinned thus adulterously but once, though he was in fact unfaithful to Jean Armour far more often. He had a child to Elizabeth Paton (though conceived before he met Jean) in 1785; possibly a child to Highland Mary in 1786; two sets of twins born out of wedlock to Jean in 1786 and 1788; in 1787 he had a child by Meg Cameron, an Edinburgh servant girl; and Jenny Clow conceived another which would be born late in 1788. All this happened before the formal marriage to Jean Armour in April 1788, as did his formal suit addressed to Margaret Chalmers in 1787; and his seemingly platonic affair with Clarinda, who was, however, Mrs. Agnes McLehose, a married woman. And he may have had fleeting affairs like one in Carlisle in May 1787. After April 1788 only one illicit amour is recorded: with Anna Park, niece of the landlady of the Globe Tavern, Dumfries, who bore him a child in 1791, out of this adulterous liaison. Altogether fourteen children, with only five born in wedlock.

For women, marriage brought increased cares. In certain respects domestic circumstances might be improving in the 18th century, but house-keeping was only a part-time occupation. The wife – like the children – had to work alongside the menfolk in the fields, in the byre or dairy, in the loomshop, or at the spinning. Even in the manses this was so: the ministers had their glebes to cultivate and in the manses there was the same spinning and sewing and dairy work as in the homes of the parishioners.

When Rev. Micah Balwhidder was left a widower he found it impossible to carry on unaided, and searched out a second wife. As Galt tells it, 'Well may I speak of her with commendation; for she was the bee that made my honey. She found the manse rookit and herrit and there was such a supply of plenishing of all sort wanted that I thought myself ruined and undone by her industry. There was such a buying of wool to make blankets, with the booming of the meikle wheel to spin the same and such birring of the little wheel for sheets and napery, that the manse was for many a day like an organ kist. Then we had milk cows and the calves to bring up, and a kirning of butter and a making of cheese; in short I was almost by myself with the jangle and din.'

Then for the housewife of those days, not only was there all this sort of work to be done besides keeping the house, but there were large families to bring up. Rev. James Lawrie of Kirkmichael had seven children; his son, Rev. George Lawrie of Loudoun, a friend to Burns, had six children; his son Archie who succeeded him at Loudoun, had twelve of a family. Large families were common to all classes of society. Among those with less respectable members, the numbers were augmented by the inclusion of their illegitimate offspring. So at Mossgiel in 1786, Mrs. Burns, already caring for six children of her own, aged from 27 to 15, had taken in two of son Robert's bastard weans–'dear bought Bess', daughter of Elizabeth Paton; and Jean Armour's first-born Robert, whose twin sister was taken by the Armours. Later at Dumfries, Jean Armour with her family of five, plus her husband's orphan cousin Fanny, took in Anne Park's child, which had been nursed for a time at Mossgiel.

Later – or sooner – to all came death, 'the Poor Man's last and often best friend.' Death was not only an ever-present threat, but an event to be prepared for, because a decent funeral was the ultimate symbol of respectability. When a wealthy person died, noted the minister of Dunlop, it was the custom 'to invite two or three parishes to attend his funeral.' Even for those of lower rank lavish funerals became 'oppressive to those who cannot afford the expense, but who, from vanity or pride, must continue the custom.' Apart from the cost of bell-money, mortcloth money, and undertaker's expenses, there was the outlay on meat and drink on the occasions of the coffining, the wake, and the funeral itself. The Kilmaurs minister lamented the 'gathering many people together and entertaining them at considerable expense when they bury their dead.' At Dundonald, 'the company are invited at 11 o'clock forenoon, but they are probably, not all arrived at 2. Till of late a pipe and tobacco were provided for every one of the company.' In

Cumnock, it was later reported the custom was 'to give half a dozen rounds or more of spirits, wine, etc. at funerals'. In January 1782 William Gibb, the Mauchline kirk officer, was drunk and incapable of performing his duties at James Smith's burial. Belatedly in June the session gave him a simple rebuke.

Death by misadventure concerned the Presbytery of Ayr when on 6th March 1777 it advised 'anent the recovery of drowned persons and seemingly dead.' Sessions were warned not to suppose death and bury in haste, for 'great numbers in such Circumstances might have been restored, had they not been treated in an improper and pernicious manner, or too harshly given up for lost.' Four rules were spelled out. The first was that the body should be carefully moved to a convenient place, avoiding rough handling, and keeping the head raised. Secondly the body should be dried, fresh air allowed free circulation, and warmth provided – either bottles or bladders of hot water, hot bricks wrapped in cloths, the skin of a sheep newly killed, or 'the Natural and Kindly warmth of a healthy person lying by the side of the Body.' These were quaintly sensible; the next was startlingly up-to-date in suggesting mouth-to-mouth resuscitation. 'Blow with force into the lungs by applying the mouth to that of the patient closing his nostrils with one hand and gently expelling the air again by pressing the chest with the other.' Meanwhile an assistant should rub the body with brandy, apply ammoniacal salts to the nostrils, and – less credible to modern minds – with a clyster or a pair of bellows 'throw the smoak of Tobacco up the fundament into the Bowels.' If a surgeon were present, bleeding might be practised, and if an obstruction, bronchotomy attempted. Finally, if signs of life became evident, the nostrils and throat should be tickled to stimulate sneezing or vomitting; a tablespoonful of warm wine or brandy and water should be offered, unless the lungs were at risk. Resuscitation methods should be continued, and even if no signs of life appeared, should be maintained for two hours or more.

To stimulate a more general concern, the presbytery offered some generous rewards. To the 'Messenger who shall first bring intelligence of a drowned person to a surgeon or minister of the parish', half-a-crown; to persons who 'during the space of two full hours shall have used the means above mentioned . . . tho' success should not follow', two guineas, and four if the person is saved; a publican or other person who will take in a body without delay ('which may be of fatal Consequence'), all expenses plus one guinea. The presbytery arranged a bulk order of apparatus from an Edinburgh firm of druggists, and kirk sessions could nominate a special church collection to defray the cost of £1 9s 6d (just under £1.50). Each set comprised one fumigator (consisting of bellows, box, tube and pipe), two flexible tubes and pipes, four wooden pipes for blowing into the nostrils, two vials of smelling salts, two vials with spirits to be applied to the wrists, and a pair of bellows. Mauchline kirk session made the purchase. Though an inland parish, the River Ayr could be dangerous, and it was no doubt noted that the apparatus was also efficacious against 'damps and noxious vapours' in such places as coal mines. Ironically enough, one of the elders who approved the purchase would himself die by drowning. William Fisher–'Holy Willie'–on his way home from Mauchline in a snowstorm in 1809 was drowned in a stream near the farm of Tongue.

CHAPTER 13

# TRADITIONS

The year in Scotland was not, as in any other Christian country, punctuated by a series of religious festivals. In the aftermath of the Reformation the celebration of all holy days was prohibited, on the argument that every day should be kept holy and to nominate certain days as especially holy implied a blasphemy that the other days were less. So in 18th century Scotland even Christmas and Easter went unmarked. But pre-christian festivals – which had sometimes become associated with Christian occasions – survived, and pagan rites were still performed as customary survivals. The solstices and equinoxes, as noticed in Anglo-Saxon and Scandinavian traditions, and recognised in England as Quarter days, received only passing recognition in Scotland: Lady Day (25 March), Midsummer (24 June), Michaelmas (24 September), Midwinter (25 December). More persistent here was the Celtic tradition based on the entry of the seasons: Candlemas (2 February), Beltane (1 May), Lammas (1 August), Hallowmas (1 November). The Scottish term days were based on these festivals.

Over many generations, adjacent festivals of diverse origin had become assimilated, and the situation was further confused when parliament reformed the calendar in 1752. The Julian or Old Style calendar was brought into line with the Gregorian or New Style, by advancing the calendar by eleven days in the month of September 1752. That there was some confusion in subsequent years is hinted at by Burns when mentioning his own birthday in 'There was a Lad was born in Kyle':

*But whatna day o whitna style,*
*I doubt it's hardly worth the while*
*To be sae nice wi Robin.* CW 267

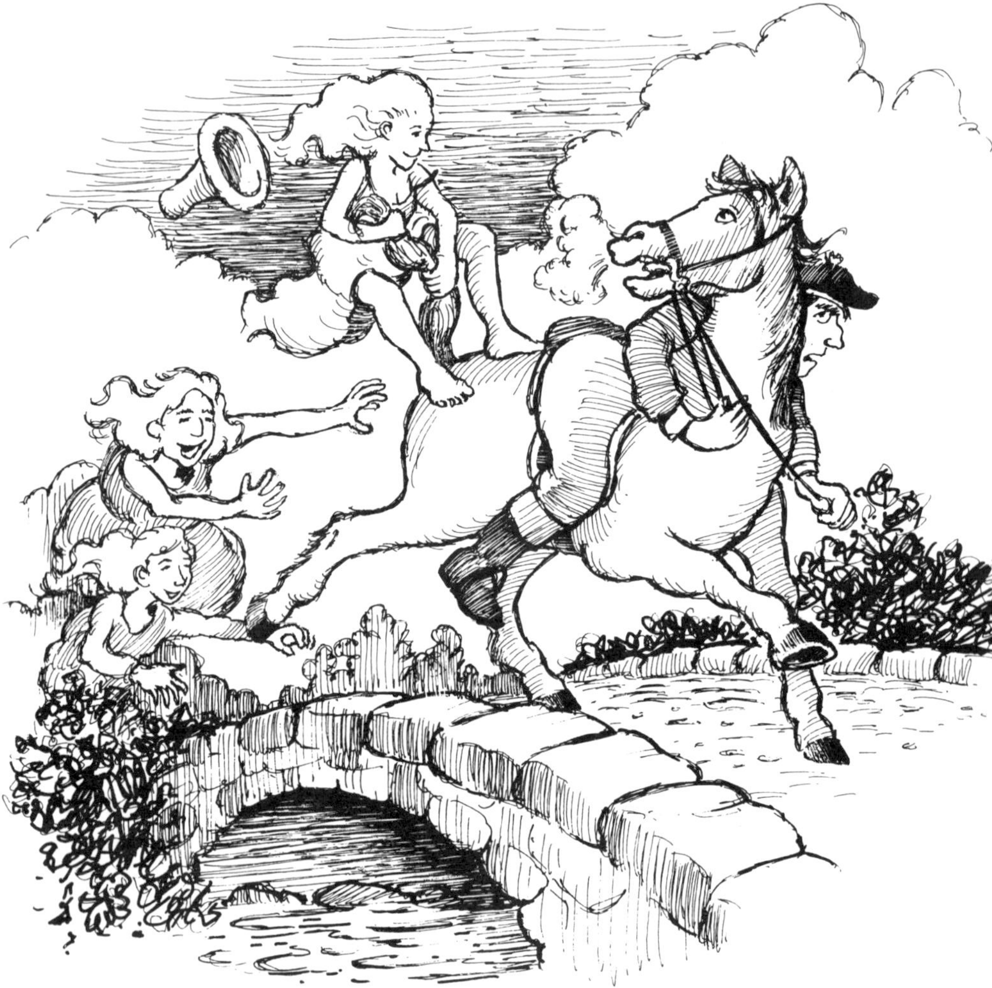

Traditionalists continued to follow the old calendar. Thus in Sorn parish as late as 1823 Beltane was commemorated on 12th May and Old Hallowe'en on 11th November. And even in 20th century Ayrshire the author's mother still noted Auld Ne'erday on 12th January.

Robert Burns' birthday on 25th January 1759 was followed by his baptism the following day. This apparent haste, Dr. A.L. Taylor suggested to me, may perhaps have been due to the imminence of Candlemas on 2nd February which, despite its Christian nomenclature, was one of the four Celtic festivals which were also occasions for the sabbaths of the witch cult, and a time when evil spirits were abroad. That the nearby Alloway 'auld haunted kirk' was – or had been – a resort of witches was embodied in local myth, immortalised much later by Burns himself in 'Tam O' Shanter'. He does not specify at which of the four festivals Tam's ride actually occurred.

Candlemas was the beginning of the Celtic year. Until 1752 in England the statutory commencement of a new year was on Lady Day in March, though in Scotland the move to 1st January had been made in 1600. But farmers still reckoned on Candlemas as marking a new beginning. After this date they yoked their ploughs and began the new season's work. Scots bairns traditionally brought offerings on this day to their dominies, though in Ayrshire this custom had been transferred to the beginning of January.

Soon after Candlemas in pre-reformation times came the beginning of Lent, with Shrove Tuesday, which could occur between 3rd February and 9th March. This night of mirth and revelry, known locally as Fasten e'en, was still celebrated. Burns was inspired to write his 'Epistle to John Lapraik' when

> *On Fasten-e'en we had a rockin,*
> *To ca' the crack and weave our stockin;*
> *And there was muckle fun and jokin.* CW 101

In Kilmarnock there were races and other amusements, for this was the apprentices' holiday. It was also a school holiday, when the children might indulge in the sport of cock-fighting, until at Mauchline in 1782 the session 'the cruel and inhuman custom of Cockfighting at Fasteneven do forbid' and abolished the school holiday.

Easter, a moveable feast within the period from 22nd March to 25th

April, passed unnoticed. Lady Day, 25th March, though forgotten as once marking the New Year, was still the period when many burghs held feeing fairs, when farm servants contracted to begin work at the May term. On 1st April children played 'Hunt the Gowk'. On the third Thursday of April old style, Mauchline had its Race fair, with a horse race along the Mossgiel road. In his 'Epistle to John Lapraik' Burns invited him to

*But Mauchline Race or Mauchline Fair,*
*I should be proud to meet you there.* CW 103

By April, the farmers had sown their oats, though sometimes it was May before they could follow with barley, and potatoes might not be planted till June. The ancient myth of the corn spirit which animates the sprouting corn was recalled by Burns when

*. . . the cheerful Spring came kindly on,*
*And show'rs began to fall;*
*John Barleycorn got up again,*
*And sore surpris'd them all.* CW 61

May 1st was the great Celtic festival of Beltane, heralding the entry of summer. The 'lifting' of cattle out to pasture had been accomplished, and the rising sun was welcomed by the herds setting alight bonfires on Beltane eve. Aiton recalled having seen about the year 1770 forty or fifty of them afire on one night. 'The herds were in use to collect whins, broom, coals, &c., and kindle fires after dark, which were attended by great numbers of the inhabitants.' They were becoming less common 'since the land was inclosed and the number of herds reduced.' After the adjustment of the calendar in 1752 the bonfires were sometimes lit rather on the eve of a local May fair, as at Ochiltree, Galston, and Kilmarnock Curd Fair. At the May fairs harvest workers were contracted. Beltane was one of the two term days, when tenants took possession of, or removed from their farms. Eventually term day (1 May O.S., 11 May N.S.) was transferred to the adjacent Whit (15 May). As with the other great festival of Hallowe'en, Beltane had its peculiar rites. Sometimes, as in Tarbolton, the young men leapt over the burning embers of a bonfire. Other occult practices followed the next morning. The state of the weather and the direction of the wind were observed as omens. And certain persons were suspected of

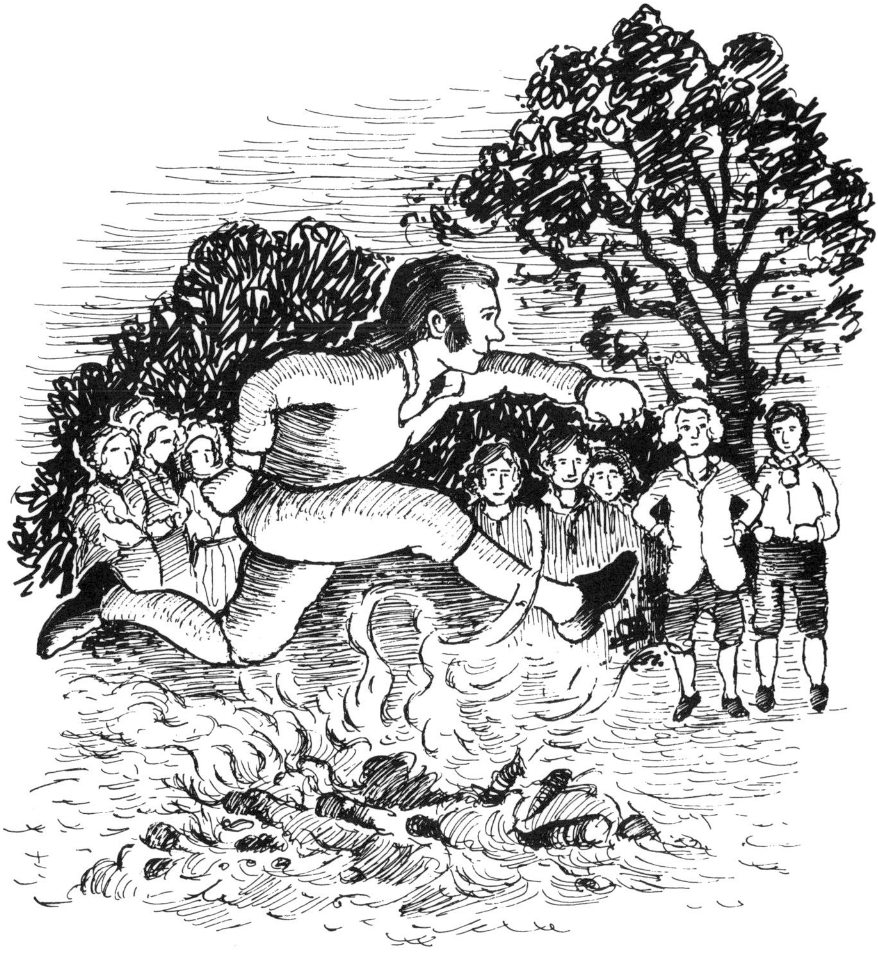

*Beltane Fire*

running over their neighbours' fields trailing a hair-tether, and thus obtaining milk from their cows in the ensuing summer months. At Tarbolton – where the ritual fire was lit annually till 1927 – the site was on the motte hill Burns passed on the occasion of 'Death and Dr. Hornbook'.

> *I was come round about the hill*
> *And todlin down on Willie's mill.* CW 96

After Beltane, the summer months proceeded at a more leisurely pace – with many children free to leave the farm to attend school. The midsummer solstice was unmarked, save in Ayr where St. John's Fair had been held on 24th June since the year 1261. With the Celtic festival of Lammas on 1st August were loosely associated the Kilmarnock Grozet Fair in late July, the Marymass Races at Irvine in mid-August, and perhaps the Mauchline Holy Fair. In two of his songs Burns noted

*Bonie was the Lammas moon,*
*Glow'rin a' the hills, aboon.* CW 312

and he recalled one incident in particular:

*It was upon a Lammas night,*
*When corn rigs are bonie,*
*Beneath the moon's unclouded light,*
*I held awa to Annie.* CW 49

Michaelmas on 29th September received no special attention, though it was followed in October by the autumn feeling fairs and the Kilmarnock Cheese Fair.

In Ayrshire's fickle climate, the progress of the crops could not effectively be correlated with any fixed festivals. Harvest – the hairst – varied from August till mid-November. After the cold stormy summer of 1782, a severe frost on 5th October blighted the unripened crops, and snow fell on 2nd November before they were cut. In more favoured years like 1774 harvest came bountifully enough to bring good cheer, so we might guess, with young Robert inspired to write his first song. Each year the crops were gathered in with the appropriate rituals–the cutting of the last sheaf, the weaving of the harvest knots, the carting home of the last load. 'That merry night we get the corn in' was the occasion for a kirn or barn dance. The cattle were now turned out on to the stubble, and the oats and barley stored in the stackyard, with luck already dried and ready for later threshing with flails and winnowed with wechts in an open-doored barn.

On 1st November was Hallowmas, but as with Beltane, the celebration was more appropriately centred in the darkness of the preceding night – Hallowe'en on 31st October. To accompany his poem on 'Hallowe'en' Burns provided notes to remind the readers of the Edinburgh edition that this was 'a night when Witches, Devils and other mischief-making beings, are all abroad on their baneful, midnight errands: particularly the Fairies, are said, on that night, to hold a grand anniversary.' As a child at Alloway he had heard from his mother and her old cousin Betty Davidson, 'the largest collection in the country of tales and songs concerning devils, ghosts, fairies, brownies, witches, warlocks, spunkies, kelpies, elf-candles, dead-lights, wraiths, apparitions, cantraips, enchanted towers, giants, dragons and other trumpery.' Young people at Hallowe'en performed various rites, and Burns noted these in his poem. Outside the house in the darkness, by pulling a stock of kail, the type of kail-runt indicated the character of one's future spouse. Throw some blue yarn into the kiln-hearth and the Devil might tell you that spouse's name. Go through the motions of sowing hemp seed, or winnowing corn in the barn, or going round the barley stack thrice, and the spouse might come as an apparition. Lasses might pull three stalks of corn from the stack to discover when their virginity would be lost. A group of them might wet their sleeves in a certain stream, and at midnight a spectre of the future husband might appear as the garment was drying before the fire. Or a lass might eat an apple alone before a looking glass, and his image be reflected in the candle-light. Around the fire a group of lads and lasses would roast nuts to divine their future, or blind-folded would select one of three dishes. And always there was sowens for supper at Hallowe'en. These were not just vanishing Carrick customs which Burns was recording from hearsay. Aiton knew them also about Kilmarnock and tells that they were still being observed a generation later. 'Many of the lower orders . . . still believe that the devil is ready at their call!'

Hallowmas (1st November) by those who still recognised the old style calendar became almost exactly identified with Martinmas (11th November). By this time all animals had been brought in from pasture, and those surplus beasts for whom there was no winter fodder were slaughtered and salted down. Martinmas became also term day. Mossgiel was rented at Martinmas 1783, though the Burns family did not move from Lochlea till the following March.

Into the winter season, and the stubble to be ploughed up, as when in November 1785 one field beside Mossgiel was ploughed and gave inspiration for 'To a Mouse'. By contrast the grassland awaited the spring: 'To a Daisy' came later in April 1786 on the adjacent field behind the farmhouse. Winter provided some leisure for recreation. For Tam Samson, the Kilmarnock seedsman and sportsman, angling for salmon, trout and eels might be over, but there was now the

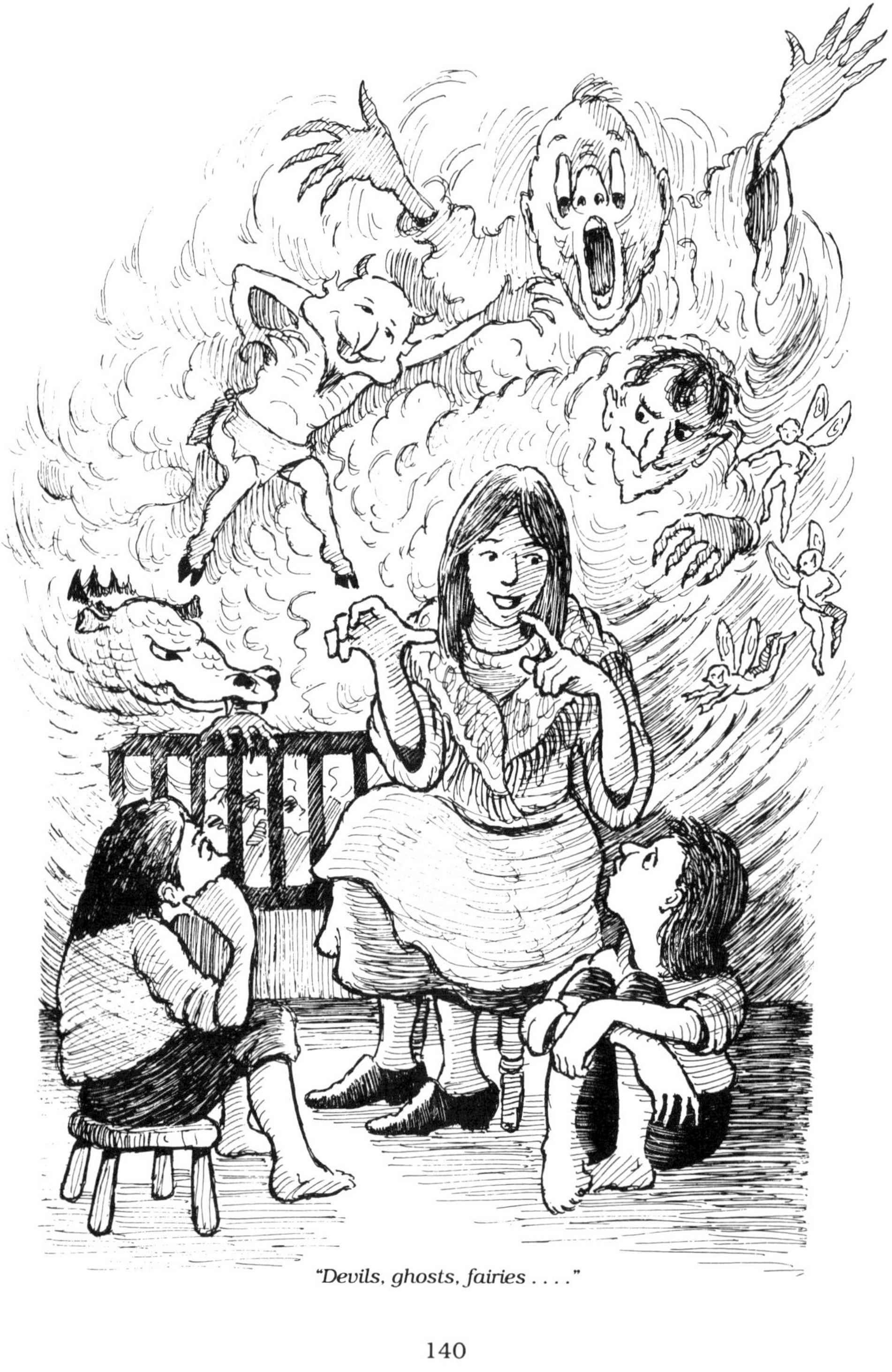

*"Devils, ghosts, fairies . . . ."*

shooting of partridges and muirfowl, and curling when the ice was bearing. In the winter evenings, neighbours visited friends' houses for rockings. The women might spin wool on the rock (distaff) while entertained by gossip and song and story.

*Duncan Gray cam here to woo,*
*On blythe Yule-night when we were fou.* CW 475

Christmas had been associated with the midwinter festival of Yule, and when the celebration of Christmas was prohibited the Yule jollifications were conveniently transferred to the 1st January, which in 1600 was nominated in Scotland as New Year's Day. The last day of the old year was Hogmanay – a word of mysterious derivation. The New Year was ushered in with 'first-footing' and visits of neighbours to share food, drink and fuel. The 'Daft Days' of Yule when children acted mummeries have disappeared, though Hallowe'en became and has continued a night for such 'guisers'. Similarly the Yule exchange of gifts was transferred to Hansel Monday, the first Monday of the New Year. If, after 1752, Auld Ne'erday was still commemorated on 11th January, Hansel Monday was not long over when

*. . . a blast o Janwar win'*
*Blew hansel in on Robin.* CW 268

Some traditional practices were upset after the Act of Union in 1707, which imposed uniform customs and excise duties throughout the United Kingdom and stipulated that coinage and other measures should be 'as are now established in England.'

Scots gold and silver coins were called in, and English currency was to become general, with one pound Sterling divided into twenty shillings, each containing twelve pence. But Scottish copper coins continued to circulate: the doit, bodle, plack or groat, and bawbee - worth respectively one, two, three and six pence Scots, the last worth only one half-penny in sterling. The pound Scots continued as a reckoning for certain payments. The cutty sark which bewitched Tam O' Shanter had been bought by Nannie's grannie 'Wi' twa pund Scots, 'twas a' her riches'. It was worth only a few shillings; for £12 Scots were equivalent to £1 Sterling.

Similar ambiguities with other measures caused confusion to people throughout the 18th century (and to 20th century commentators). The 'lang Scots miles' mentioned in 'Tam O' Shanter' were indeed of greater length than the English Statute miles, covering nearly two thousand Statute yards. With lesser lengths, each Scots inch equalled 1.003 Statute inches, and proportionately throughout the range with 37 Scots inches = 1 ell; 6 ells = 1 fall; 4 falls = 1 chain; 10 chains = 1 furlong; 8 furlongs = 1 Scots mile. In measuring land, the Scots acre was equivalent to 1.26 English acres; and, for smaller divisions, 36 ells = 1 fall, 40 falls = 1 rood; 4 roods = 1 acre.

Grain in Scotland was measured by the table of 4 stimparts, lippies or forpets = 1 peck; 4 pecks = 1 firlot; 4 firlots = 1 boll; 16 bolls = 1 chalder. The firlot approximated to the English bushel, but there was no uniformity anywhere in 18th century Britain. The firlot for measuring oats, barley, and malt was a different capacity from that for wheat, rye, peas, beans, and salt; and measures might be heaped, sometimes straiked. A tendency was for meal to be sold by weight, as were potatoes and groceries. For these, English avoirdupois measure was accepted, with 16 ounces = 1 pound; 14 pounds = 1 stone; 8 stones = 1 hundredweight. But for cheese, butter, meat , hay, and straw there was a trone or county weight, with one Ayrshire pound = 26 ounces avoirdupois, and 16 Ayrshire pounds = 1 Ayrshire stone.

If all this was complicated for persons buying and selling, there was for liquid measure a (fairly) uniform Scots gallon, as compared with four differing English gallons. There was a scale of 4 gills = 1 mutchkin; 2 mutchkins = 1 choppin; 2 choppins = 1 pint; 8 pints = 1 gallon. The Scots gallon was nearly four times as great as any of the English gallons, so that 'Go fetch to me a pint of wine, And fill it in a silver tassie' provided a generous measure. A tappit-hen, that lidded drinking vessel, contained two Scots pints.

If traditional measures were slowly being superseded as the 18th century advanced, another feature of everyday life was threatened, with language becoming anglified.

In 1603 Scotland had lost its royal court when King James VI went south to become also King James I of England; and after the Act of Union in 1707 Scotland lost its own parliament. Edinburgh, however, retained some characteristics of a capital city, with its law courts, its annual meetings of the General Assembly of the Kirk, its cultural and social circles, its authors and publishers who earned it the title of

'Athens of the North'. But though efforts were made to retain the national consciousness, the English connection made its influence felt in such things as outlook, manners, and language. Most directly affected were those members of the upper class who went south for politics, business, pleasure, who sent their sons to England for schooling, and who prospected in the English matrimonial market. Their model was copied by other members of the gentry and many of the middle rank, especially in language. Everyone was familiar with the English of the Authorised Version of the Bible, and for the many who read more widely whether in theology, history, literature, or agriculture, the books were all written in English standard prose. Though the traditional lowland Scots remained the speech of everyday life, and echoes of the vernacular expression can be noted in the formal, sometimes stilted writing of the schoolmasters who recorded the minutes of the kirk sessions, the ideal was southern English. Aiton in 1811 complained that 'Every thing, which is not exactly according to English pronunciation, is now generally termed illiterate and vulgar.'

Lord Auchinleck was one of those who conservatively retained the traditional speech. He was not impressed by Dr. Samuel Johnson–'an auld dominie! he keeped a schule and caud it an acaadamy' and told him that Cromwell 'gart Kings ken they had a lith in their neck.' By contrast, his son James Boswell the biographer aped English fashions and was terrified of Scotticisms in his speech and writings.

By the end of the century most people were speaking what the Dunlop minister defined as 'a mixture of Scotch and English.' Rev. William Auld of Mauchline made plain his own attitude to the change when he wrote that 'The Scots dialect is the language spoken, but it is gradually improving, and approaching nearer to the English.' Sometimes the lesser gentry, like the laird of Logan, unconcernedly continued to speak Scots always. A schoolmaster like William Simson of Cumnock argued that Scots was less 'provincial' than English by citing French and classical derivations in a glossary he supplied as an appendix to Aiton's *Agricultural Report.* But for those who had a humble respect for book-learning, and pretensions for advancement, English was the model.

One of the reasons why John Murdoch, sometime English master at Ayr burgh school, admired William Burnes was this: 'He spoke the English language with more propriety – both with respect to diction and pronunciation – than any man I ever knew, with no greater advantages. This had a very good effect on the boys, who began to talk and reason like men, much sooner than their neighbours.' John Tennant, another acquaintance of the young Robert and Gilbert, also noticed that 'Their style of language was quite above that of their compeers.' Professor Dugald Stewart remarked of Burns the 'purity in his turn of expression' and how he 'avoided more successfully than most Scotchmen, the peculiarities of Scottish phraseology!'

Robert Burns, under his father's admiring tutelage, assiduously copied the epistolatory style of Mrs. Elizabeth Rowe's *Moral Letters;* while Arthur Masson's *Collection of Prose and Verse* introduced him to the English poets whom he later sometimes imitated. With practice he became a skilled practitioner in the art of letters, and – had he written nothing else – might have earned some small note in the field of English poetry.

But from his mother, from Betty Davidson, and from the lasses in the harvest field, he learned the tales and songs of the Carrick border, which introduced him to the different and separate Scottish tradition. At Irvine, 'meeting with Fergusson's *Scotch Poems*, I strung anew my wildly-sounding rustic lyre with emulating vigour.' A year later he wrote: 'However I am pleased with the work of our Scotch Poets, particularly the excellent Ramsay, and the still more excellent Ferguson ... yet we have never had one Scotch Poet of any eminence, to make the fertile banks of Irvine, the romantic woodlands & sequestered scenes on Aire, and the heathy mountainous source, & winding sweep of Doon, emulate Tay, Forth, Ettrick, Tweed, &c.' Or, as he put it in his 'Epistle to William Simson':

*Ramsay an famous Fergusson*
*Gied Forth an Tay a lift aboon;*
*Yarrow an Tweed, to monie a tune,*
*Owre Scotland rings;*
*While Irwin, Lugar, Ayr an Doon*
*Naebody sings.*
*But, Willie, set your fit to mine,*
*And cock your crest!*
*We'll gar our streams an burnies shine* CW 108
*Up wi the best!*

Later in the same poem he expressed his new credo of the validity of Scots as a language for all who

*. . . spak their thoughts in plain, braid Lallans,*
*Like you or me.* CW 110

Burns discovered himself as a member of a fraternity of local enthusiasts for the preservation of Scots, and he later found there were many more in other parts of Scotland as well. It was not the case that others began only afterwards to write Scots verse in imitation of Burns. Some did, but in Kyle several were writing contemporaneously: including Saunders Tait, John Lapraik, William Simson, David Sillar, Thomas Walker. What inspired him (as he later wrote to 'The Guidwife of Wauchope House') was the patriotic wish

*That I for poor auld Scotland's sake*
*Some usefu plan or book could make,*
*Or sing a sang at least.* CW 271

So in April 1786 he issued 'Proposals for publishing by subscription Scotch Poems by Robert Burns' and this appeared on 31st July of that year from John Wilson's Kilmarnock press as *Poems Chiefly in the Scottish Dialect.* Most of the poems were in fact in Scots or Scots-English, padded out by some purely English pieces upon which he obviously set less store. A glossary was added as a kind of manifesto to emphasise the richness of a rural vocabulary that seemed under threat. The price was three shillings (15p), and the edition of 612 copies was sold out in little more than a month after publication.

The Kilmarnock edition received enthusiastic reviews – in the *Edinburgh Magazine* in October, *The Monthly Review* in December, and one by Henry Mackenzie in *The Lounger* also in December – so that Edinburgh was ready to welcome him. Disciples of Rousseau's philosophy would be impressed by Mackenzie's praise of 'this heaven-taught plough-man, from his humble and unlettered station'. The *New London Magazine* might regret 'that the Scottish dialect, in which these poems are written must obscure the native beauties with which they appear to abound.' But in fact it was Burns's vigorous use of Scots which ensured the success also of the Edinburgh edition of 1787, a third edition in 1793, and by 1815 at least eighty-two editions of his works, both complete and selected, had appeared. Some of his poems also came out separately as cheap broadsides, witness to their wide popular appeal.

Allan Cunningham wrote: 'I was at that time resident in Galloway, contiguous to Ayrshire, and I can well remember, how that even ploughboys and maidservants would gladly part with the wages they earned the most hardily and which they wanted to purchase the necessary clothing, if they might but procure the works of Burns.' James Hogg, the 'Ettrick Shepherd,' recalled: 'The first time I ever heard of Burns was in 1797 . . . One day during the summer a half daft man named John Scott, came to me on the hill, and to amuse me repeated Tam O' Shanter. I was delighted!' A century later, George Douglas Brown, who would become Ayrshire's greatest novelist, received as a boy from an old herd a copy of Burns, which was the first book Brown ever owned. So Burns contributed to the survival of the 'plain, braid lallans.'

## CHAPTER 14

# TOWNSCAPE 1796

Within a generation Ayrshire's appearance had visibly changed. The agricultural revolution had wrought alterations in the landscape. Plantations of trees were growing up to banish the memories of bleakness. New hedges of thorn and beech were tidily enclosing fields where more bountiful harvests were promised. Well-made roads were traversing the countryside. Many farm steadings were looking more trig. Imposing new mansion houses with spacious policies had replaced bare old tower houses. Yet, here and there, empty and dilapidated cottages marked rural depopulation, for most of the swollen population were now living in towns and villages.

By the 1790s most of Ayrshire's 75,000 inhabitants – an increase from 59,000 in 1755 – were resident in sixty-eight nucleated settlements. The Statistical Account records Kilmarnock (5670) followed by Ayr (3871) and Irvine (3500) now joined by Saltcoats (2325) and other ten towns with more than a thousand inhabitants. There were seven villages with between five hundred and a thousand inhabitants. There were twenty-two places whose population must have been somewhere between one and five hundred. In addition there were twenty-five clachans of assorted sizes with fewer than a hundred people in each. Nearly all these were creations of the 18th century. Some were deliberately planned by improving landlords. Most grew up haphazardly beside parish churches or at other convenient centres.

'Auld Ayr, wham ne'er a town surpasses' – the county town had enjoyed only modest growth and still retained much of its medieval aspect. In the Statistical Account, Rev. Dr. William McGill (who had baptised Burns) and Rev. Dr. William McGill (of 'The Kirk's Alarm') remarked that 'the inhabitants have been increasing sensibly, though not rapidly, for more than 30 years past.' Ayr had hardly extended beyond the confines of the back dykes which marked its traditional bounds. Armstrong's town plan of 1775 gives us a close-up view. The town layout was based on the converging High Street and Sandgate. The former was built up along its length, extending into Townhead (now Smith Street) and Cowgate (now Alloway Street). From the High Street there led off towards the river the short Bridgegate and the Mill Vennel; and to the west on its opposite side the Carrick Vennel and the tree-lined Newmarket Street which had been laid out in 1767. The shorter Sandgate had on its seaward side the Boat Vennel leading to the Ratton quay at the harbour, the School Vennel (later Academy Lane), and what is now St. John's Lane; with Cathcart Street a new addition. On the landward side, Newmarket Street led to the High Street and a new road (now Boswell Park) linked up with Carrick Vennel.

At the meeting of the two principal thoroughfare stood the imposing Malt Cross. Up High Street were the Fish Cross and Meal market, beside the site of the old tollbooth. Opposite, beside the river, was the Auld Kirk built there in 1654. Further up High Street was the Auld Tour, otherwise the Wallace Tower, and nearby in Mill Street was a new brewery, the Moravian church, and the poorshouse opened in 1756. After 1700 shops began to replace the old booths in High Street. This was now the commercial centre. Sandgate was the 'west end' where some of the local gentry still maintained town houses. Near the corner of the two main streets was a town hall or assembly room. In the centre of the Sandgate stood the New or Over Tollbooth, with the town gaol below the council chamber. This had been rebuilt in 1754. On the Wallace Tower and on the Tollbooth steeples there had been public clocks since 1731 and 1740 respectively:

*The drowsy Dungeon-Clock had number'd two,*
*And Wallace Tower had sworn the fact was true.* CW 245

Somewhere in the High Street may have been the inn where Tam O' Shanter and Souter Johnnie enjoyed the 'reaming swats, that drank divinely.' But there is no evidence that the 'Tam O' Shanter Inn' was in business before mid-19th century.

West of the burgh proper was the Fort area. Here were the remains of the Citadel built in the 17th century during the Cromwellian occupation; the Tower of St. John which was all that remained of the original parish church; the Schoolhouse adjacent to the Sandgate; the brewery of 1734 which was turned into a soap-boiling business; the Sugar house where refining was done for a time after 1770; fishermen's cottages near the harbour; some small coal workings; and the sand dunes leading down towards the Low Green.

Definitely outwith the control of the royal burgh was the area north of the river, where freedom from vested corporate interests allowed much more spectacular development.

Newton-upon-Ayr was a burgh of barony whose land belonged to a group of forty-eight freemen. This agrarian community was being transformed by the development of new trades – cotton weaving, coal mining, shipbuilding and ropemaking. From about three or four hundred early in the 18th century population grew to 1600, making Newton on its own one of the biggest townships in the county. Most lived in the one long thoroughfare called Main Street, composed largely of handloom weavers' but-and-bens, set wide enough apart to accommodate the lade or stream running down the street to a corn-mill on the bank of the River Ayr. In 1777 a town house and church were erected – with 'Peebles frae the water-fit' as the first minister. Another sign of significant advance – two years later in 1779 Newton was disjoined from Monkton and Prestwick and became a separate parish.

Just to the east, about 1760 Sir Thomas Wallace of Craigie, father of Burns' correspondent Mrs. Dunlop, began to feu out houses and gardens. By the 1790s this had developed into the township of Wallacetown with nearly a thousand inhabitants. Some were respectable grain merchants and retired farmers. At the other extreme were disorderly vagrants who found free scope in this unpoliced area. Most of them were labouring folk from the West Highlands or Ireland, finding employment at the lime kiln, in the Blackhouse pits, on the coal wagon way leading to the harbour, or in the cotton weaving. Wallacetown was served but inadequately by the remote St. Quivox parish church, and appropriate to the immigrants' lack of respect for the establishment, two seceders' congregations were formed, with an Anti-burgher kirk in 1770 and Burgher kirk in 1799.

By the last decade of the 18th century the county town was thus extended into a conurbation of more than six thousand inhabitants: rather more than half crowded into the limited confines of the old royal burgh, and almost as many now living in the two new conjoint communities which had so quickly grown from minuscule beginnings across the river.

For long enough the only link between the two almost separate entities was the narrow 15th century Auld Brig of Ayr; and the Ducat ford some way upstream. Increased traffic however required something better than a bridge which was a

*. . . poor, narrow foot-path of a street,*
*Where twa wheel-barrows tremble when they meet,* CW 246

The creation of a New Bridge was the work of John Ballantine. Born in 1743, the son of an Ayr merchant, he became a partner in Hunter's bank and in his later years was able to purchase the old family estate of Castlehill. He died, a bachelor, in 1812. He was provost of Ayr 1787-89, 1793-95, 1796-98, and left behind as monuments to his memory the New Bridge and the Academy. Soon after he became a councillor in 1780 he had a report prepared on the condition of the auld brig, secured a private bill for a new bridge, commissioned Robert Adam to design it, and arranged for Alexander Steven, a local mason to build it along suitably-modified lines. The New Bridge was opened in 1788, just downstream from the auld brig, which was retained as a pedestrian way. A new main thoroughfare was driven into the heart of the royal burgh. On the Newton side the Main Street was improved, the mercat cross moved aside, and the corn mill demolished. On the Ayr side, a New Bridge Street was opened, the old Malt Cross removed, and eventually (in 1825) the tollbooth in the Sandgate was demolished. The New Bridge (which, as Burns prophesied, would become 'a shapeless cairn') was replaced by the present new bridge after the disastrous flood of 1877.

But when Robert Burns was in Ayr on his last recorded visit at the end of September 1786 the New Bridge had not yet donned its 'braw new coat'. Work on it was only beginning when from Simpson's Inn at the north end of the Auld Brig he sent his poem on 'The Brigs of Ayr' to John Ballantine, to whom it was most appropriately dedicated.

Burns had much less to say about the other royal burgh of Irvine, where he stayed for the short spell from about midsummer 1781 till early the following year. Irvine, on the north bank of the river which gave it its name, lay along a very wide High Street with its Town House in the centre of the thoroughfare. To the north the highway headed for Kilwinning and Greenock. In the other direction it swung east to

Kilmarnock. One road branches off west across the river and down the coast towards Ayr. Opposite, the Glasgow Vennel took traffic towards Stewarton and Glasgow. This last had become a very busy route till Atlantic shipping by-passed Irvine for up-river ports. In mid-18th century Irvine with some three thousand inhabitants was the county's chief town. Signs of prosperity were the new bridge of 1746 and the rebuilding of the parish church in 1774. It was, said Aiton much later, 'a clean, open, fine-looking town' and he indicated that its streets were cleaner and more elegant than those of Ayr. Yet its promise was not maintained. Rev. James Richmond in the Statistical Account confessed that 'manufactures, as yet, are not carried on here to any extent.' As in Ayr the incorporated trades were not enthusiastic about new businesses. Weaving and other trades were carried on 'in the suburbs' but even across the river, Fullarton remained a mere clachan. Alexander Peacock, perhaps a relative of Burns' mother, had a typical small flax-heckling shop in a but and ben in the Glasgow Vennel. Burns lodged in another house nearby. But Peacock was 'a scoundrel of the first water' and it has been suggested that Burns moved to another heckling shop in High Street. The disastrous fire on New Year's Day brought near an end his stay in Irvine. While there, Burns became acquainted with the family of Provost Charles Hamilton, made a close friend of Richard Brown the sailor, knew some of those involved in the Buchanite disruption at the Relief Kirk, and made good use of Templeton's bookshop in High Street. 18th century Irvine produced two literary figures of its own. James Montgomery, who before he died at the age of eighty-three earned some renown as poet and hymn writer, was born here on 4th November 1771, the son of a poor Moravian missionary; but he left Irvine in 1775 while still a child. Also in Irvine was born, on 2nd May 1779, the enterprising colonist and famous novelist, John Galt. The son of a sea captain, he was growing up in the royal burgh during Burns' stay. The Galt family moved to Greenock in 1790, but Irvine was the model for 'Gudetown' so vividly depicted in his novel *The Provost.*

Kilmarnock was thriving more than Irvine, and it is tempting to speculate how Burns' life might have been altered if he had gone instead to learn a trade in Kilmarnock. Rev. James Mackinlay – whose arrival Burns recorded in 'The Ordination' – was moved to enthusiasm for his adopted town in the Statistical Account. 'Among the advantages may be reckoned its situation in the midst of a populous and fertile country, where provisions of all kinds are to be had in abundance, and at moderate prices. Coal, so necessary in almost every branch of manufacture, is found close to it in vast abundance, and may be had easier and cheaper than in any other town in the neighbourhood. The town is furnished with a meal-market, plentifully supplied with good and wholesome grain; and always a penny or three halfpence a peck cheaper than in the Glasgow or Paisley markets. Indeed all sorts of provisions, especially meal, butter, eggs, and poultry, are so much cheaper in this part of the country, that they are constantly carried to the Glasgow and Paisley markets, not merely to supply the demands of these populous towns, but to bring greater prices than can be got for them at home. The town is also provided with an excellent market for all sorts of butcher meat, which is reckoned by far the best in the neighbourhood; in so much that many families in Glasgow, at the distance of 21 miles, are supplied from it; induced, partly by the superior quality of the meat, and partly by an addition to the weight of an ounce and a half to the pound.'

This burgh of barony had had a meteoric rise from its late inception in 1592, reaching about 1,000 in 1700; 2,500 by 1750; and near 6,000 by the end of the century. The two ancient royal burghs were eclipsed, and there was a particular satisfaction in surpassing the county town – 'the wicked town of Ayr' as Burns chose to refer to it in 'The Ordination'. Kilmarnock had acquired new facilities to match its growth – five churches, two public and several private schools, fifty inns and ale houses, a post office, a printing shop, three masonic lodges, and a bowling green.

Burns was intimately acquainted with the 'streets an' neuks o' Killie'. From the Cross on the north bank of the Kilmarnock Water, the old cramped main highway squeezed west through Cheapside and past the Laigh Kirk on its way to Irvine; from Cheapside the auld brig over the water led south to Begbie's tavern (the Angel Inn) in the Sandbed on the road to Ayr. From the other side of the Cross the Foregate and Soulis Street led north by the meal market, Sandy Patrick's public house, the bowling green, and the new High Church of 1731, on the way to Glasgow. Also from the east side of the Cross went Nailer's Close, leading to the town green, the green ford – or after the 1750s a bridge – leading past Braehead and Tam Samson's house on the way to Crookedholm and Hurlford and thence east to Edinburgh or south to Mauchline and Dumfries. From the south side of the Cross

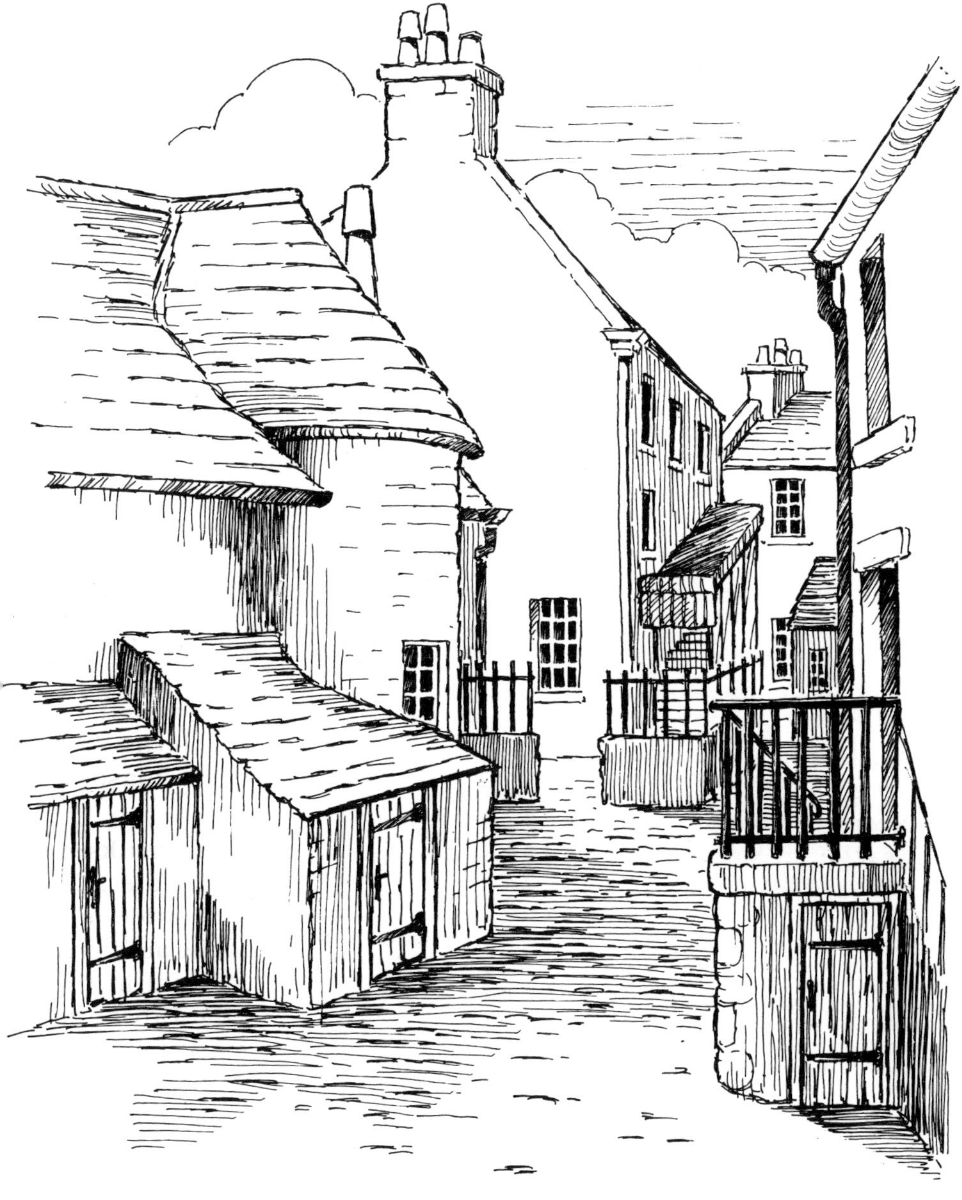

*The Star Inn Close, Kilmarnock*

was a fourth exit, a narrow lane (later Waterloo Street) containing the Star Inn Close where John Wilson had his printing shop. This lane also led to the river, and in 1770 a third bridge was erected to provide an alternative route to the south and west.

Archibald McKay, the local historian, described the old town centre: 'The streets were crooked and narrow; the houses were low and poorly lighted; and to many of them that were two storeys high were attached outside stairs, that not only confined the already limited thoroughfares, but gave to the houses themselves a rude and clumsy aspect.' The old Town House at the corner of Cheapside was 'a gloomy-looking structure, two storeys high, with a small bell-house, and shops on the ground floor, facing the street . . . At the west end of the building was the Thieves' Hole . . . and above were two dungeon-like apartments, called the Tollbooth, at the stairhead of which hung the juggs or iron collar, in which petty delinquents were doomed to stand for a given time, exposed to the gaze of the multitude. The part of the upper flat nearest the Cross formed the Hall or Court-house, the entrance to which was by a broad outside stair faced with a parapet.'

The expansion of the town was partly to the north (with the High Church to provide for that corner of the parish); on the green to the east; and southwards towards Riccarton. About 1765 the Earl of Glencairn improved the road between Kilmarnock and Riccarton and laid out a new community at Glencairn Square. The banks of the Kilmarnock and Irvine waters as they approached their confluence at Riccarton provided admirable sites for new industries. Thus Burns exhorted 'Black' John Russel, minister of the High Church and preacher at Mauchline Holy Fair

*. . . to the Netherton repair,*
*And turn a carpet weaver,*
*Aff-hand this day.* CW 193

The centre of Kilmarnock retained what Aiton called 'a despicable appearance' till the labyrinth was pierced by a network of new wide thoroughfares allowing freer passage to the increased through traffic. King Street was opened to provide an outlet to the south; Portland Street north from the Cross; and later Duke Street to the east. And in 1805 new Town Buildings were erected in King Street. The growth of the burgh of barony was not inhibited by its feudal superiors. The last

Earl of Kilmarnock - whose Jacobite sympathies found no support in Kilmarnock - was executed in 1747; his son sold off the estate to Glencairn, whose pretensions the town council successfully resisted in the Court of Session in 1771; after 1786 ownership passed to Henrietta Scott, later marchioness of Titchfield and Duchess of Portland, and there was a common enthusiasm for commercial expansion. One isolated incident exemplifies the town council's open outlook. When James Boswell visited the town with Pasquale Paoli, the Corsican patriot, and Count Bursynski, the Polish ambassador, the two were presented with the freedom of the burgh, on Sunday 12th September 1771.

In a lively community like this, Robert Burns found kindred spirits and boon companions. His associates in Ayr, like Robert Aitken and John Ballantine, were patrons and good friends. But in Kilmarnock he joined a circle of cronies: Tam Samson, who had established his seedsman firm in 1759; Robert Muir, wine merchant; John Goldie, cabinet-maker, then wine merchant, also freethinker, author and speculator; Gavin Turnbull, carpet weaver, poet, later professional actor; and Major William Parker, banker, laird of Assloss, and master of St. John's masonic lodge. Their influence no doubt helped persuade John Wilson to undertake the printing of Burns' poems in 1786, and Robert Muir himself took 72 copies. Significantly enough, Kilmarnock folk did more than most to perpetuate his memory. In 1808 the first Burns club in his native county was formed in the Angel Inn, Kilmarnock. (It was preceded by clubs formed in Greenock, 1801, and Paisley, 1805). In 1879 a Burns Monument was erected in Kay Park. And in 1885 the Burns Federation was instituted in Kilmarnock. The Burns Monument had been inaugurated at Alloway in 1823, and the Burns Cottage converted from a public hostelry into a museum in 1881. But the royal burgh of Ayr erected a statue only in 1891, following five other Scots towns, London, and six foreign cities. The Burns Monument in Mauchline came only in 1896 on the centenary of the poet's death. Very appropriately, on the roll of the eight hundred clubs affiliated to the Burns Federation, Kilmarnock heads the list as No. 0.

The three chief towns of Ayrshire lay on the periphery of Burns' everyday existence. Tarbolton, and later Mauchline, was the centre of a life which was literally parochial. Tarbolton was in some ways a lively enough place to have two rival congregations - parish kirk and burghers – two rival masonic lodges, two agricultural associations, and sufficient hostelries to accommodate social assemblies of all kinds including a dancing school and a bachelors' club. But the village was – and still is – off the main traffic routes. Manufacturing never became important. Traditional markets were organised by the burgh council – which has survived to become unique in Scotland, still holding its annual Yule meeting. The population of the parish of Tarbolton actually declined from 1,365 (in 1755) to 1,200 (in 1796) and the village itself did not rise beyond some 500 inhabitants. 'Auld Wodrow' – Rev. Dr. Patrick Wodrow – had been parish minister since 1738, and died in 1793 at the age of 80. His assistant and putative successor, Rev. John McMath, gave up in 1791 and enlisted as a private soldier.

Mauchline, on the other hand, was a busier place. The parish kirk stood beside the so-called Abbot Hunter's Tower, a 15th century building from which the monks of Melrose had administered their wide Kylesmuir estates until they passed into Loudoun hands at the Reformation. Already in the 16th century Mauchline had ten hostelries and by the 18th century thirteen fairs annually, as one would anticipate at the intersection of the highways from Ayr to Edinburgh and from Kilmarnock to Dumfries. It was an obvious site for development, and though the burgh charter of 1510 had lapsed, the village grew from less than 500 population in mid-century to more than 1,000 by the 1790s.

This was one of those villages which Aiton would describe as 'extremely irregular, the streets narrow, very crooked, ill paved, often dirty, and the general aspect mean.' The old road from Kilmarnock came down the hill from near Mossgiel, passed the Elbow Inn and the Knowe into what became known as the Back Causeway or Castle Street. Here in an upstairs single-end apartment of a two-storey house, Robert Burns and Jean Armour lived between February and November 1788. They looked out to Gavin Hamilton's house beside the Castle, and Netherplace estate beyond. In front, skirting the kirkyard, was the old burgh gaol, and Hugh Morton's inn with its ballroom. They were both there at a dance after the Mauchline fair, soon after Burns had come to Mossgiel. Later, so the tradition continues, they met on the bleaching green which ran down from near the Elbow Inn to the burn beside the Castle . . . The Back Causeway continued past the Burns house into the Cross, with Nanse Tinnock's changehouse opening its back door into the kirkyard. From the Cross the road twisted round the kirkyard and passed between Poosie Nansie's and Johnnie Dow's Whitefoord Arms into the Cowgate where the Armours lived. Then past Beechgrove cottage into the country again, skirting Ballochmyle and by the Howford across the River Ayr to Cumnock and Dumfries. Or from the Cowgate one could pass down the Tanfield towards Barskimming bridge, the only way over the River Ayr till James Armour's father built the Howford bridge. The Ayr-Edinburgh road also found its way through Mauchline. One could approach from Tarbolton via Willie's Mill and Mossgiel, or come up by Failford where Burns had his farewell meeting with Highland Mary. There was a choice of routes out of Mauchline. From the Knowe a road went up Burnside to the Loan Green and Townhead; reached also from the Cross by Bellman's Close; or from Cowgate past the manse and through the glebe – all leading towards Welton, Montgarswood, Sorn, Muirkirk, and then towards Edinburgh.

Here, on a smaller scale than in Ayr and Kilmarnock, increased traffic forced drastic surgery on the old huddle of buildings. The 1766 Turnpike Act required the improvement of both main highways through Mauchline. The Kilmarnock–Cumnock road took a direct route downhill and a New Road would be driven into Mauchline with a continuation (later Earl Grey Street) leading out towards the Howford bridge. Though this was not completed till the 19th century – removing James Smith's house at the Cross – work was under way by the 1770s, with a toll-house on the road opposite Netherplace gate, and the new Black Bull Inn and adjacent buildings erected in what would become Earl Grey Street. Certainly the new highway towards Ayr was in being. Loudoun Street is mentioned in the session records in 1778 and its continuation, the 'new street of Mauchline' in 1779. On the opposite side of the Cross, High Street was on the new turnpike road up to the hill-top. Here in 1791 John Richmond and his wife Janet Surgeoner set up in the 'new house of the Kiln Knowes.' But when Robert Burns came to Mauchline in 1784, and moved into the village as a married man in 1788, the modern street pattern had not yet been formed.

Mauchline was growing. Even the kirk session toyed with the idea of building a house for letting on its land of Braefoot. In 1776 Thomas Fisher, mason, offered to build one measuring 30 feet by 15 feet by 6 feet for the sum of £12. The Burns house in the Back Causeway was a nearly-new house, and the upper apartment must have offered more scope than the cramped conditions on the farm at Mossgiel. That was only a but and ben with an upstairs garret in which three small apartments had been formed. The end room had a small window in the gable facing Mauchline. The mid-apartment (where Robert and Gilbert slept) had only a sky-light. And there was a small lumber room reached by a ladder from the kitchen. Here lived Mrs. Burns with four sons (three after John's death in 1785, two after Robert's departure), three daughters, at one time three of Robert's weans, herdboy (William Patrick), and possibly a servant lass. The new houses in a growing village were much more attractive.

Village life in Mauchline was a source of fascination for Burns in two respects – as a bachelor in his twenties seeking personal and social gratification, and a poet whose genius was just reaching maturity. William Patrick later recalled some of the local persons who were immortalised by their association with or mention by the poet. Rev. William Auld was 'much respeckit.' The elder, William Fisher, 'Holy Willie', was 'neither very bad nor very good, to outward appearance; he was blamed for taking the kirk bawbees. When standin' at the plate on Sabbath, fowk said, he would boo doon to pat his boots richt, as it were, and slip in a bawbee or so.' Gavin Hamilton was 'the poor man's friend', said Patrick echoing Burns. Johnnie Dow of the Whitefoord Arms was a 'rough, swearin character, muckle gi'en to the bottle.' Nanse Tinnock was 'auld, douce, and pawkie.' Other characters mentioned by Burns were James Humphrey, mason–the 'blethran' bitch'; 'Godly' James Bryan, tenant in Welton, otherwise 'Auld Whitrick'; the village herd, 'Laird McGaan' alias 'Auld Tootie'; 'Auld Clinkum' or 'Clinkumbell', the kirk officer, gravedigger, and bellman, Robert Gibb who succeeded his brother William in 1784; Mrs. Gibson–'Poosie Nansie'–and her sluttish daughter 'Racer Jess'. There was the 'Mauchline wag' who was 'Clockie' John Brown the clockmaker. Patrick remembered Burns' two closest friends. James Smith, an elder's son, had a 'high character . . . worth knowing'. He left Mauchline in 1788 and died over forty years later in Jamaica. John Richmond was at that time a 'rough chap . . . wild . . . fond o' company.' But after his return from Edinburgh he became staid, respectable and rather ashamed of his former association with Burns. The fourth member of the 'Court of Equity' was William Hunter, a shoemaker. With Smith and Richmond, Burns helped form in Mauchline an association like the Tarbolton Bachelors' Club – the Young Mens' Conversation Society meeting in Ann Orr's tavern in the Cowgate; and he also belonged to a Reading Society meeting in McLelland's inn, now the Loudoun Arms.

Then there were the 'Mauchline belles.' Helen Miller, whose father was landlord of the Sun Inn, later married Dr. John Mackenzie. Jean Merkland, a merchant's daughter, married James Findlay, the Tarbolton excise officer who trained Burns. Jean Smith, sister of Burns' friend, married James Candlish from Edinburgh. Betty Miller, sister of Helen, and Christine Morton both married local merchants. And there was Jean Armour–'the jewel for me o' them a''. William Patrick had grown up as a next-door neighbour to the Armours in Cowgate. James Armour, the master builder owned his own house and several others. Jean was 'a decent well-doin' lass' who was full of sprightliness and fun. Patrick also remembered Mary Campbell, whom Burns met at Gavin Hamilton's in July 1785 before she moved to Coilsfield to take charge of the dairy there.

From Mauchline, Robert Burns set off – on a pony borrowed from George Reid, son-in-law of 'Guid Auld Glen' John Tennant – for Edinburgh. He stayed there from November 1786 till May 1787; for three short spells between his holiday tours and a trip to Mauchline; a second long stay from October 1787 till February 1788 when he had his affair with 'Clarinda', Mrs. Agnes Maclehose; then two brief final visits in 1788 and 1789.

The Old Town of Edinburgh was built high along the narrow ridge extending from the Castle on its rocky eminence towards the palace of Holyrood at the other end of the Royal Mile. Tall 'lands' of eight storeys or more bordered the Lawnmarket; High Street, which had St. Giles church, Parliament House, and Edinburgh Cross; the Netherbow; and Canongate. Running parallel to these, on the southern edge of the ridge, were the other old streets of the Grassmarket and Cowgate. The whole area within the old town walls was honeycombed with lesser wynds and closes. But Edinburgh was expanding. The new commercial and industrial city of Glasgow was growing more rapidly, it is true, from 27,451 in 1755 to 77,385 in 1792: but the city on the Clyde remained still the second city of Scotland. In the same period Edinburgh's population increased from 52,720 to 82,560. Suburban development took place to the south in the first instance, with George Square laid out after 1760. But the major extension followed the ambitious plans made in 1767 for the New Town to the north. The draining of the Nor' Loch which lay between was commenced. In 1772 work was completed on a North Bridge to link the Old Town with the New, and in 1788 a South Bridge made closer contacts possible with the southern areas. The enlarged city acquired enhanced facilities of varied kinds. It had, for example, by 1790 two theatres and four newspapers. The university, with 500 students in 1763, began the New College in 1789 and the roll increased to 1,300.

When Burns arrived in November 1786 he found lodgings with his Mauchline friend, John Richmond, in Baxter's Close in the Lawnmarket, near Lady Stair's House. William Creech's bookshop was at the Luckenbooths down High Street, opposite Parliament House. William Smellie's printing shop was further down, in Anchor Close. When he returned to Edinburgh the following October, he found accommodation with William Cruikshanks, a new acquaintance, in St. James' Square in the New Town.

William Creech supplied the Statistical Account with a long series of notes to show how life in Edinburgh was changing. For example: 'In 1763 – People of fashion dined at two o'clock, or a little after it; business was attended to in the afternoon. It was a common practice to lock the shops at one o'clock, and to open them after dinner at two. In 1783 – People of fashion, and of the middle rank, dined at four or five o'clock: No business was done in the afternoon, dinner of itself having become a very serious business.

'In 1763 – Wine was seldom seen, or, in a small quantity, at the tables of the middle rank of people. In 1791 – Every tradesman in decent circumstances presents wine after dinner; and many in plenty and variety.

'In 1763 – It was the fashion for gentlemen to attend the drawing rooms of the ladies in the afternoons, to drink tea, and to mix in the society and conversation of the women. In 1783 – The drawing rooms were totally deserted; invitations to tea in the afternoon were given up; and the only opportunity gentlemen had of being in ladies company, was when they happened to mess together at dinner or supper; and even then, an impatience was sometimes shewn, till the ladies retired. Card parties, after a long dinner; and also after a late supper were frequent.'

Edinburgh society was ready to welcome Burns. Though the young poet Robert Fergusson had died un-noticed so recently as 1774, the new Ayrshire poet found Edinburgh awaiting him. The Earl of Glencairn was acquainted with him through his relations, James Dalrymple of Orangefield and Robert Aiken of Ayr, and extended his patronage. Through him the Caledonian Hunt took the lead in sponsoring the Edinburgh edition. Literary circles has been introduced to Burns' poems as a result of Rev. George Lawrie of Loudoun's contacts with the blind scholar, Dr. Thomas Blacklock; and the *Edinburgh Magazine* for October, November and December carried extracts from the Kilmarnock edition. Professor Dugald Stewart lent Henry Mackenzie a copy he had brought from Ayrshire, which inspired Mackenzie's enthusiastic review in the December issue of *The Lounger*. Mrs. Cockburn (author of 'The Flowers of the Forest') wrote that 'The town is at present agog with the ploughman poet.' The Duke and Duchess of Gordon, leaders of Edinburgh polite society, offered their patronage.

So Burns became at once an accepted member of the literati, making the acquaintance of Henry Erskine, Dean of the Faculty of Advocates; Dr. Hugh Blair, the preacher and poet; Rev. Dr. William Greenfield; Professor Adam Ferguson, at whose home the young Walter Scott made brief contact with Burns; William Tytler; James Gregory; Dr. Blacklock; Henry Mackenzie; but just missed meeting the ailing Adam Smith. Those with Ayrshire connections joined the earl of Glencairn and Dugald Stewart in seeking him out, notably Sir John Whitefoord, formerly of Ballochmyle; Sir James Hunter Blair; Professor Josiah Walker. As well as patrons and fellow-writers, he found new friends: Alexander Cunningham; the printer William Smellie who introduced him to the Crochallan Fencibles club he had founded; Peter Hill the bookseller; Robert Ainslie, the law student who went with Burns on his Borders tour; William Nichol, the Latin master at the High School who was his companion on the Highland tour; James Johnson the engraver and Stephen Clarke the organist with whom he enthusiastically co-operated in editing the *Scots Musical Museum*.

Like so many of his contemporaries, Robert Burns was born in the country, but ended his life as a townsman. He moved in November 1791 into Dumfries, where he died less than five years after, on 21st July 1796.

Dumfries had much to commend it. As 'Queen of the South' it was – as it still is – a kind of regional sub-capital. In the Statistical Account, Rev. Dr. William Burnside, writing just about the time of Burns' arrival, summed up what it was like. 'The town, together with the neighbourhood a few miles around it, furnishes a society, amongst whom a person of moderate fortune may spend his days, with as much satisfaction and enjoyment, as, perhaps, in any part of these kingdoms.' And Burns, already familiar with Dumfries while resident at Ellisland, must have found much to remind him of Ayr, with which it had many close similarities.

Dumfries lay near the mouth of the River Nith. Nearly parallel to its eastern bank stretched the High Street and its extension, the Kirkgate.

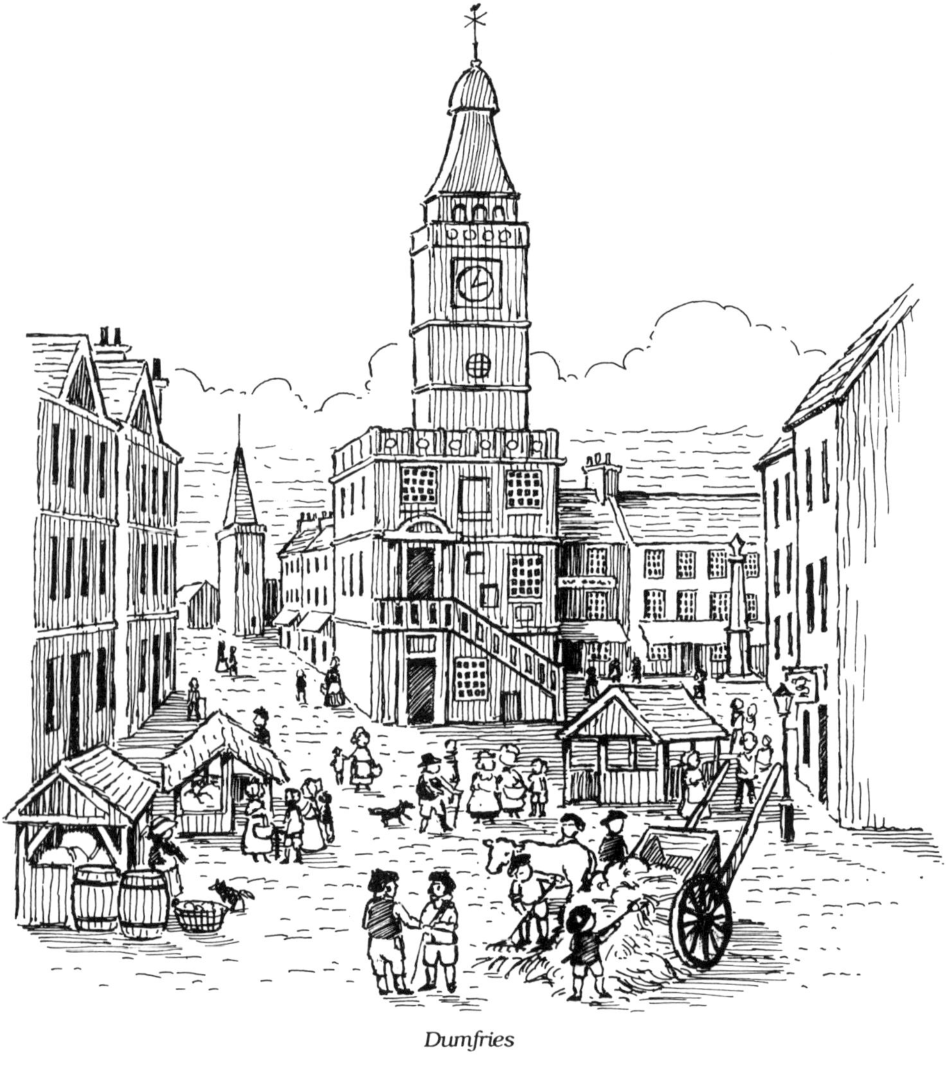

*Dumfries*

The river was crossed by a 15th century stone bridge, with a new bridge added upstream between 1790 and 1794. On the opposite bank and outwith the burgh Maxwelltown was growing up. The royal burgh of Dumfries owed its origin to William the Lion, created in 1186, nineteen years before Ayr. It had a town council of twenty five members, with a new council being elected annually by its predecessors. The council met in the tolbooth which was situated in the middle of the wide High Street. Dumfries had seven incorporated trades - hammermen, squaremen, tailors, weavers, shoemakers, skinners and fleshers. This was a community of traditional crafts; and busy markets and fairs where cattle and horses were bought and sold; with some coastal and a little foreign shipping. New manufactures were not significantly affecting its traditional character. Town population had grown from perhaps 3,000 in mid-century to around 5,600 in the 1790s. The facilities were compatible with those of Ayr. The parish church of St. Michael's (rebuilt 1745) was supplemented by the New Church (1727) and there were also congregations of the Relief Kirk, Anti-burghers, Episcopalians, Methodists, and occasional visits from a Roman Catholic priest. There were assembly rooms; libraries; a good burgh school which became an academy in 1802; two or three boarding schools for young ladies; three banks; an infirmary opened in 1777; a theatre built in 1790; and a printing shop publishing a *Weekly Journal.*

The Burns family moved first of all into a three-roomed second-floor tenement rented from Captain John Hamilton in what was then Friar Vennel, otherwise the Wee or Cawart's Vennel, now Bank Street. In the spring of 1793 he could afford to rent from the same proprietor another house in Mill Vennel (now Burns Street). This was something much better: a substantial, detached, two-storey residence, in one of the upstairs bedrooms of which Burns died, and which was occupied by his widow till her death in 1834.

Burns was easily accepted into the Dumfries community. Indeed, in 1787 the council had been enthusiastic enough to make him a freeman of the burgh and in 1793 accepted that this entitled him to appropriately-reduced fees for his children in the burgh school. In turn he participated in the work of the new theatre, in the formation of a public library, and joined the Volunteers when they were instituted. He became known in the Globe Inn and several other hostelries. Among his excise colleagues he made good friends with his immediate superior, Alexander Findlater, and also with John Lewars. James Gray and Thomas White of the burgh school also became associates. So too did Dr. William Maxwell, fellow-radical, and his medical adviser. Closest of all perhaps was John Syme, one of those whose fortunes had been shattered by the collapse of the Ayr Bank, but who was successfully recouping himself as Distributor of Stamps for the Dumfries area. And not far away was Robert Riddell of Friars Carse and his sister-in-law, Mrs. Maria Riddell of Woodley Park. Besides this circle of local acquaintances, he had his correspondents, added to whose number was George Thomson, for whose *Select Scottish Airs* he was now the major contributor.

On Thursday 21st July 1796 Robert Burns died, aged 37, at his home in the Mill Vennel. At the weekend his coffined corpse was taken to the Trades House. On Monday 25th July there was an impressive funeral, arranged by his friend John Syme, and conducted in military manner by the Dumfries Volunteers, the Cinque Port Cavalry, and the Angus-shire Fencibles. He was buried in St. Michael's churchyard, on a spot marked by a plain tombstone, and in 1815 the body was transferred to the Burns Mausoleum erected in the same cemetery.

# BIBLIOGRAPHY

There are several accounts written by contemporaries: Andrew Wight, *The Present State of Husbandry in Scotland*, 4 vols., 1778-1784; Colonel William Fullarton, *General View of the Agriculture of the County of Ayr*, 1793; a second agricultural *General View* by William Aiton, 1811; Sir John Sinclair, *Statistical Account of Scotland*, 21 vols., 1791-1799; 'Memories of Ayrshire about 1760' by Rev. J. Mitchell written in 1842, in *Miscellany* of the Scottish History Society, 1939; George Robertson, *Topographical Description of Cunninghame*, 1820, and his *Rural Recollections*, 1829. The published *Journals of James Boswell*, 12 vols., 1950-1989, and volumes of his *Correspondence* in progress since 1966 provide the views of that illustrious Ayrshire laird. There are three sets of maps: William Roy's manuscript 'Military Survey of Scotland, 1755-1767' in the British Library, London; A. & M. Armstrong's *Map of Ayrshire*, 1775, reprinted 1959; Taylor and Skinner's *Survey and Maps of the Roads of North Britain*, 1776. Though fictional in some respects, John Galt's *Annals of the Parish*, 1821, and *The Provost*, 1822, are informative. Manuscript sources include county, burgh, and parish records (especially Mauchline kirk session minutes) and various estate papers.

Some information on Burns' associates and background can be had from his biographers: James Currie, 1800; amplified (and corrected) by later writers, especially Robert Chambers, 1851-1852; William Scott Douglas, 1877-1879; William Wallace, 1896; Hans Hecht, 1919; Franklyn Bliss Snyder, 1932; James Mackay, 1992. The best studies of his works are by David Daiches, 1950, and Thomas Crawford, 1960. The most authoritative edition of the poems is by James Kinsley, 3 vols., 1968; for the letters J. De Lancey Ferguson, 2 vols., 1931, and G. Ross Roy, 2 vols., 1985. These are complemented by James Mackay's *Works*, 1986, *Letters*, 1989, and *Word Finder*, 1989.

*The Burns Chronicle*, annually since 1892, is a storehouse of informative articles; *Ayrshire Collections*, published by Ayrshire Archaeological and Natural History Society in 12 vols., 1950-1983, and subsequent monographs, provide much 18th century material. There is a range of diverse studies: William Boyd, *Education in Ayrshire Through Seven Centuries*, 1961; Robert Chambers and John Wilson, *The Land of Burns*, 1840; J.D. Carrick, *The Laird of Logan*, 1835; Andrew Edgar, *Old Church Life in Scotland*, 2 vols., 1885, 1886; R.T. Fitzhugh, *Robert Burns, Associates and Contemporaries*, 1943; William Jolly, *Robert Burns at Mossgiel*, 1881; James Paterson, *History of the County of Ayr*, 5 vols., 1863-1866; Charles Rogers, *The Book of Robert Burns*, 3 vols., 1889-1891; John Service, *The Memorables of Robin Cummell*, 1913; Graham Smith, *Robert Burns the Exciseman*, 1989; and C.A. Whatley, 'Industrialisation in Ayrshire', Strathclyde University unpublished thesis, 1975. Essential reference works are Maurice Lindsay, *Burns Encyclopedia*, 1959; Andrew Boyle, *Ayrshire Book of Burns Lore*, 1985; James Mackay, *Burns Lore of Dumfries and Galloway*, 1988.

The present author has, among various contributions to Ayrshire history, the following specifically concerned with Burns. He has edited *Ayrshire at the Time of Burns*, 1959; *Mauchline Memories of Robert Burns*, 1985; *Grose's Antiquities of Ayrshire*, 1991, these published by Ayrshire Archaeological and Natural History Society. Also articles relating to Burns in *Ayrshire Collections*, Vol. 3, 1955, and Vol. 4, 1958; *Burns Chronicle*, 1961, 1980, 1981, 1985, 1991; *Scottish Literary Journal*, 1981; introduction to *Statistical Account, Ayrshire*, 1982 reprint; contributor to *A Sense of Place*, ed. Cruickshank, 1988, and *Burns Now*, ed. Simpson, 1994. John Strawhorn has also included studies of Burns in several of his local histories: *Ayrshire, Story of a County*, 1975, Chapter 12; *Irvine*, 1985, Ch. 10; *Ayr*, 1989, Ch. 10; *Discovering Ayrshire*, 1988, Ch. 8.

---

***Most of the illustrations in this book are also available as black and white or hand coloured prints direct from the artist:***

*CHRISTY DANIELLES,*
*Arkyleglen Cottage, 8 Main Street, Dalrymple Ayr KA6 6DF*